PARTNERING *Dance* AND *Education*

Intelligent Moves for Changing Times

Judith Lynne Hanna, PhD

University of Maryland

Human Kinetics

Library of Congress Cataloging-in-Publication Data

Hanna, Judith Lynne.
    Partnering dance and education : intelligent moves for changing
times / Judith Lynne Hanna.
       p. cm.
    Includes bibliographical references and index.
    ISBN 0-88011-511-4
    1. Dance—Study and teaching—United States. 2. Interdisciplinary
approach in education—United States. 3. Dance—Social aspects–
–United States. 4. Dance—United States—Psychological aspects.
I. Title
GV1589.H35   1999
762.8'071'073—DC21   98–34340
                                             CIP

ISBN-10: 0-88011-511-4
ISBN-13: 978-0-88011-511-7

Acquisitions Editor: Judy Patterson Wright, PhD; **Developmental Editor:** Christine Drews; **Assistant Editor:** John Wentworth; **Copyeditor:** Amie Bell; **Proofreader:** Kathy Bennett; **Graphic Designer:** Nancy Rasmus; **Graphic Artist:** Brian McElwain; **Cover Designer:** Jack Davis; **Printer:** United Graphics

Cover: Rasta Thomas performing "Nostalgia." Choreographer: Vladimir Anguelov; photographer: Chris Dame

Printed in the United States of America   10 9 8 7 6 5 4

Human Kinetics
Web site: www.HumanKinetics.com

United States: Human Kinetics, P.O. Box 5076, Champaign, IL 61825-5076
800-747-4457
e-mail: humank@hkusa.com

Canada: Human Kinetics, 475 Devonshire Road Unit 100, Windsor, ON N8Y 2L5
800-465-7301 (in Canada only)
e-mail: info@hkcanada.com

Europe: Human Kinetics, 107 Bradford Road, Stanningley
Leeds LS28 6AT, United Kingdom
+44 (0) 113 255 5665
e-mail: hk@hkeurope.com

Australia: Human Kinetics, 57A Price Avenue, Lower Mitcham, South Australia 5062
08 8372 0999
e-mail: info@hkaustralia.com

New Zealand: Human Kinetics, Division of Sports Distributors NZ Ltd.,
P.O. Box 300 226 Albany, North Shore City, Auckland
0064 9 478 1207
e-mail: info@humankinetics.co.nz

To my musician parents, Lili and David Selmont, who took me to see my first dance performances and gave me my first dance lessons; my wonderful husband and colleague, William John Hanna, who introduced me to research; and my two beloved sons, Shawn Harrison Hanna and Aaron Evan Hanna—whose K-12 and university education did not include dance!

Contents

Part 11 Learning In, About, and Through Dance

PHOTO CREDITS

Acknowledgments

Partnering Dance and Education could not have made its debut without the contributions of many people in different places over half a century. Indeed, this book speaks in voices far too numerous to mention them all.

I am grateful to my musician parents, Lili and David Selmont, who took me to see the St. Louis Municipal Opera Company's ballets and musicals. Then at age 8, when my pediatrician diagnosed me as being *pes planus* (flat-footed) and said dancing would make my feet strong, my parents took me to ballet class. This first dancing experience inspired me go on to study different forms of ballet, modern, and creative movement, followed later by study in Afro-Caribbean, African, Indian, jazz, and flamenco dance. (By the way, I am not sure if dance helped my feet, but it unquestionably challenged me intellectually, emotionally, and physically; and it helped me cope with stress.)

Partnering Dance and Education would not have materialized in the manner it has without the dance artists, teachers, and fellow dancers who helped me experience the love, joy, and knowledge of dance. These people who widened my horizons include dance teachers in private studios, in public education, and in informal settings. I am indebted to my alma mater, University High School, West Los Angeles, for offering modern dance, as did the colleges I attended later.

I also thank my dance students in camps, community centers, public and private schools and universities, and my social studies and English students in middle school, high school, and university education. My work with these young people catalyzed my reflection on dance and dance education.

I wish to acknowledge the Gill School, Bernardsville, New Jersey: In 1972 it offered me the opportunity to develop, teach, and evaluate a dance-centered interdisciplinary program in New York City. With guest teachers I introduced students to several dance techniques and their historical backgrounds, using the New York Public Library Performing Arts Research Center at Lincoln Center as a resource. Students attended dance performances and wrote critiques (which strengthened their skills in English and movement analysis) and compared their own opinions with reviews in the *New York Times*.

I am indebted to informants from African villages to American urban theaters. They taught me their dances and gave me new angles of vision about the significance of dance.

To my friends in Africa, especially Nigeria and Uganda, thank you for opening my eyes to the potential of dance as a medium of education for young and old alike. It was here that I first witnessed dance education, dance in education, and the relationship of dance to other aspects of life.

I appreciate the opportunity the U.S. Department of Education provided me as a civil servant. I met people nationwide who called attention to current issues and trends that helped shape this book. Likewise, I am grateful for the opportunity to serve on the ArtsPartnership (supported by the National Endowment for the Arts, the U.S. Department of Education, arts organizations, representatives from the states, and business people), which, since 1996, has kept me abreast of developments in arts education.

For generously sharing their knowledge and responding to mine, I am indebted to Jane Bonbright, Ed.D., of the National Dance Education Association (NDEA), and Susan W. Stinson, Ph.D., Dance at the University of North Carolina, Greensboro. I have been discussing dance with Sue since 1978.

Special thanks go to the following people: David Alexander, Boston Ballet, Center for Education; Darrell Ayers, Amy Nordin, Patty Laing, and Barbara Shepherd, Education Department, the John F. Kennedy Center for the Performing Arts; David Bach, formerly of the Minnesota Alliance for Arts in Education; Vidya Bheindaiker, communication specialist; Deborah Brzoska, Vancouver School District; Loren Bucek, dance program, City Center Theater Foundation; Ralph Burgard, North Carolina A+ Schools; Susan Cashion, Ph.D., Dance, Stanford University; Chris Dame, photographer; Leilani Lattin Duke, Getty Education Institute for the Arts; Rima Faber, Ph.D., Primary Movers and NDEA; Richard D. Frey, Ph.D., formerly of Human Kinetics; Hortensia Fonseca, Maryland Youth Ballet; Susan Gingrasso, Dance Department, University of Wisconsin, Stevens Point; Diana F. Green, Dance Department, Huntingdon College; Doug Herbert, Director, Arts in Education, National Endowment for the Arts; Samuel Hope, National Association of Schools of Dance; the Kennedy Center Alliance for Arts Education Network (KAAEN); Connie Kieffer, Ph.D., Highland Park High School; Debra Leigh, St. Cloud University; Susan McGreevy-Nichols, Roger Williams Middle School; Barry Oreck, ArtsConnections; Lynnette Overby, Ph.D., Michigan State University; K.C. Patrick, former editor for *Dance Teacher Now* and writer for *Dance Magazine*; Pamela Paulson, Ph.D., Minnesota Center for Arts Education; Amy Polovick, dance specialist; Karl Schaffer, Ph.D., mathematician and dancer; Michael Sikes, Ph.D., arts consultant; Tomi Short, dance teacher, former New York City Ballet dancer; Southern Arts Education Connections; Pamela Squires, dance critic, *Washington Post*; Joan Stahl, librarian, Smithsonian Institution; Daniel Thomas, M.D., Ph.D., and father of prize-winning dancer, RastaThomas; Elena White, dance educator; Hannah C. Wiley, Dance Department, University of Washington; and Jannas Zalesky, Outreach Education Director, City Center Theater Foundation.

I am grateful to the following publishers for helping me to shape the presentation of some of this work: University of Texas Press, University of Chicago Press, AMS Press, *Anthropology and Education, Dance Teacher Now, Interethnic Communication, Phi Delta Kappan,* and *Practicing Anthropologist.*

Finally, I thank Human Kinetics editors, Judy Patterson Wright, Ph.D., Christine Drews, John Wentworth, and Amie Bell for their guidance in bringing this book to fruition.

Prelude

Dance is an art form that links mind and body in a society that tends to view the body with distrust; an art form that celebrates process in a society that values product; an art form that in its person-to-person transmission serves as a kind of "cultural DNA," particularly for groups who historically have been denied access to political power; an art form that empowers women in a society that tends to diminish the value of "women's work," and finally, an art form that affirms the essential function of kinesthetic intelligence in a culture that tends to measure knowledge in words and numbers.

— MINDY L. LEVINE (1994:11)

Dance is about life, creativity, people, and being flexible, open to change, and having experience in decision-making.

— MARTHA MYERS, DEAN OF THE AMERICAN DANCE FESTIVAL AND FORMER CHAIRPERSON OF DANCE AT CONNECTICUT COLLEGE (QUOTED IN DANCERS IN CAP AND GOWN, 1995, P. 83)

WHY A BOOK ON DANCE EDUCATION?

As we look to the future and see educators, politicians, and parents desiring to improve and reform the education system, we must assess how dance fits within this reform and especially how dance can be used to improve the education of our children. Education in kindergarten through 12th grade and in colleges and universities is about developing intelligence (Sternberg 1996), and dance can be used to develop certain types of intelligence. The renowned Harvard University professor of education, Howard Gardner, has identified kinesthetic intelligence, including dance, as one of several kinds of intelligence, such as linguistic, musical, logical-mathematical, spatial, intrapersonal, and interpersonal intelligence.

Path-breaking milestones in the United States bear witness to the increasing recognition of the value of the discipline of dance: Dance has been included in the National Education Goals, National Standards for Dance Education have been offered, national assessment of dance education is being projected, and teacher certification in dance is required by more and more states. A search is underway for improved teaching methods in all subjects, including dance, in order to make students more competitive in the world economy.

With its magical potential, dance can help meet the needs of individual youth as well as help nations reach their education goals. Without dance education—the wellspring of dancers and dance audiences—the field of dance is in jeopardy.

Dance is meritorious as an end unto itself and needs no outside excuse or pretext for its presence in school curricula. For this reason, dance warrants in-depth attention apart from its relationship to other education goals. Dance, however, can also facilitate learning other academic disciplines and life skills. Not only can students learn the discipline of dance, but they can also learn about dance and through dance. Through dance education students can discover and address personal and public concerns about health, gender, ethnicity, self, and their national identity.

As a result of the education reform movement, the U.S. federal and many state governments now consider dance education to be a core subject. We are at a critical threshold, and dancers, educators, policy makers, and concerned citizens must begin to look at dance with an enlightened perspective. To quote Martha Myers,

> Because we are in the middle of an enormous cultural change [what some call a "culture war"], we need new models and sources in a world where there might not be grants to sustain a career. . . . our best talking point . . . is that we train students for life, not just dance. (*Dancers in Cap and Gown* 1995:83)

With a vision of the future of dance education, I present key issues and trends that illuminate the potential of dance in preparing our youth for life in a competitive global environment. This means revisiting what dance is and can be. Dance education need not be ghettoized in past history (Brown 1994). Because dance and dance education are part of a larger whole (art, society, and education in general), *Partnering Dance and Education* takes a unique broad perspective, with the intention of filling in some gaps in the dance literature.

If dance education is to fulfill its potential, awareness of changing possibilities in schools, communities, and the nation is essential. Knowledge of this context, that is, the landscape or ecology of dance education, can guide our retention of useful traditions while it also aids our development of new ways of learning and teaching.

In this book I try to take into account the diversity of dance education, from dance curricula that are severely lacking to the ideal vision presented in the National Standards for Dance Education for K-12. I discuss illustrative current programs and studies, and I also include reports from unique studies conducted years ago as well as discussion of programs no longer in existence. Several worthy dance curricula have been discontinued either because of a shortage of funds or poor educational leadership. Discussing these "oldies but goodies," however, should help us flesh out our understanding of contemporary developments.

This book presents current thinking relevant to dance; models of delivering dance education; and practical resources for teaching in, about, and through dance. A scaffold for gaining understanding and garnering theoretical and practical knowledge is interlaced with some useful "how-to" suggestions.

YOU'RE THE AUDIENCE

This book is primarily for future and practicing dance educators and for dancers interested in better understanding the potential of dance. You can apply the ideas presented here whether you work in public or private schools, universities, special arts schools, or dance studios or as a professional performer.

Educators in disciplines other than dance will also find this book enlightening. These educators will gain important information about dance to enhance student learning in their respective disciplines. One approach is to integrate dance into other academic classes; another approach is to offer problem-centered curricula using dance as one way of knowing, teaching, and learning.

If you are an administrator or member of a dance company or an owner of a dance studio, this book may advance your knowledge of dance by itself or in relation to the performer–audience connection. Many dance organizations are creating partnerships between dance artists and schools, and this book may help you to do the same.

Partnering Dance and Education provides useful information as well for education decision makers, including administrators, parent–teacher associations, school boards, legislators, and foundations. These individuals can make positive decisions about dance education when armed with an understanding of current issues and trends.

And concerned citizens can learn what to expect from dance education. By action or inaction, the public influences decisions about realizing the possibilities of dance education. Although the book's focus is on developments in the United States, much of the information is also applicable to educators, dance artists, decision makers, and the public in other countries.

ITINERARY

Part I focuses on "Understanding Dance Education." Chapter 1, "Is Dance a Distinct Body of Knowledge?" explores the appropriateness of dance for academic schools. The chapter asks what is dance, its elements, its sensory, emotional, and cognitive processes, and what is the potential for transferring learned dance skills to other domains? Is dance a performing, liberal, physical, or applied art?

Chapter 2, "The Power of Dance Well Taught," notes potential benefits of dance education by drawing upon reports and formal research. Here, I discuss some key ways of offering dance education that suggest the range of viable options and possible combinations.

Chapter 3, "Survival of Dance Education," places dance education in its historical context. The chapter questions whether dance education is taking advantage of recent milestones that place it on a challenging threshold.

Chapter 4, "Who Should Teach Dance?" examines how professional companies promote education, ponders the appropriate background and competencies for dance educators, and addresses the criteria for successful teaching. I discuss the numerous ways in which collaboration among academic and dance school teachers, dance organizations, communities, and local and touring dance artists can benefit students.

Part II, "Learning In, About, and Through Dance," addresses how dance education, although meaningful in itself, has broader relevance. Chapters 5, 6, 8, and 10 describe how dance can teach academic and workplace skills, benefit at-risk youth, promote national identity yet preserve cultural diversity, and both dispel and create stress. In addition, chapter 7 describes how teachers can use their observations of children's dance at play to assess where students are in dance and in their understanding of the world, and chapter 9 looks at dance and gender by examining how dance educators may deliberately and inadvertently teach students about sex roles.

The "Finale: Overcoming Obstacles and Moving Forward" discusses hurdles to dance education's success. Promising pathways to overcome these obstacles are put on the agenda.

Appendixes at the end of the book include a set of discussion questions prompted by each chapter for use in courses or in self-reflection; the Outline of National Dance Education Standards, which describes the content of sequential dance education; and a thorough list of resources for dance educators, including addresses of leading dance organizations, programs, and schools as well as selected readings cross-referenced to the bibliography.

As do the other arts, dance embodies the human imagination, records human achievement, and distinguishes us as human beings. Creating dance helps form human communities and cultures. Every flourishing culture and civilization has provided for its children the necessary formal instruction to create the arts and to understand their meanings.

Part 1

Understanding Dance Education

Chapter 1

Is Dance a Distinct Body of Knowledge?

To understand the culture, study the dance. To understand the dance, study the people.

— CHUCK DAVIS, DANCER, CHOREOGRAPHER, AND TEACHER (QUOTED IN LEVINE 1994:7)

To me, the body says what words cannot. . . . Dancing is very like poetry. It's like the poetic lyricism sometimes, it's like the rawness of dramatic poetry, it's like the terror, or it can be a terrible revelation of meaning.

— MODERN DANCE GENIUS, MARTHA GRAHAM (1985:H8)

I had been dancing for 30 years before I felt I knew the depth and scope of dance; its historical and cultural roots, its enriching and transforming aspects, its force as a preeminent tool for communication.

— JACQUES D'AMBOISE, FORMER PRINCIPAL DANCER, NEW YORK CITY BALLET; FOUNDER, NATIONAL DANCE INSTITUTE (1996:1)

*A*n overview of the essence of dance helps us understand its role in the "21st-century" education reform movement. For the first time, the United States has National Education Goals, and dance, as one of the arts (which include dance, music, theater, and the visual arts), is included in the goals as a core subject for all children. Another first is the development of voluntary National Standards for Dance Education that offer a vision of what students kindergarten through twelfth grade (K-12) should know and be able to do (see appendix 2).

A distinct, coherent body of knowledge must have a dominant concept with interrelated concepts. Dance as a discipline in this sense is like a diamond with radiant karats. It is beautiful to look at, and, at the same time, it is highly valued for its instrumental hardness. I will now explore the concepts that make dance a field of study.

WHAT IS DANCE?

Just what is dance? This central question has numerous answers. Is a child's somewhat automatic rhythmic reaction to strong emotion, such as joyously jumping up and down, dance? No. Is it the same as communicative, dancelike displays by animals? No. Ethologists call these ritual performances *fixed action patterns*, or *programmed motor sequences*, which appear as animals mature and interact with their own species in a natural setting. These animal "dances" appear to communicate immediate feelings, (e.g., fear, hunger, well-being, aggression, reassurance, submission, sexual arousal), drives, and autonomic rhythms. The "dancing" chimpanzees, horses, dogs, bears, parrots, and elephants we see in the circus "dance" on human cue through conditioning constrained by an animal's biological capabilities.

Is dance physicality and emotion? Yes. The instrument of human dance is the body unmediated by other material, such as the artist's brush, paint, and canvas. Dance is often emotionally arousing, eliciting peak experiences, transcendent moments, spirituality, and "magic."

The Western cultural heritage from biblical and early Greek times divides mind and body, the body supposedly undermining the integrity and purity of the mind. Plato and Lucan feared that common dancing could arouse passions and undermine the civil society. Salome's dance was linked to eroticism, temptation, sin, and destruction. Later, within the Protestant ethic, dance, like play, was permitted only to children. Adult dancing was considered the devil's handiwork and is still suspect among some people today.

The often-told joke on the folk dance circuit is, "Why don't the Baptists have sex standing up?" The answer: "They might be accused of dancing." Yet after ruling against it for 151 years, Baylor University, the largest Baptist institution in the world, located in Waco, Texas, permitted dancing on campus. President Robert B. Sloan, Jr., noted there are several dances, what Baptists call "foot functions," described in the Bible. Foot functions include the dance of the elders in Jesus's presence at the Feast of Lights, as related in the Gospel of John (Myerson 1996).

It is useful to conceive of dance as encompassing knowledge in the arts, humanities, and social and behavioral sciences; this conceptualization of dance is relevant particularly to the United States, which is becoming increasingly diverse (multicultural). As an anthropologist, I have talked to dancers and dance scholars of many cultures and surveyed the literature on behavior generally called dance. From this work I have come to view dance as follows: Dance is human behavior composed (from the dancer's perspective, which is usually shared by the audience members of the dancer's culture) of purposeful (individual choice and social learning play a role), intentionally rhythmical, and culturally influenced sequences of nonverbal body movements mostly other than those performed in ordinary motor activities. The motion (in time, space, and with effort) has an inherent and aesthetic value (the notion of appropriateness and competency as viewed by the dancer's culture) and symbolic potential.

A dancer's purpose may be to play with movement itself, to provide an emotional experience, or to conceptualize through movement. Renowned dancer Isadora Duncan is widely reported to have said, "If I could *tell* you what I mean, there would be no point in dancing." Jack Anderson, a dance critic for the *New York Times*, refers to "dance as a form of speaking, and words as a dance of thoughts" (Anderson 1997:B10).

If purpose, intent, cultural influence, aesthetics, and symbolism are integral to dance, then dance is surely more than physicality and emotion. The mind, that is, cognition, is at the helm. As scientist Stephen Jay Gould points out in *Creating the Creators*, humans are "the paragon of neural advance," with the capacity to originate novel structures and functions (1996:43).

Movement is the medium of dance; it originates in ordinary but distinct motor activities. For example, there are movements used to actually wash clothes and movements used in dance to symbolize washing. These motor activities may be culturally specific.

An individual's own creativity and culture influence her or his dance making, performing, and viewing. *Culture* refers to the values, beliefs, norms, and rules shared by a group and learned through communication. Individuals in a group acquire cognitive or mental "maps" that enable them to act appropriately in the group. Individuals usually interpret the dance they make, perform, or view within the confines of the group perspective. Culture affects who dances what, why, how, when, where, and with and for whom, in addition to affecting the role of the dance audience. Moreover, culture shapes the permissible gestures, locomotion, and posture, the different body parts moved in time and space and with energy, and the associated meaning.

A people's basic cultural assumptions and orientations, the proscriptions and prescriptions, as well as the seeds of their destruction or alteration, emerge in the dance, which can serve as a mode of communication. Dance may be a vehicle for purposeful communication or an open channel that could be used in this way. History attests to dance as a means of sending messages of grievance and remedy as dancers rebel against and offer alternatives to the status quo. Effective communication, of course, depends upon the shared knowledge of the dancer and the audience. Skilled dancer expression and sensitive audience perception interplay. Embedded in culture and society, dance reflects, and often influences, social values and beliefs, how people are socially organized, and how they move in other activities.

Abstract, or nonrepresentational, dance, a "play with form," is also part of Western culture. But as Jennifer Dunning, also a dance critic for the *New York Times,* points out, "There has never been a purely abstract, plotless dance. . . . put two human beings on a stage, or even one, and all sorts of narratives suggest themselves" (Dunning 1997a:B1). About "abstract pieces," Alessandra Ferri, one of American Ballet Theatre's most beloved stars, said,

> Even if you are not telling a story, you are playing a character. You are playing yourself. You are bringing something of yourself into the dance. You *are* telling a story. The human body cannot be abstract. No matter what you do . . . you are telling the story of your life in your body. And a dancer's body is extremely expressive. (quoted in Dunning 1997b:B1)

Dance forms of a particular historical time are often a response to previous ones. Our dance contributes to what defines us as a nation, a generation, a gender, a person. As a part of the big picture of what is happening at a particular time and place, what has happened, and what might happen, a dancer does not exist in a vacuum. An African proverb is applicable to the dancer onstage: "It takes an entire village to educate a single child."

THE BODY IN SPACE, IN TIME, AND WITH EFFORT

Students usually begin their dance education by learning the building blocks of dance. The human body moves through space, in time, and with effort, constrained by its anatomical and physiological characteristics. Through dance students learn the following basics:

- ❧ Space has direction, level, amplitude, focus, grouping, and shape.
- ❧ Rhythm has tempo, duration, accent, and meter.
- ❧ Effort, or dynamics, is force or energy, tension, relaxation, and flow.
- ❧ Locomotor means of moving from place to place include a walk, run, leap, hop, jump, skip, slide, and gallop.
- ❧ Gesture, movement that does not carry weight, can be rotation, flexion, extension, and vibration.
- ❧ A phrase movement is a group of sequences that cohere and make a distinctive statement.
- ❧ A movement motif is a portion of a dance that can be presented in different ways, such as fast or slow, with more or less force.

Students gain insight into how these elements of dance combine. They explore such concepts as abstraction, representation, symbolism, imagery, communication, expression, transition, mirroring, style, improvisation, performance, perception, acquisition, call-and-response, solo, duet, and ensemble. Because the body is the instrument of dance, students learn how the body works. They learn the names of body parts, kinesiology, physics, and nutrition.

DANCE INVOLVES THE SENSES AND THE EMOTIONS

Sensory awareness expands our access to the ways of the world, both inner and outer experience. Dance is multisensory: the sight of dancers moving in time and space; the sound of physical movement; the smell of the dancers' physical exertion; the tactile sensation of body parts touching the ground, other body parts, people or props, and the air around the dancers; the proxemic sense of distance between dancers and audience; and the kinesthetic experience (feeling of bodily movement and tension). Audience members may empathize with the dancers' sensory experience.

Feelings and emotions tend to imbue dance. Feeling is a person's physiological response to experiencing a strong stimulus. Emotion is the individual's perception, interpretation, and evaluation of what influences the feeling (Goleman 1995). This process manifests itself in dance. In response to an immediate or recollected stimulus (such as an immediate threat or a remembered pleasurable image), a dancer responds physiologically and makes cognitive inferences about the stimulus. A dancer may try to escape the feeling by creating fantasy dances, or he or she may confront the feeling by creating dances about it.

A powerful source of human motivation, emotion constrains or inspires us as we create dances and relate to one another. Because emotions and their movement expression convey meanings that influence special and everyday activities, we traffic in clues to distinguish different emotions.

Psychologist Rudolf Arnheim thought the beginning dancer learning the "the art of muscle sense" gives up "the safe control of reason and modesty in favor of an indecent yielding to instinct" (1966:261). Dance theorists such as François Delsarte (Shawn 1974), Rudolph Laban (North 1972), and Curt Sachs (1937) asserted that body movement and gesture reveal inner feelings. Modern dance pioneer Mary Wigman and modern dance critic John Martin wanted the audience to view dance not from an intellectual point of view but instead from an emotional perspective. Spectators, Wigman urged, should empathize with the dancer's ecstatic emotional experience. Other anti-intellectual responses to dance appear in old proverbs: "The greater the fool, the better the dancer"; "never was a dancer a good scholar"; and "good dancers have mostly better heels than heads."

Anti-intellectualism also appeared in my study of the performer–audience connection (Hanna 1983). Of four American and four Asian concerts of different kinds of dance, the American modern dance performance had the lowest audience participation in filling out a questionnaire. A spectator said, "I am just *enjoying* this performance, and I don't want to spoil the joy of this by *thinking*." Dance teachers often encourage this attitude by remarking to their students, "Just do it, don't think about it."

In contrast with the view that dance reveals inner feelings, philosopher Susanne Langer (1953, 1957) argued that dance conveys symbolic emotion. Recalling an experienced emotion, the dancer conveys this recollected feeling in performance.

The controversy about whether dancers convey immediate or symbolic feelings revolves around discovering what actually occurs in dancer–audience encounters. Empirically studying dancers, performances, and audiences, I found that earlier unidimensional views of emotion in dance were incorrect (Hanna 1983).Choreographers and performers reported more than one way of expressing emotion through dancing. No one way is more important than another, and more than one manner of expression may occur during a performance. Here are some of the ways that choreographers and performers express emotions through dance:

1. Feeling a particular emotion, the performer may immediately express it through dance.

2. A dancer may recall an emotion from earlier personal experience and use the memory as a stimulus to express the emotion in dance.

3. The dancer may recall emotion and express it symbolically, using the illusion of the emotion rather than its actual presence.

4. Dancing may induce emotion through energetic physical activity or interaction between or among dancers during a performance. Kinesthetic stress, overexertion, and fatigue increase susceptibility to a dancer's altered state of consciousness through, for example, altered brain wave frequencies, adrenalin, and blood–sugar content. Giddiness may occur through high speed or sensory rhythmic stimulation in more than one sensory mode.

5. Audience reaction to an ongoing performance may evoke the performer's emotions, which may or may not be expressed in dance.

6. However the dancer expresses emotion, through immediate or recollected feeling, the dancer attempts to evoke emotion (although not necessarily a specific one) in the audience.

Are emotions expressed in dance universally understood, as commonly thought? No! For example, at a concert by the postmodern dancer Douglas Dunn, spectators offered opposing views on whether or not the dancers conveyed emotion in the dance. Nearly half of the respondents saw no feeling. The other half perceived a wide range of emotions. Fifty-five percent of the audience respondents observed eroticism, a strong emotion. Perceiving this feeling in the intertwining and rolling of the couple on the floor, a male engineer said it made him feel "horny." Another person viewed the dancing as "x-rated." Seeing ecstasy as the dancers were "lying as if spent," a male lawyer felt "excited." Remember that half of the audience reporting their perceptions saw no emotion. Some of the people described the movement style as mechanical, stilted, robotlike, and computerized. "It made me feel like I was watching androids or mechanical mannequins," said one respondent.

Chris Dame

Are emotions expressed in dance universally understood, as commonly thought? No!

At the performances in my study, there were perceptual differences among the audience members in recognizing dancers' emotions and clues to indicate them, which were based on the individual spectator's ethnic group, gender, occupation, and knowledge about dance. For example, East Indians overwhelmingly identified anger, whereas less than a third of the American respondents did the same. The Indians saw anger in the dancers' faces, eyes, and hands. They were better informed about the classical Indian tradition of emphasizing the face and eyes both in gesture and makeup and of articulating the hands in distinct signs and symbols. Moreover, the Indians were more familiar with the mythological stories and personalities of the characters who appeared in the dances they were viewing.

Dance Intelligence

Is the mind (cognition) integral to dance? Is there a mentality of matter? Prior to the last quarter of the 20th century, laypersons, scholars, and dancers considered dance to be merely physical and emotional, as noted earlier. This narrow view of dance, however, is falling by the wayside; educators in the United States have widely espoused psychologist Howard Gardner's concept of multiple intelligences articulated in *Frames of Mind* (1983; see also Gardner 1991, 1992, 1994). Intelligence is more than just one's performance on an IQ test; it is a biopsychological potential that manifests in various ways. Gardner posits seven intelligences (linguistic, musical, logical–mathematical, spatial, bodily–kinesthetic, intrapersonal, and interpersonal) that appear within some kind of symbolic system. Gardner refers to dance as bodily–kinesthetic intelligence, a form of thinking and an ability to solve problems through "control of one's bodily motions" (1983:207). Surgeons, too, exhibit highly developed bodily–kinesthetic intelligence (Gardner 1993:9).

While dancers and their audiences can sense the feel and command of the majestic human body, the intellect tells us how to move and makes sense of feeling. The mind stirs the imagination; it ignites and perceives the dynamics of dance. "The eye hungers to make sense of what lies before it," says David Perkins (1994:8), a researcher in the field of cognition.

We have learned that dance communicates concepts symbolically, that dance is a form of one of the multiple intelligences, that individuals learn in different ways, and that cognition and emotion are intertwined. The sensuous aspects of the aesthetic experience mesh with cerebral processes. Dance is seemingly the most physical and lively of all the arts in expressing, communicating, and manifesting and/or feeling emotions. Children can learn the cognitive aspects of dance, including symbols (see Greenberg 1979; Gardner 1998).

The Director of the Center of Cognitive Studies at Tufts University, Daniel Dennett, author of *Consciousness Explained*, discusses why we are often unaware of the processes involved in dancing and watching dancing: "There's attention, there's the capacity to think thoughts, there's self-monitoring, there's being alert, there's sentience. All of these things come apart in various ways. You can have one without the other" (quoted in Achenbach 1995:C5).

One's knowledge, of course, affects the degree to which one is conscious of dance phenomena. Dancers think about their craft when learning technique. Gradually the body performs increasingly complex movements without mediated instruction from the conscious mind. Dancers rely on what is called "muscle memory." Muscle memory is involved in many everyday activities, such as driving a car or tying a shoelace.

DANCE IS LANGUAGELIKE

Cognition, the process of knowing, is part of intelligence. We know through language, and dance is languagelike (Barko 1977; Goellner and Murphy 1995). Literacy goes beyond verbal and numerical skills. Through physical movement, we can make dances with concepts found in verbal language: words, sentences, phrases, and so on.

Dance requires the same underlying faculty in the brain for conceptualization, creativity, and memory as does verbal language in speaking and writing as well as in the nonverbal American Sign Language. Both dance and verbal language have vocabulary (e.g., steps and gestures in dance). They have grammar (i.e., rules for putting the vocabulary together and how one movement can be justified as following another). And they have semantics (meaning).

Dance, however, assembles these elements in a manner that more often resembles poetry, with its multiple, symbolic, and elusive meanings, than it resembles prose. Martha Graham, who first described dance as emotional expression in the 1930s, later described dance as language, similar to poetry, in the 1980s. She recognized that dance is more than the physical externalization of inner feeling, that it is also a cognitive activity (Graham 1985). Words express in sequential form what is there simultaneously in reality. Dance images often offer density of information and an immediate insight into what is depicted. Dance critic Jennifer Dunning explains, "Dance, like poetry, is an art of metaphor and abstraction, though it whisks by and cannot easily be reread" (1998).

Dance can communicate meaning about form. Choreographer Merce Cunningham, who danced with Martha Graham for a short period, made abstract dances that paralleled 20th-century writers such as Gertrude Stein, James Joyce, and T.S. Eliot. These writers challenged earlier linear and representatoinal ways of writing poetry and prose (Dalva 1988).

Dance critic Anna Kisselgoff describes ballet as being about its own classical lexicon. The classical attributes of ballet are harmony and balance. She further describes ballet as "a codified centuries-old grammar of movement" (1997:B10).

IS DANCE A UNIVERSAL LANGUAGE?

Contrary to conventional wisdom, we now know dance is not a universal "language." Dance is many languages and dialects. Peter Martins, co-director of the New York City Ballet, believes classical ballet and modern dance are the same language with a different dialect (Solway 1988:40). By contrast, classical Indian dance, with its ancient elaborate system of codified gestures, is a different language, at times more similar to prose than poetry.

DANCE KNOWLEDGE AND CREATIVITY

In much linguistic behavior an individual creates sentences and responds to them without being conscious of how he or she is doing so. Similarly, dance processes sometimes operate without a dancer's or spectator's awareness of the vocabulary, grammar, and semantics of a dance idiom. Trained dancers are able to create and perform novel sequences of movement within a particular style. Similarly, educated viewers understand sequences they have never seen before. They can recognize the innovative as well as the familiar. For example, we identify ballet by its codified basic positions; outward rotation of the hip joint; pointed toes; moves and steps with the feet turned sideways and parallel to each other; sustained leg extensions; and distinctive phrases and transitions. However, the Kirov, Bournonville, and Balanchine ballet schools are stylistically, dialectically, distinct.

American modern dancers often develop their own movement vocabularies and points of view. The Martha Graham idiom is recognizable in movements with percussive contractions and re-leases and dramatic stories. In his own choreography, Erick Hawkins (who danced with Martha Graham for many years and was actually married to her for a short time) based his technique and choreography on tensionless, lyrical vocabulary; serenity; harmony in the opposi-tion of resisting and yielding to gravity; and thematic abstraction. Alwin Nikolais created relatively balanced arrangements of human movement, sound, light, and visual and kinetic objects.

An important contrast in dance exists between the choreographer, or improviser within a style, and the dancer. Sometimes they are one and the same. Choreographing set dances and improvising within a style require a knowledge (usually tacit) of rules for matching move-ment with appropriate meanings. These rules are usually left-hemi-sphere brain functions, emphasizing digital, analytical, and sequential processing of information as in language or mathematics. Dance imitation, or dancing someone else's choreography, depends on learn-ing a set pattern, which is generally a right-hemisphere function, involving analogic and spatial abilities. When a dancer goes beyond merely replicating a choreographed dance and interprets, that is, re-creates, it, this process draws upon left-hemisphere functions.

DANCE CONVEYS MEANING

Turning to semantics, or meaning, in dance, here, too, dance can convey meaning that the dancer does not intend. Spectators construe meaning from their own personal and cultural experiences. Because the media of conveying meaning in dance condense a myriad of affectively linked associations, dance has an affective charge. Perhaps this is why dance has long held pride of place in religion, ethnic identity, gender marking, and social stratification. The optical array of danced messages may lead to reinforcing ongoing patterns of social behavior, acquiring new responses, or weakening or strengthening inhibitions over fully elaborated patterns in a person's repertoire. Dance messages may also facilitate performance of previously learned behavior that was unencumbered by restraints.

In the course of analyzing field research notes and films of dances of the Ubakala Igbo people of Nigeria, I realized this: Although tools exist to analyze the physical movements of dance, for example, the notation systems of Laban, Benesh, and Eskhol, no tool existed for probing for meaning in the movements. In response to this need, I have developed a semantic grid to serve as a tool for discovering *and* creating movement. This grid evolved through the efforts of numerous dancers and researchers attempting to make sense of dances in different parts of the world. The grid includes some dimensions of meaning in movement (see figure 1.1). The devices and spheres represent various ways in which dancers embody the imagination.

Dancers create meaning in one or more "boxes" of the grid formed by the intersection of the vertical and horizontal lines separating devices and spheres (Hanna 1979c has a full explication). Seeking meaning in a dance, the observer can impose the grid on the dance as a whole and then zoom in on smaller units of the dance to ask if meaning could be related to one or more of the boxes. For example, looking at the intersection of stylizaton and discursive performance, it is possible that a dancer's stylizaton (device of a prancing horse) would be meaningful in a carnival story (sphere of discursive performance).

Dimensions of Meaning in Dance

Spheres

Devices	Event	Body in action	Whole performance	Discursive performance	Specific movement	Intermesh with other medium	Vehicle for other medium	Presence
Concretization								
Icon								
Stylization								
Metonym								
Metaphor								
Actualization								

Figure 1.1 Semantic grid—a tool for discovering and creating meaning in movement.

Devices for Conveying Meaning in Dance

At least six symbolic devices are used for conveying meaning that dancers may utilize in dance: concretization, icon, stylization, metonym, metaphor, and actualization. I describe these devices next in terms of my work on dance, sex, and gender (Hanna 1988b).

Concretization. Concretization is movement that produces the outward aspect of something. Examples are courtship dances showing potential lovers' flirtation, warrior dances displaying advance and retreat battle tactics, and Nigeria's Ubakala women mimetically cradling an infant in dances celebrating birth.

Icon. The icon represents most properties or formal characteristics of something; icons are responded to as if they actually were what they represent. An icon would be the Haitian dancer who manifests the presence of Ghede, the god of love and death, through a specific dance and whom his fellow Haitians treat with genuine awe and gender-appropriate behavior as if the dancer were actually the god himself.

Stylization. A stylization encompasses arbitrary and conventional gestures or movements, as in the Western ballet *danseur* pointing to his heart as a sign of love for his lady. In Ghana, an Akan dancer says, "I look to God," when he points either his right hand or both hands skyward. "If you bind me with cords," he continues, "I shall break them into pieces." As he states the latter, "he rolls both hands inward and stretches his right arm simultaneously with the last beats of the music" (Nketia 1974:208). Ubakala youth move the pelvic girdle and upper torso vigorously to highlight secondary sex characteristics; women symbolize fertility stylistically with torso undulations and hip shifts to mark a woman's elevated prestige and status with the birth of a child, what the Ubakala consider to be the rebirth of an ancestor.

Metonym. A metonym is a motional conceptualization of one thing representing another, of which it is a part, or with which it is associated in the same frame of reference. An example is a romantic duet representing a more encompassing relationship, such as a marriage. Ubakala dance seems to be a pervasive metonym. As specialized cultural motion, dance is metonymical to the motion of life and the Ubakala ethos of action.

Metaphor. The expression of one thought, experience, or phenomenon in place of another that it resembles is a metaphor, the joining of different domains in often unexpected and creative ways. Illustrative is a fairy tale love story between animals to denote the situation between human lovers. Likewise, contrastive movement patterns for men and women are metaphors for their distinct social roles. The device of metaphor may be the most prevalent form of conveying meaning in dance. Among the Ubakala, dancing to celebrate the birth of a child serves as a metaphor for safe passage to different villages, achieving wealth and prestige, and fruitful parent–child and husband–wife relations. In the past, one obtained protection to visit and trade in villages other than one's own through marriage. Otherwise, strangers were liable to be captured and sold into slavery or buried to accompany a prestigious deceased individual in the journey to the ancestor world.

Actualization.   Actualization is a portrayal of one or several of a dancer's usual roles. This device occurs in performance settings without rigid boundaries between performer and spectator, when a dancer expresses a romantic interest in an audience member who through dance accepts or rejects the dancer. Dance may reflect a performer's individual, group, and national identity.

DANCE DEVICES OPERATE WITHIN SPHERES

The devices for encapsulating meaning in dance seem to operate within one or more of eight spheres: event, body in action, whole pattern of performance, sequence of unfolding movement, specific movement, intermesh of movement with another medium, vehicle for another medium, and presence. These spheres are described next.

Event.   An example of the meaning of dance being in the dance event itself is when people attend a social dance to be seen socially, perhaps as a participant in a fund-raising charity ball or to signal sexual or marital availability and find partners. In the event, the dancing itself is incidental to the social purpose behind it.

Body in Action.   The meaning of dance may be in the sphere of the total human body in action. For example, meaning is found in a woman's or a man's self-presentation.

Whole Pattern of Performance.   The whole pattern of performance, which may emphasize structure, style, feeling, or drama, may be the locus of meaning for participants and observers. Focus is on the interrelation of parts of a dance that give it a distinctiveness, as in a sacred dance.

Discursive Performance.   Meaning may be centered in the sequence of unfolding movement, including who does what to whom and how in dramatic episodes. Narrative ballets like "Sleeping Beauty" and "The Nutcracker" are illustrative.

Specific Movements. Specific movements and how they are performed may be significant, as when a male dancer parodies a woman by dancing en pointe. Like words, some movements have definitions.

Intermesh of Movements With Another Medium. The intermesh of movements with other communication modes, such as song or costume, may be where meaning lies. The dance movement for a masquerade becomes significant when the performer dons the mask.

Dance as a Vehicle for Another Medium. Meaning may be in the sphere of dance as a vehicle for another medium. For example, in Tonga dance serves as a backdrop for a performer's poetry or rap recitation.

Presence. The sphere of meaning may be centered in presence, the emotionality of projected sensuality, raw animality, charisma, or "the magic of dance." Presence is the electrical energy among dancers and audience.

COMMENT ON THE MEANING OF DANCE

The meaning of dance warrants further comment: Dance may be a sign of love, through any of the above devices. However, dance may simply be, for example, love itself, in terms of a performer sensing in physical action the quality of love. Moreover, dance may be an instrument, such as a means to develop love and effect what it signifies. The question of the representation of reality lies in the belief of the viewer or doer (Hanna 1987).

Some members of the dance world argue that abstract contemporary dance movement has no referent beyond itself. Yet the movement may refer to other genres of dance and the historical development of dance. In addition, dance viewers may read meaning into a performance irrespective of choreographer or dancer intention.

DANCE AND OTHER TYPES OF INTELLIGENCE

Not only is dance a form of kinesthetic intelligence, but it also draws upon other kinds of intelligence. For example, the dancer uses musical and spatial intelligences. And linguistic intelligence makes use of kinesthetic intelligence. Vernacular and literary writers, for example, use dance metaphors to illuminate aspects of their work (Hanna 1983). Different dances are associated with different milieux, historical eras, characters, emotions, and life stages. The punch of dance performance in its first flesh-and-blood incarnation carries over to metaphoric transformations. Our frequent use of dance terms and expressions in speech, song, news headlines, and other print media suggests its impact. For example, "he waltzed around the subject";

Dance as a Field of Study

What Is Dance?

Human behavior

Purposeful

Intentionally rhythmical

Culturally influenced

Nonverbal body movements in time, in space, and with effort

Aesthetically valuable

Having symbolic potential

Related Concepts

Motor activity

The senses and emotion

Intelligence

Language

Creativity

Meaning

Approaches in Teaching Dance

Aesthetics (philosophy)

Anthropology

Biomechanics

Business/management

Choreography

Experience

History

Kinesiology

Pedagogy

Physics

"they choreographed the battle." Re-creation of dance as a metaphor in plays, novels, and poetry has a long history. Shakespeare, for example, allows lovers to speak indirectly to one another by using dance as a metaphor for love in "Much Ado About Nothing" (e.g., Beatrice speaks of the "hot and hasty" quality of the jig).

IS DANCE A PERFORMING, LIBERAL, PHYSICAL, OR APPLIED ART?

If dance is a distinct body of knowledge, then what type is it? Controversy rages over the place of dance in education and its form of delivery. Yet dance has multiple possibilities in different combinations. First, dance has intrinsic value, meritorious in itself. It is a performing art, pleasurable as an end, and needing no outside excuse or pretext. It warrants in-depth attention apart from any relationship to other purposes. As a performing art, students may be trained to be competitive in the professional world as performers or in other dance-related careers.

In addition, dance has a context, or ecology, and a history. These facets of dance make it a liberal art, part of the humanities and social and behavioral sciences. For example, dance is located within the domains of psychology and philosophy when individuals learn to critically perceive, respond to, and judge the elements of dance and their connections, and to realize the qualities of dance that contribute to the aesthetic response. The business of dance places dance within the sphere of economics and arts administration and law.

The liberal arts offer general education and intellectual development as opposed to professional or vocational skills. Consequently, dance majors study the anthropology, economics, history, philosophy, and psychology of dance. They explore, for example, what is dance, what are the intentions of dancers, the language of dance, and the meaning and importance of dance to individuals and society. Dance majors are concerned with the historically particular, the unique, and the culturally specific as well as the commonality of all of dance as human behavior.

Dance is corporeal. As such it is a physical art within the science domains of anatomy, biomechanics, health, physiology, and physics. Dance can be experiential and academic at the same time.

Dance also has instrumental values and can be used to accomplish many purposes. Dance expresses and communicates emotions, ideas, values, and beliefs that reinforce or change what is; dance teaches and persuades; dance entertains; dance promotes appreciation of other cultures; and dance teaches students attributes and skills that they can transfer to other aspects of their lives. Thus dance can be an applied art when the intrinsic and utilitarian intertwine. Professional performing artists tend not to accept art as a means to a nonart end. Linkages, however, can produce a whole more powerful than each of its parts.

One potential application is the transfer of ways of learning in dance and what is actually learned to other academic subjects and aspects of life. This topic is explored next.

POTENTIAL TRANSFER OF DANCE LEARNING

The world-famous dancer Rudolf Nureyev recognized the transfer of dance learning to other situations; this transfer is one of the great potentials of dance education. Dance education gives students experiential and other knowledge in dance, enhances learning in other subjects, and can be applied to other areas of life. Nureyev himself not only crossed over into other dance genres but also into other artistic disciplines (theater and film acting). Nureyev explained, "If you know one subject very well, then you have a key to every other subject. If you know one language very well, you know structure, syntax, grammar. With all that, you can quickly assimilate another language" (Lemay 1990:35-36).

EXPLICIT TEACHING TO PROMOTE TRANSFER OF DANCE LEARNING

The transfer of thinking and skills acquired through dance to other contexts, however, is by no means automatic. Rather, teachers need to teach explicitly for the transfer to occur (Perkins and Salomon 1988). They need to help students build relational webs. Here are some general ways for teachers to encourage the transfer of what is learned in dance education to other subjects and situations (see chapter 5 for specifics):

- Make explicit to students the rationale of what you teach.
- Explain to students how they can use the processes, skills, and concepts they master through dance education in other academic subjects, the world of work, and other aspects of life.

The potential of transfer centers on the contrast between meaningful and rote learning. Class instruction, student discovery, apprenticeship, or coaching require students' reflection to gain an awareness that what they did and learned; this creates transfer potential to other settings.

There are two main types of transfer: *Low-road transfer* is the automatic triggering of well-practiced activities in new circumstances that are similar to the original learning context. An example of transfer to dance is opening a dance history book that triggers reading habits acquired elsewhere in English class. An example of transfer from dance is thinking spatially in dance making (such as moving in different directions and at different levels) to enhance understanding geography, organizational hierarchy, information flow, and transportation.

High-road transfer depends on the intentional abstraction of skill or knowledge from one context to a new one. This means reflecting on what is learned and actively making connections between contexts. For example, in forward-reaching high-road transfer, a dance student learning mathematical skills through dance movement and phrasing might anticipate how the design elements of dance, which is three-dimensional, can be used to represent multidimensional problems. An illustration of backward-reaching high-road transfer is a student who, while confronting a mathematics problem, thinks reflectively and searches for relevant knowledge already acquired in earlier dance classes to discover that an understanding of rhythmic patterns learned in dance is applicable to solving a math problem.

Following educational theorist Bloom's taxonomy to help teachers teach new information sequentially (Bloom et al. 1956), Beech's (1997:32) illustrative dance questioning strategies for the cognitive (remembering knowledge, comprehension, application, analysis, synthesis, and evaluation), affective (receiving material, responding, valuing, organization), and psychomotor (perceiving correctly, ready to learn, mastering mechanics of movement) domains can help promote the transfer of learning.

ENCORE

Our current knowledge challenges long-held assumptions about dance. Dance is more than emotional and physical experiential expression. Dance is a mental phenomenon, too. It is nonverbal, languagelike communication. There is no "universal language" of dance. Several distinct (though sometimes overlapping) relationships exist between dance and emotion. Dance is part of culture, with a history and an aesthetic. The various aspects of dance are not at odds.

Knowledge of the complexity of dance can enhance teachers' explanations as they ask students to create dances based on the movement concepts of space, time, and effort; to integrate the formal aspects of dance, emotional concepts, and ideas; to perform dances; and to view dances, critique them, and analyze their place in culture and history. Learning in, about, and through dance has unlimited possibilities for personal growth.

Awareness that dance is more than an important physical and emotional activity makes dance education in the schools more acceptable to many parents and school faculty. Of course, challenges to traditional thinking in the discipline of dance, as with any field, create resistance. Nonetheless, dance is, indeed, a distinct, coherent body of knowledge.

Chapter 2

The Power of Dance Well Taught

Dance is the most immediate and accessible of the arts because it involves your own body. When you learn to move your body on a note of music, it's exciting. You have taken control of your body and by learning to do that, you discover that you can take control of your life.

– Jacques d'Amboise (1989:5)

*D*ance allows humans to express, communicate, and understand ideas and feelings in an engaging manner. The physical body, the senses, feelings, emotions, and mind of the dancer interweave. This complex interrelationship makes dance a unique experience. In dance education at its finest, students feel the magic, or transcendence, of dance.

Dance education, offered in many different formats, has numerous academic- and workplace-related benefits that are not mutually exclusive. An important issue is the outcomes of dance education—they determine the place of dance education in public education. The importance of any outcome of quality dance education, be it professional dance competence or intellectual, emotional, social, or physical development, depends on one's views and needs.

In dance education, as is the case with most educational practices, rigorous empirical research has not been undertaken on cause-and-effect relationships between certain dance education practices and student outcomes. Why? Few resources have been available for research in dance education, and even fewer have been available for systematic assessment. So, we must rely on theory (an integrating scaffold, web, or tapestry), case studies, and practitioner observations. Teachers, administrators, parents, observers, and students themselves have provided testimony on the various benefits of dance education. Research further validating these outcomes is on the agenda.

WHAT ARE SOME POTENTIAL BENEFITS OF DANCE EDUCATION?

In this section I look back through time at varying cultures for examples that illustrate the persistence of some of the outcomes of dance education. Next I draw upon the reports of teachers, administrators, parents, and students. Then I refer to some suggestive research that shows a positive association between students being educated in dance and academic achievement and other measures of school success.

HISTORY REVEALS POTENTIAL OF DANCE EDUCATION

Anthropologists and historians have documented the educative role of dance in numerous cultures (Hanna 1988a-c). The widespread use of dance to perpetuate, modify, and create culture for young and old alike points to the efficacy of dance.

Many African dances—like opera, musicals, and performance art in the West—combine music, movement, costume, song, and message to instruct the populace. Traditionally in Africa exposure to dance begins perhaps as early as life in a dancing mother's womb and continues until death. History attests to a similar use of dance by Christians and Hindus.

In fact, many totalitarian and authoritarian systems control dance because of its significance and potency. Politicians have banned certain dances that could undermine their power. The power of art in people's lives was explained well by actor Ron Silver in the Public Broadcasting Service production of "A Tribute to Vaclav Havel" (March 2, 1990 WNET-13). Silver underscored that Havel was being honored not because he is a president or a playwright but because he has dedicated his life to reminding us of something timeless and universal, "that art matters. . . . that artists speak to people in ways that politicians cannot. . . . that art has the power to define us, to challenge us, and to make us explore the frontiers of human existence."

China has used the European elitist classical ballet to instruct its people about the virtues of the workers. Cuba's African-derived rumba dance of the lower classes is a national symbol of efforts to teach egalitarianism (Christopher 1979; Daniel 1995). India and Mexico also draw upon their respective dances to convey messages to the people.

Interestingly, some writers and advertisers in the United States have recognized the educative potency of dance (Hanna 1983). They use dance metaphors to comment on politics, science, and social relations and dance images to promote their products in print and on television. In one print ad, Bankers Trust Company advertised its philosophy as follows: "Excellence is achieved only through consistency and innovation. And Subtlety." The statement is adjacent to a photograph of "Swan Lake," a classical ballet that has been staged and restaged countless times. With a magical immediacy, and with explicit or symbolic messages, dance conveys values by telling truths, revealing perceptions, and unveiling secrets. Dance meaning may be multilayered like an onion; like verbal language, dance can also lie, obscure, or hide reality.

Dance education also has outcomes for science, as scientist Root-Bernstein explains,

> Various artistic insights have actually preceded and made possible subsequent scientific discoveries. The arts thus can stimulate scientific progress, and we dismiss them at our peril. . . . These skills include the abilities to observe acutely; to think spatially (what does an object look like when I rotate it in my mind?) and kinesthetically (how does it move?); to identify the

essential components of a complex whole; to recognize and invent patterns (the "rules" governing a system); to gain what the Nobelist Barbara McClintock called "a feeling for the organism"—empathy with the objects of study; and to synthesize and communicate the results of one's thinking visually, verbally, or mathematically. (Root-Bernstein 1997:B6)

ANECDOTAL REPORTS

Often anecdotal material is the best evidence we have of the benefits of dance education. Over the past half century, observational and experiential assessments of the benefits of dance education by teachers, administrators, parents, and students include the following:

1. *Dance education aids the development of kinesthetic intelligence.*

2. *Dance education creates opportunities for self-expression and communication within the constraints of the medium of the body.* Dance, used as a mirror of the dancer's being, may help students understand themselves as a whole person and to discover and express their identities, values, and beliefs, whether personal, ethnic, gender-related, communal, or national.

3. *Dance, whether representational, thematic, or abstract, is a repository of civilization that changes through time.* Because cultural data is imploded within dance, dance is a way to define, share, and inscribe our lives and times. Learning set dances and creating new ones are venues to understanding past and present human experiences.

4. *Dance education teaches the values and skills of creativity, problem solving, risk taking, making judgments in the absence of rules, and higher-order thinking skills.* The need for such skills is heard in business discourse on U.S. competitiveness in the world economy. Dance achievement can help students gain the self-esteem and confidence needed to apply themselves in other areas.

5. *Dance provides an opportunity for students to recognize that there are multiple solutions to problems.* Elliot Eisner, professor of education and art at Stanford University, says there is no single correct answer in art. Dancers "can affix their own individuality onto their work in a way that many of the other subjects [such as spelling and computing] do not provide" (quoted in O'Neil 1994:2).

6. *The study of dance fosters an individual's ability to better interpret interpersonal nonverbal communication.* Shortcomings in this arena often lead to difficulties in social relations (Nowicki and Oxenford 1989).

Chris Dame

The study of dance fosters an individual's ability to better interpret nonverbal communication.

7. *Dance education provides a strong base from which to analyze and make informed judgments about corporeal images.* These images permeate our lives through the media and cultural products. Dance education urges students to pay attention to relationships and nuances of time, space, and effort in dance as well as a dance's musical accompaniment, costume, and stage set.

8. *Learning the dances of other cultures helps students to develop an understanding and respect for them.* Students can examine

the unique history, heroes, and elements of different dances and compare them with dances embraced, incorporated, or transformed into a shared culture.

9. *Through stimulating all the senses, dance goes beyond verbal language in engaging dancers and promoting the development of multisensory beings.* What is learned in multisensory ways tends to be remembered longer.

10. *Dance provides options to destructive alternatives in a world that is unpredictable and unsafe for children.* Dance can empower some students who are otherwise disempowered and disenfranchised.

11. *Dance education frequently prepares people for careers in dance and other fields.* These careers can be in dance, dance-related fields, and fields that draw on the skills and knowledge acquired through dance education. For instance, Linda Hamilton became a clinical psychologist after dancing with the New York City Ballet. Michele Simmons became a chiropractor specializing in dance and sports injuries in California following study at the High School of Performing Arts and the Martha Graham School; performance as a lead dancer with such companies as Alvin Ailey, Donald McKayle, and George W. Faison; and appearances in such films as "The Wiz" and the video, "Thriller," where she flanked Michael Jackson. Jacques d'Amboise, former dancer with New York City Ballet, set up the National Dance Institute to work with K-12 students in school, linking dance to the requirements of other disciplines. Ballet dancer Anya Peterson Royce became an anthropologist and senior academic administrator.

12. *Dance enhances an individual's lifelong quality of life.* Personal fulfillment often comes in doing and viewing, whether in vocational settings or avocational pursuits. Early dance education leads to adult participation in dance through continuing to take class in dance or other exercise and attending performances. Dance education helps develop poise for business and community situations and the facility to learn new social dances easily.

13. *Participation in dance benefits our communities economically.* Nonprofit arts organizations, alone, generate more than $36.8 billion of business within their communities, according to a 1994 study conducted by the National Assembly of Local Arts Agencies (now part of Americans for the Arts). The three-year study surveyed 789 arts organizations in 33 communities, excluding New York City (it alone generates $1.3 billion per year), Chicago, and Los Angeles. Spending by local arts organizations produces local, state, and federal revenue. Moreover, the nonprofit arts industry supports about 1.3

How Dance Education
Contributes to Goals 2000

Goal 1: **All children ready to learn**—Dance is a natural means of learning for young children.

Goal 2: **Ninety-percent graduation rate**—Dance provides a route for academic success for some disenfranchised or disempowered students and encourages them to stay in school.

Goal 3: **Competency in core subjects**—Dance, within the arts, is a core subject. In addition, dance enhances learning in other core subjects. Dance instruction and interdisciplinary teaching combine to produce a synergistic effect, each form of teaching and learning reinforcing the other.

Goal 4: **First in the world in math and science**—Dance facilitates learning in these subjects by giving concrete expression and meaning to abstract concepts. The creation of art is what scientists do when they hypothesize and create.

Goal 5: **Adults literate and skilled**—Dance is a medium of education.

Goal 6: **Safe, disciplined, and drug-free schools**—Dance helps students develop self-discipline as they learn technique. Dance performances can connect them to their community in ways that prevent violence and drug use.

Goal 7: **Professional development for educators**—The dance field is striving to offer preservice and in-service training to engage teachers, educate them in dance, and facilitate learning in other areas.

Goal 8: **Increased parental involvement in learning**—Parents can be asked to assist in the production of dance performances in which their children are performing.

---

million jobs in the United States. The bottom line is that public investment in the arts brings back a return several times its value in state, county, and local tax revenues according to the 1996 study of New York City conducted by McKinsey & Company (see Lyman 1997).

14. *Dance education helps students develop physical fitness, appreciation of the body, concern for sound health practices, and effective stress management approaches.* Dance shares many of the health benefits of other athletics.

15. *Dance education contributes to the National Education Goals* (Goals 2000: Educate America Act of 1994 PL 103-227), as noted above.

Research Evidence

Some studies show a positive association between students being educated in dance and academic achievement and other measures of school success. Why? We do not know for certain, but this section offers some possible explanations. First, I look at evaluations of dance programs. Next, I look at studies that evaluate the benefits of the arts as a whole. This research varies in degree of rigor. The case studies presented make no claim to being universal but provide insight and understanding nonetheless.

Benefits of Dance Programs

The ArtsConnection Young Talent Dance Program for New York City Public Schools (see chapter 6) examined the impact of its dance education program on the motivation, academic performance, and personal development of inner-city youth. The evaluation included standardized test scores and other measures (BrooksSchmitz 1990b). Youngsters felt an increased sense of specialness, capability, achievement, and empowerment to make changes in their lives; they acquired self-discipline and new learning strategies; their attendance improved; they exhibited more mature behavior, including caring about others, a sense of responsibility, and an acceptance of deferred gratification; they were willing to work hard and complete tasks; their achievement, as measured by standardized reading and math tests, was equal to or better than that of their peers; and they had a new understanding about the arts and the commitment required for a career in them. It is possible that the tutoring included as part of the program, rather than the arts experience, was responsible for the student gains; or it may have been a combination of the two.

A two-year study of high school students' views of school (Stinson 1991, 1992) showed that students disliked "boring" classes in which teachers talked in a monotone about material the students did not see as being useful in their lives. In contrast, students liked dance classes that actively involved them in exploring ideas and feelings in embodied form and gave them a sense of power and control through creative accomplishment. Dance education may be the elixir for some students' alienation from school.

Heather Fletcher, a ballet student since age five and now at Yale University, became a semi-finalist in the Westinghouse Science Talent Search with her study of the relationship between ballet training and academic performance (Fletcher 1998). Among 100 ballet dancers, between 11 and 17 years, in intensive summer ballet programs, she found that highly motivated dancers work harder and perform better academically than less motivated dancers who devalue hard work and perform less well. To excel at ballet requires high-level concentration, memory, and dedication to achievement. Dance training instills disciplined work habits. Motivation in dance was the best predictor of grade point average.

Frances Rauscher et al. (1997) found a causal connection between piano keyboard music training and preschool children's improved spatial–temporal reasoning abilities. This type of reasoning, necessary for mathematics and science, may also be applicable to dance training. Abstract concepts of interval and proportion were more highly developed in the student piano players, probably because they had learned to manipulate the geometrically divided keyboard to produce a musical scale that was divided in a regular way. The study suggests that "music training . . . produces long-term modifications in underlying neural circuitry . . . in regions not primarily concerned with music" (1997:7). Like piano players, dancers using parts of the body learn to count out rhythms to sound accompaniment; couple that with visual and aural information; and use fine motor coordination, memory, sight reading, or movement analysis to manipulate the body in geometrically divided spatial patterns.

BENEFITS OF ARTS EDUCATION AS A WHOLE

An indicator of the positive impact of arts education courses comes from the National Center for Education Statistics (1995). The grade averages of secondary students who concentrate in the arts (defined as earning more than three credits in any combination of courses in dance, dramatic arts, design, graphic and commercial arts, crafts, fine arts, music, and creative writing) are generally higher than those of the student body as a whole.

The 1987–1997 profiles of college-bound high school seniors compiled by the College Board revealed that students who take arts courses tend to have higher scores on the Scholastic Aptitude Test (SAT) than do those who do not. Furthermore, the more arts courses a student takes, generally speaking, the higher his or her SAT scores. In 1995, students who studied the arts for 4 years scored 59 points higher on the SAT's verbal portion and 44 points higher on the mathematical portion (Boston 1996:8).

A study of effective desegregated schools, using statistical data from 200 southern high schools, found that courses in the arts contributed to desegregation, positive self-esteem, and academic achievement (Crain et al. 1982). More cross-racial interaction occurred in performing and visual arts classes than in other subjects.

Schools with an extra teacher in the arts posted scores for the self-esteem of male students that ranged between 5 and 10 percentage points higher than schools without the extra teacher; students improved academic achievement scores by 14 to 15 points on a scale similar to the SAT.

Learning to Read Through the Arts (LTRTA) began as a remedial program for underachieving youngsters in reading and writing in the second through seventh grades, then expanded to serve K-12 (see chapter 6). As evidenced by standardized test scores, academic achievement for most LTRTA students eliminates their need for special reading services.

In Sampson County, North Carolina, standardized test scores went up two years in a row. The only thing that had changed in the county during those years was the introduction of arts education (Zullinger 1990). St. Augustine School—located in the South Bronx, New York, the poorest congressional district in the nation—faced closure because of underenrollment and bankruptcy. When the school became St. Augustine School of the Arts enrollment soared. Its students, grades K-12, were gaining proficiency in the arts; and, according to principal Thomas Pilecki, 98 percent met New York State academic standards (not including the arts). At the same time, in a public school a few blocks away from St. Augustine School of the Arts, fewer than half of the youngsters from the same neighborhood could read at grade level (Hanna 1991b).

Ashley River Creative Arts Elementary School, in Charleston, South Carolina, is a public arts magnet school for grades K-5. (Magnet schools attract students outside the neighborhood, usually to achieve desegregation.) Ashley River is a model for other schools, including the numerous A+ (arts plus) schools in six states, which apply some practices developed by arts magnet schools to traditional nonmagnet schools. Ashley River students receive daily arts instruction: two 40-minute periods covering in a week visual art, music, dance/movement, and drama/creative writing. A Suzuki string program and ballet classes are also provided. In addition, classroom teachers work in teams to plan interdisciplinary thematic study units. The school serves a lower middle-income, blue-collar neighborhood with a student body that is about 40 percent African-American and 60 percent Caucasian. Students are admitted on a first-come, first-served basis; the waiting list holds over 1,000 names. In just five years, Ashley River became the second highest academically ranked school in the Charleston public school system. Test scores in the sciences, language arts, math, and social studies were consistently 10 to 20 points above local and state averages. Equally important, the students like their school.

There are 27 A+ Schools in North Carolina—one of the largest school improvement efforts in the state. The network received more than $1 million in Goals 2000 funds to support the integration of the arts into the schools. The evaluation is developing baseline data for summative assessment of the program after four years of operation (Wilson et al. 1996).

Sunset Park Elementary School in Wilmington, North Carolina, with 84 percent of its students participating in the free lunch program, followed the Ashley River model in the A+ Schools Program. After one year, student disciplinary actions fell from 130 to 50, suspensions dropped from 70 to 3, and PTA attendance rose from an average of 100 to over 400 parents attending each meeting.

The SPECTRA+ (Schools, Parents, Educators, Children, Teachers Rediscover the Arts) program in the Hamilton and Fairfield school districts in southwestern Ohio places the arts in elementary school curriculum at a level equal in significance to the other academic subjects. One hour of each school day is dedicated to art, music, dance, drama, or media arts for each student. SPECTRA+ students, from 1992 to 1993, showed greater improvement in total reading achievement, vocabulary, and comprehension. They scored higher over the control groups in terms of creative thinking, math comprehension, and reading achievement (Luftig 1994).

The School for Creative and Performing Arts, a public school, grades 4 through 11, in Cincinnati, Ohio, admits students based on interest and audition. In the year 1989–1990, the student body was 46.7 percent African-American, 52.7 percent Caucasian, 0.3 percent Asian American, and 0.4 percent Hispanic; 24 percent received free or reduced lunch. The average daily attendance was 92.9 percent. At the elementary level, the school ranked first in the school district in all three areas of the California Achievement Test. At the secondary level, only one school ranked higher. The American College Testing program scores increased steadily over 5 years from 18.9 in the year 1985–1986 to 21.9 in 1989–1990. In 1995–1996, the statistics were similar.

The Galef Institute's Different Ways of Knowing in the Classroom (DWok) is an education-reform initiative that from 1995 to 1996 included nearly 801,000 students; 3,354 teachers; and 376 schools in seven states. With a multiple intelligences conceptual base, DWok offers students multiple ways to learn (including dance) and to demonstrate what they know. Galef promotes teacher collaboration, professional development, and an arts-infused curriculum. The program integrates the study of social studies and history with reading, writing, math, science, and the arts.

A three-year independent evaluation of 1,000 DWok students, in four school partnerships in diverse pilot settings across the United States, showed that on nationally normed tests, participants made significant strides over nonparticipants (Catterall 1995). DWok participants' achievement in vocabulary, comprehension, and other measures of language arts for each year of participation exceeded the accomplishment of nonparticipants. Sustained participation in DWok reversed patterns of deterioration of children's attitudes about learning and school.

Clearly evidence points to the positive outcomes of dance education. These benefits are realized in a palette of offerings, some of which I discuss next.

WHAT ARE SOME KEY WAYS OF PROVIDING DANCE EDUCATION?

Some students' sole dance education is in private sector dance studios (dance schools). Even students in K-12 schools and colleges that offer dance courses, or even full dance programs, often take studio classes after school, on the weekends, and during school vacations.

Many colleges and universities offer a dance major, which comes in many different forms. Some colleges offer rigorous preprofessional training, others offer dance as part of their physical education courses, dance masters and doctoral programs in dance, and masters and doctoral programs in nondance disciplines (e.g., anthropology, comparative literature, communication, education, history, performance studies, psychology, sociology, women's studies) in which the students can focus specifically on dance (see appendix 3).

Here I present some dance formats that can be considered for dance education in grades K-12 because this seems to be the area that educators know the least about. "Dance" education in K-12 nationwide continually surfaces in multifarious models. "Dance," Jane Bonbright of the National Dance Education Association reports,

> may consist of technique classes, ethnic/cultural dance, choreography, improvisation, the learning of dance history and culture, aesthetics and criticism; or it may be considered cheer leading, line dancing, and drill team. . . . It can be taught in 30 minute slots once every two weeks or in 50-90 minute slots taught weekly or daily. (1995)

Schools are subject to economic and political winds, and education leadership turns over. Sometimes dance education programs are never institutionalized, and longevity may be less than five years.

Consequently, dance education offerings often change. The following sections describe illustrative preprofessional programs, arts magnet schools, arts organizations, dance companies, and other types of programs in dance education at a point in time.

PREPROFESSIONAL TRAINING

Preprofessional training is offered in dance schools with competitive admissions policies (Hanna 1998d). Academic offerings are separate from dance education. Emphasis is on dancing or what is called "studio work."

The private residential and commuter Kirov Academy of Ballet (KAB) of Washington, D.C., founded in 1991, is under the tutelage of Oleg Vinogradov, the artistic director for 20 years at the Kirov Ballet of St. Petersburg. KAB offers the Agrippina Vaganova method of ballet training in the rich Russian tradition of the Kirov Ballet studied by many of the world's most famous dancers, including Rudolf Nureyev, Mikhail Baryshnikov, and Natalia Makarova. The KAB encompasses three levels of preprofessional dance education: a preparatory program for students ages 8 to 11 years who want to develop their skills for professional dance; a preprofessional program for students in academic grades 7 through 12 who study academics and dance in the same facility; and an apprentice program for high school graduates. Students come from many countries.

Forty-five KAB alumni now perform with major dance companies. Two KAB students, Rasta Thomas (see page 9) and Michele Wiles (see page 157), who completed KAB's full 6-year program and joined professional dance companies, reflect KAB quality. Each dancer achieved one of the highest honors in the world of dance at the highly prestigious International Ballet Competition of Varna, Bulgaria, in 1996. For the first time in the competition's 32-year history, American dancers won the gold medals in both the men's and women's junior divisions. In 1998, at age 16, Rasta received special dispensation to compete in the USA International Ballet competition in Jackson, Mississippi, in the senior men's division, and he won the gold medal!

The Ballet Tech organization, under choreographer Eliot Feld's direction, spans a continuum that begins with an introductory program of one to two free classes a week for children of nascent talent in third and fourth grades from public schools all over New York City. Its preprofessional Ballet Tech school (formerly The New Ballet School, Joyner 1996) auditions about 35,000 children each year from 450 public schools in New York City and accepts about 800. Classes, transportation, shoes and leotards are provided to students free of charge. The

New York City Public School of Dance is an on-site academic school for grades 6 to 12. These students make up Kids Dance, a performing troupe. Graduates perform in the Ballet Tech company.

Dance programs in schools of the arts (art-based schools) also have competitive admissions policies. Students take dance courses with an emphasis on studio work and separate academic courses. The High School of Performing Arts, established in Manhattan, New York, in 1948, was the first public secondary school to develop preprofessional training in the performing arts. Duke Ellington School of the Arts, for grades 9 through 12, is a citywide Washington, D.C. public school with an extended school day of 8:30 A.M. to 5 P.M. Admission is by audition or portfolio review. The school received a Blue Ribbon Award in the U.S. Department of Education nationwide competition for school growth and achievement.

Some arts schools are residency programs, such as North Carolina School of the Arts and Interlochen Arts Academy, which include high school- and college-level training. Walnut Hill School, a preprofessional program for grades 8 through 12, is affiliated with the Boston Ballet Institute for Dance Education, which also has programs for other schools.

Arts Magnet Schools

Between 300 and 400 magnet performing arts schools are in existence nationwide. Dance programs in arts magnet schools often forgo entry requirements based on dance talent or competency, such as Ashley River Creative Arts Elementary School mentioned earlier. Interdisciplinary learning may be part of the curriculum.

Jefferson High School has a Performing and Visual Arts Magnet program for full-time or part-time students (those who take their academic courses at their home school). Jefferson High accepts middle-school students for advanced placement and Portland Community College students through a concurrent enrollment system.

Dance programs offer dance and other academic subjects separately and also integrated. Integration is approached in two ways. One is like the approach taken by the Vancouver School of Arts and Academics, Vancouver, Washington, for grades 6 through 12, in which dance is integrated with other arts. Another approach is that taken by the Minnesota Center for Arts Education High School, discussed in chapter 5, in which dance is not only integrated with the other arts but also with other academic subjects.

ARTS ORGANIZATION OFFERINGS

In partnership with schools, educational arts organizations sponsor dance programs in and outside the school. The SPECTRA+ education reform/school renewal four-year pilot program involving all students in the arts on a daily basis is one example mentioned earlier. The Hamilton Fairfield Arts Association, a community-based organization operating the Fitton Center for Creative Arts in Hamilton, Ohio, coordinated the SPECTRA+ program. The Galef Institute, also noted previously, is another example.

The goal of the three-step Lincoln Center Institute for the Arts in Education in New York City is to promote aesthetic education through partnerships with school districts. It tries to develop skills of perception in the transaction between the person and the work of art, rather than the history, traditions, and technical nature of the art form. The spotlight is on "breakthroughs and new beginnings in the kind of wide-awakeness that allows for wonder and unease and questioning and the pursuit of what is not yet" (flyer of the Association of Institutes for Aesthetic Education). Following is a description of the Institute's three-step program.

> ❧ Step 1: Teachers participate in a program at Lincoln Center to explore aesthetic concepts of performed works. Teaching artists direct participatory activities. Teachers view a work, identify and explore its characteristics, view other works of art that have similar characteristics, view the work again, and discuss changed perceptions. Then teachers discuss the design of constructing comparable experiences for their students.

> ❧ Step 2: Teams of teachers in each participating school work with the Institute's teaching artists to plan programs for their students.

> ❧ Step 3: Teachers carry out the education units with the students.

About 300 schools with 2,000 K-12 teachers and administrators in the arts and other subjects in the New York metropolitan area participate in the program. Educators have access to the Heckscher Foundation Resource Center. The Institute model is now being replicated in other cities.

Although the John F. Kennedy Center for the Performing Arts is located in Washington, D.C., its Arts Education Program offers resources for educators nationwide, giving it the mystique of a national model. The education programs for teachers are applicable toward graduate credit through the University of Virginia and toward inservice credit in the District of Columbia, Maryland, and Virginia public school systems. The Kennedy Center's "Community Initiative

in Dance" involves the center, local schools, and New York's renowned Dance Theatre of Harlem. The outreach activity targets area
dance students, teachers, and the public through lecture–demonstrations, workshops, live performance, and training programs in the
District and in Maryland and Virginia suburbs.

Building on local programs for teachers developed over nearly two
decades, the Kennedy Center's Performing Arts Centers and Schools
partnership program has national repercussions. Participants have
come from more than 24 states. An institute brings together partnerships of arts presenting organizations and their neighboring school
systems to create new learning opportunities for teachers and students. Follow-up consultation assists in program development.

Young Audiences, founded in Baltimore in 1950, has become a
national network of 34 chapters in 28 states. The affiliate reinforces
the curriculum of schools in its area with in-school performances
accompanied by curriculum guides and audience participation.

DANCE COMPANY PROGRAMS

Dance companies sponsor dance education programs in partnership
with schools. The Dance Theatre of Harlem's educational outreach
"spreading the wealth" program provides classroom and other instructional services to public school children through the
ArtsConnection program and to homeless children through the program, HELP I, Inc. Arts Exposure introduces thousands of students
from inner-city neighborhoods to dance through 90-minute demonstration performances. This program has been presented in more than
13 cities nationwide.

Alvin Ailey American Dance Theater sends dancers out to public
schools and community centers and invites young people into the
theater for special performances. Ailey's interest in dance-in-educa-
tion programs stemmed from his first exposure to dance when his
junior high school English teacher took his class to see the Ballet
Russe de Monte Carlo. The following year another teacher took his
class to see Katherine Dunham, who was to become an important
inspiration for Ailey's work.

The 1996–1997 Ailey dance education program served over 30,000
public school children in the New York metropolitan areas and
100,000 youth nationally. Artistic Director Judith Jamison encourages young people to "think big . . . take a chance. Reach out. Go
further than you've ever gone before. When you get lost, focus. Believe
that the gift is in you. Accept it. Let your light shine."

Some dance companies offer dance programs in which students participate in the professional company or take classes at the company school. In their spare time, students take academic classes to complete their high school diplomas.

Dance courses or programs within public or private schools may require students to apprentice or intern with a professional arts organization, including the possibility of working for a professional company by helping with fundraising activities, ushering at performances, and so forth.

OTHER SCHOOL INSTRUCTION IN DANCE

Dance activity in studio, recreation department, and community center dance classes outside school may be taken for school physical education credit (Maryland's Montgomery County Public Schools has offered this choice). Dance programs exist for "cluster schools." For example, Fillmore Arts Center serves K-8 public school students each week from five Washington, D.C., public schools in the immediate area.

Dance is offered as part of general education courses in many different ways. Some schools have dance programs that offer dance classes and also dance integrated with classes in other disciplines. Duxbury Park Arts IMPACT Elementary School and Roger Williams Middle School Dance Program (discussed in chapter 5) are two examples. Other schools offer dance activity for all students with variable time and frequency; for example, 20 or 30 minutes every other week or an hour a day for a number of days. A school may have its own dance specialist or several schools may share a dance specialist among them.

Dance education is also offered in integrated arts programs (dance is integrated with other curricula). Dance and other disciplines may focus separately on a common theme (such as the American Revolution) in thematically organized schools. A school may provide dance activities in the school itself or in an arts center that interested students from the regular school classrooms may attend. Dance may also be taught as part of physical education courses (commonly folk and ethnic dance).

Dance courses may be school electives. For example, Highland Park High School, Highland Park, Illinois, offers two or three courses within its fine arts department. The curriculum centers around the discipline-based arts education model.

Dance may be combined with theater as an elective course. Neshaminy High School, Langhorne, Pennsylvania, has an integrated

Karen Daniels

First graders at Fillmore Arts Center.

course taught by a team made up of faculty from fine arts, language arts, and physical education departments as well as a resident dance artist.

Dance activity is provided for youngsters with disabilities. For example, Alvin Ailey American Dance Center has offered a New Visions Dance Program for the blind and visually impaired. The National Dance Institute (discussed in chapter 6) serves youngsters with learning disability or behavioral problems, deaf and hearing-impaired, blind, and visually-impaired youngsters. Initiating programs or responding to needs from schools and teachers, Very Special Arts supports a range of dance programs serving physically challenged youngsters.

Note that dance activities offered by arts organizations or dance companies may be exposure programs, that is, a one-time activity or short series of activities that serve as "enrichment" for other parts of the curriculum. Outreach programs are ongoing activities for interested public school students that are similar to the programs they customarily offer on-site in their own facilities. Integrated programs offer ongoing instruction during the day to entire classes, grades, or schools.

Another point to mention is that creative dance, based on natural movement rather than formal styles such as ballet, predominates in the academic setting K-12. In the higher grades creative dance is called improvisation and choreography. Creativity can be teacher-initiated, where teachers specify how the assignment is to be done, or student-centered, where students are given varying degrees of independence in choosing how to implement the assignment. In performing arts schools, students generally study in depth the technique of different forms of dance, such as ballet, jazz, or tap, in addition to classes in choreography and production. Other areas of study in dance, such as history, criticism, and analysis, are also becoming part of public school dance offerings.

ENCORE

Dance education in the schools is important because it develops kinesthetic intelligence. This intelligence is echoed in other aspects of students' lives. Sometimes dance permits humans to express, communicate, and understand ideas, feelings, and things they could not say or understand in other ways. When students receive dance education, they learn information and ways of thinking that complement other subjects. The outcomes of dance education can contribute to education reform and the achievement of the National Education Goals as students learn in, about, and through dance. Some students, through exposure to dance in their school, will go on to obtain the preprofessional training needed to become successful dancers or to have dance-related careers.

Dance education is offered in a variety of ways. Students may get a brief taste of dance or participate in a sequentially rich program. In the curricular context, dance may be a discrete subject area or a component within another subject such as music, social studies, literature, language, science, and physical education. In some schools, the only dance education available is offered through arts partnerships, education organizations, or dance companies in the community context.

Chapter 3

Survival of Dance Education

Despite the evidence of their importance from every time and culture, the arts do not now have a firm place in American education.

– GORDON CAWELTI,
EDUCATIONAL RESEARCH SERVICE,
AND MILTON GOLDBERG,
NATIONAL ALLIANCE OF BUSINESS (1997:2)

*D*ance is the least taught of the arts. Long the stepchild of school and university education, dance education now has a unique window of opportunity in which to remedy this situation. Dance only requires a teacher and students and a space in which to move; no additional instruments or materials are needed. By contrast, music requires instruments, and visual arts need supplies (David Bach, former Executive Director of the Minnesota Alliance for Arts Education, personal communication, March 18, 1996).

In previous chapters I have discussed what students can learn from dance education in various formats. Current milestones create a place for dance education in the latest education reform movement. Since the early 1990s a surge has taken place in dance education discourse, and collaboration among disciplines and organizations has increased to help bring lode- stars to the fore. Challenging benchmarks create a new context—unimaginable just a few years ago—for the development and expansion of dance education. The critical issue for educators is how to take advantage of this new landscape. Let us begin to address that question by first taking a brief look at the historical context surrounding dance education.

WHAT IS THE FOUNDATION FOR NEW STEPS IN DANCE EDUCATION?

History helps us understand how we got to where we are; it is the springboard for new directions. This section looks back at developments and key figures in culture and education (Faber 1994; Hanna 1987, 1988b, 1989a, b; Kraus et al. 1991).

SETTING THE STAGE

The roots of dance education in the United States are primarily Western in origin. Despite its central role as a social grace in genteel education in 16th-century Europe, dance was not seen as requiring serious use of the mind; dance had only a marginal role in ideological education. Later, the heritage of Puritanism and the Industrial Revolution further diverted attention from the significance of dance.

Why was dance excluded from education? Because its instrument, the body, had to be denied or harnessed in service of a chilling morality and economic productivity. At times disparaged and held in disrepute, dance bears the weight of being prohibited or apologized for. So dance did not merit inclusion in schools, universities, or scholarly research.

By the 20th century, however, the fine arts came to be seen as an area in which imagination and creativity were especially cultured. Yet dance, taught in a few colleges since the early 19th century, was considered merely to be training for physical fitness or social grace.

Beginning about the 1920s, the work of dancers, dance educators, philosophers, and psychologists contributed pivotal theoretical and practical building blocks toward new perspectives on dance. These groups influenced each other at different times, blurring a more concise chronology. Also, the historical progression varied nationwide. More like a web or woven cloth than a linear progression, influences on various streams of dance were uneven, with overlapping impact. Time lagged between a pioneer's work and its dissemination and consequences, and in some places newer work leapfrogged earlier forms of dance education. New developments in dance, however, did not necessarily eliminate previous ones.

One can recognize four key influences in contemporary dance education. First, creative self-expression and modern dance became the dominant focus in school and university dance education. This creativity in dance overshadowed the traditional folk and national dances taught in the schools when folklorists published their collections in the early 20th century. Second, European pioneering thinker–practitioners influenced the climate for dance education. Third, a ground-breaking academic, Margaret Newall H'Doubler, helped make dance respectable in academia. Fourth, scholars in other fields cultivated a milieu in which dance in schools and colleges could begin to flourish.

CREATIVE SELF-EXPRESSION AND PIONEER MODERN DANCERS

At the turn of the century, dancer Isadora Duncan, among others, changed the concept of dance in the Western world. As a performer and educator, she was instrumental in catalyzing the acceptance of dance as self-expression. Creative movement came to be called modern dance at the collegiate level and creative dance in K-12. Modern dance broke with ballet and manifested itself in highly individualistic and diverse artistic expressions.

Ballet, the standard for dance in the United States until Isadora Duncan, had evolved over the past 400 years into a highly disciplined, codified tradition. Ballet has five positions for the body, arms, and legs. Turnout from the body center with the feet pointed out to the sides in an unnatural stance is *de rigueur*. In the air, only pointed toes were acceptable.

In marked contrast with ballet, Duncan danced barefoot and barelegged in a filmy, short Greek tunic. She applied her notion of free, expressive, rhythmic natural movement and use of weight and gravity both in concert and in educating her students. She inspired other dancers, some of whom developed their own dance techniques and styles. Many dance educators were to draw upon these new dance techniques, modifying them to meet changing educational concerns.

Dance, at first taught by physical education teachers, offered girls traditional dance forms to imitate, not stimuli to evoke creative movement of their own. Young children learned dances based on nursery rhymes and folk dance styles. Then what was called "natural dancing" became an aspect of some teacher training in physical education.

The evolving technique, choreography, and performance of innovative professional dancers were especially critical to the evolution of dance education and its infusion into the schools. Early modern dancers were crusaders as they sought to create vital, unique American forms of dance. They often had thriving schools in studios; community centers; and, later, universities. Since the 1930s, these dance centers have served as meccas for dance educators. The pioneering dancers also attracted physical education teachers who wanted to learn the new movement forms. In the 1950s university and other writers began to disseminate pedagogy by translating the nonverbal into the verbal.

Pioneers Ted Shawn and Ruth St. Denis laid the groundwork for multiculturalism. Opening the Denishawn school in 1915, they drew upon Asian dances to develop their modern dance styles. Their inauthentic Indian, Japanese, and Egyptian dances still approximated the dance styles of the non-Western world more closely than had ballet.

Schooled by Denishawn, Martha Graham went on to create a seismic wave with both a distinct repertoire and dance technique. Over her obituary at the age of 96 was this headline: "Choreographer Hailed for Creating a Language" (Safire 1991). Graham gave dance a new vocabulary. Considered the greatest single figure in American modern dance, she, too, drew upon both non-Western and Western traditions. Graham introduced the tension of contracting and releasing the torso, revealing the effort of movement continuously unfolding and radiating from the pelvic central core. She created falls and recoveries and use of movement on the floor, including balancing on bent knees and hinging backward. Graham shaped the body into spirals.

The *New York Times* language specialist, William Safire, raises this question:

Why were *language* and *vocabulary* so often used to describe [Graham's] contributions to dance? In this case, we deal with a lexicon of wordlessness, which seems to be an oxymoron; however, it is apt to treat the art of dance as silent speech.

. . . We have words to bridge the spoken and unspoken languages. One is *expression*. When some bit of dialect we use is met with a blank look, we say, "that's an expression" meaning "That's a figure of speech" to express a meaning; another sense of *expression* is "a suggestion of emotion," as when a face adopts a pained "expression.". . . The point is that language, most often used in the sense of a system of words, also has a sense of "communication by means other than words"—by signs, movements, touches, sounds, tastes . . . and . . . smells. (Safire 1991:16)

Janet Eilber, a former soloist with the Graham company, said that Graham "developed a vocabulary of movements to describe emotion in physical rather than verbal language, using the torque of the body to show the twist and pull of pain or desire" (quoted in Safire 1991:16).

Another Denishawn student, Doris Humphrey, designed a technique based on the rise and fall of human breath. Her theory was that dance movement represents an arc between fall and recovery, the pull of gravity and equilibrium. In 1928, with Charles Weidman, Humphrey began offering intensive summer courses for teachers.

José Limón, Helen Tamiris, Jane Dudley, Sophie Maslow, William Bales, and Agnes de Mille were among those who introduced social themes as dance content and drew upon Americana folklore and rhythms. Erick Hawkins promoted movement that was natural to the human being and probed the roots of dance in numerous cultures. Donald McKayle, Talley Beatty, Alvin Ailey, George Faison, Eleo Pomare, and Pearl Primus are renowned for portraying the life of African-Americans in the United States. Katherine Dunham brought to the American stage and classroom movements of the Caribbean.

The American Dance Festival at Bennington College emerged as the center for modern dance and its offshoots. The festival later moved to Connecticut College and then to Duke University. In the 1960s practitioners of the avant-garde called postmodern dance introduced everyday movement more fully into performance (Banes 1980). Whereas modern dance rebelled against ballet, postmodern dance challenged modern dance. Blasting open traditional concepts of what dance should be, postmodern dance broke down the boundaries between art and life experience, offered a sense of immediacy, and used strategies of monotony and repetition. The projection of emotion or personality, appreciation of physical beauty, virtuosic technique, and a focus on literary ideas or music forms were downplayed.

Social dances permit some of the creative self-expression that has become part of dance education. A recent shift in dance education is toward greater inclusion of world/ethnic forms to reflect the nation's increasing cultural diversity and new social dance forms to attract young people. One finds the dances of Ballet Folklorico being taught in the schools in place of square dancing; country/western dance supplants folk dance. And street, house, and hip hop dance substitute for modern dance (Professor Susan Cashion, Dance Program, Stanford University, reports this scene on the west coast in the 1980s).

EUROPEAN THINKERS—PRACTITIONERS

Several European thinker–practitioners had a great influence on the acceptance of dance as education in the United States. In the 19th century, the German educator Friedrich Froebel founded the concept of kindergarten, promoted physical training for child development, and championed education for girls. In the early 20th century, Emile Jaques-Dalcroze, a Swiss musician, developed a movement approach to music education called Eurythmics (1930:5). He designed exercises that drew upon the spontaneous rhythms of the body that he believed had synchronous mental rhythms. Musical rhythms and phrases were transformed into dance, and the resulting body movements were, in turn, transformed back into music. He trained many dancers, including Mary Wigman, who later became prominent in the German and United States modern dance movement.

François' Delsarte, a French music and acting teacher of the 19th century, influenced Ruth St. Denis, Ted Shawn, and German and central European dancers, and subsequently dance educators in the United States. Delsarte expounded on free, individualistic expression and developed a system of expressive movement and gesture based on how the body moves in response to emotional stimuli. This "aesthetic gymnastics" or "aesthetic calisthenics" as it was called entered physical education. Delsarte's concepts of oppositions, parallelisms, and successions were to appear later in modern dance vocabulary (Kraus et al. 1991:114, 296).

Dancer and educator Rudolf Laban (who was Hungarian born but worked mainly in France, Germany, and England) emerged as a leading movement analyst and a stimulus for dance education (Foster 1977). He and his disciples have created concepts that influence the observation, evaluation, and notation of dance known as Labanotation (Hutchinson 1970) and Effort Shape (Dell 1970). Some dance educators introduce their students to the notation but far more use Labanotation's conceptual framework to teach creative movement and to analyze movement and dance.

Laban (1948) systematized dance education using structure: Students should learn the movements of the body (what moves), space (where the body and its parts move), dynamics (how the body moves, the quality or effort), and the relationship among these as well as with what or whom the body moves. Laban was concerned with the benefits of the creative activity upon the student's personality.

His students, Joan Russell and Marion North, further contributed to dance education in the United States. Applying Laban's theoretical work on movement, Russell defined a course of study for different elementary school age groups. She believed that students should explore the elements of dance; once they have gained familiarity with this material, they can create movements of their own (1965:12).

Marion North considered dance to use archetypal symbols of body movement to express ideas or feelings (1971). Although we know that many symbols are not universal but instead are culturally specific (Hanna 1983; 1988c,d), North was consonant with current knowledge that the term "vocabulary" has similar meaning in both dance and verbal language. She believed in the importance of understanding children through observing their movement patterns (a point elaborated in chapter 7).

DANCE ENTERS THE U.S. ACADEMIC SETTING

Seminal to the development of dance education, Margaret Newall H'Doubler established the first dance major at the University of Wisconsin in 1926. Dance was then part of the physical education department. H'Doubler's background as a biology major helped her couch dance within a scientific framework of the time and give credibility to the study of dance in a university setting (1925). She built on the work of her mentors, Gertrude Colby and Bird Larson at Teachers College, Columbia University, and went on to train several generations of dance teachers.

H'Doubler focused on expressing emotional life through dance, believing that it contributed to full human development. The process of creativity was more significant than the performance, the focal point of her mentors.

Outside of physical education, students' exposure to dance was largely through the "Artists in School" program of the late 1950s. It presented one or more performances in a school auditorium or performance space in the community. Then, in the 1960s, the program sent individual artists or groups into the classroom to conduct workshops for students and offer professional development for teachers. The next decade featured staff and curriculum development teams of dance artists and teachers working together.

Over a 15-year history, with the primary activity occurring in the 1970s, the National Institute of Education-supported Central and Midwestern Regional Education Laboratory (CEMREL) Arts and Humanities Project created and evaluated arts and aesthetic education curriculum units for schools. Reports in the *Yearbook Series on Research in Arts and Education* and various journals indicated that aesthetic education promoted student self-expression, creativity, performance, intuitive and sensory-oriented learning, an understanding of discipline, emotional development, and appreciation (evaluation/criticism).

In the 1980s, dance education at the college level partially splintered off from the shadow of physical education. Dance educators found new homes in departments of dance within schools of fine art or education. Here they could explore more fully the creative and aesthetic aspects of dance. More important, dance began to earn credibility as a serious independent discipline. (See Cashion 1989, Ferdun 1990, and Hilsendager 1989 for different perspectives.)

The break from physical education, however, has had negative consequences for teacher education in dance, according to Sarah Hilsendager, a university professor of dance:

> Dance is unique among arts disciplines in that is both "of" and "distinct from" its historical parent—physical education. Highly specialized conservatory and degree-granting programs have proliferated; most give scant attention to formal teacher preparation. Yet the vast majority of dance being taught in the nation's schools is through physical education. . . . As dance has separated itself further and further from its parent discipline, that discipline has expanded into any number of specializations, leaving the area of preservice preparation in dance far behind. (1992:1-2; see also BrooksSchmitz 1992)

The National Dance Association (NDA) of the American Alliance for Health, Physical Education, Recreation and Dance (AAHPERD) has provided a support network for dance educators and advocacy and has worked on national partnerships forged in arts education toward developing standards and assessments. In 1998 the National Dance Education Association (NDEA) was formed outside the Alliance to continue serving the national agenda of a comprehensive approach to dance as an art form in education (see below, dance as a core subject). NDA has had to refocus its mission on dance education as it relates to the disciplines of health, physical education, and recreation so that it is more congruent with the mission of its AAHPERD umbrella organization. "The whole is truly greater than the sum of its parts," said Jane Bonbright (1998).

OTHER SCHOLARS STIMULATE DANCE EDUCATION IN AMERICA

Early in the 20th century, philosopher John Dewey's work was seminal to the development of dance education in academic settings. Although Dewey did not address dance directly, his prolific writing and teaching at Columbia University, Teachers College, were, nonetheless, pivotal in preparing school systems to offer dance for all children. He believed that children learn by doing, that "action is the test of comprehension," and that physical health promotes mental activity (1915:120). Opposing the static, factory model of education requiring rote learning that had evolved, Dewey proposed child-centered education (1913, 1915).

The field of developmental psychology alerted dance educators to youngsters' changing needs. Gladys Andrews (1954) was one of the first American dance educators to base her teaching on child development and recognition of individual growth differences. Addressing the needs of the whole child, she used creative and expressive aspects of movement to catalyze personal development.

Later, cognitive psychology led to a rethinking of dance and dance education. Jean Piaget (1929, 1955, 1962), biologist, brought to center stage the thought and learning processes of children. He reported that children experience their world concretely. Recognition of children's physical expression of thought and ideas ignited the effort to give children the opportunity to learn in, about, and through dance. It should be noted, however, that critics disagree with Piaget's view that as soon as children can use symbols, concrete experiences become unnecessary for logical thought. His narrow view of imagination is also considered by some to be problematic (e.g., Stinson 1985).

Since the 1950s a significant body of research has developed outside dance that has important implications for dance and dance education. Innovation in the fields of nonverbal communication

(Hinde 1972; Wolfgang 1984), socio- and psycholinguistics (Hymes 1974), semiotics (the study of signs) (Sebeok 1986), therapy (*American Journal of Dance Therapy*), cognition (Dennett 1991; Eisner 1982b; Gardner 1983, 1991, 1998; Gazzaniga 1985; Resnick 1989), and the transfer of learning from one domain to another (Cormier and Hagman 1987; Salomon and Perkins 1989; Singley and Anderson 1989) has led to new understandings of dance.

The work of psychologist Howard Gardner (1983) has gained widespread acceptance in the arts and education communities. Posited as bodily–kinesthetic intelligence and a cognitive skill, dance is a way of knowing as well as something to know about. The cognitive aspect of dance complements the physical educator's concern for motor activity and health and the dancer's and dance educator's concern with technique, style, and dance as an inner experience of emotional expression and growth.

Gardner's colleague, David Perkins (Perkins and Salomon 1988), suggested the potential reverberation of dance education. He argued convincingly for the transferability of knowledge and skills from one subject to another.

Thus far I have discussed the beginnings of dance education in Western dance as social grace and exercise. The evolution from ballet and folk dance to modern dance and creative self-expression had the undergirding of new philosophies and new developments in the social and behavioral sciences. Academics linked knowledge of dance to knowledge in other fields, permitting dance education to grow within a supportive web. Now there is a new web of support involving the education reform movement, which is discussed next.

CAN DANCE EDUCATION DEVELOP WITHIN THE EDUCATION REFORM MOVEMENT?

The current education reform movement in the United States, the "dance ecology" or environment for dance, has generated new demands and different expectations for all students and subjects—including dance—at all grade levels. Education reform efforts ignited in the 1980s by several states provided a national wake-up call (see National Commission on Excellence in Education 1983).

The current clamor for change includes school restructuring, national and state subject-matter standards, emphasis on interdisciplinary curricula, and different modes of assessment. These modes include using the qualitative ways the arts have assessed achievement in contrast to, for example, multiple-choice questions.

Representatives of over 100 national arts, arts education, education, higher education, business, foundation, parent, and government groups have joined forces. Their action plan is to incorporate the arts into ongoing education reform efforts at the state and local levels (National Endowment for the Arts 1995). Dance is certainly an underutilized resource for education reform. Components of the education reform movement that offer dance education an opportunity to flourish are federal legislation recognizing the arts as a core subject, voluntary world-class standards, assessment and teaching needs, business concerns, media and cyberspace growth, and an arts research agenda.

A CORE SUBJECT

Dance, along with music, theater, and the visual arts, is included as a core subject in the bipartisan education reform legislation, the Goals 2000: Educate America Act (1994). This legislation mandates that "All students will leave grades 4, 8, and 12 having demonstrated competence over challenging subject matter, including English, mathematics, science, foreign languages, civics and government, economics, the arts, history, and geography" (p. B3).

School curricula, standards, and resources, however, are determined by state and local districts, including the decision of whether dance is included and how. At least 47 states are participating in the national education goals. The arts are a "new form of educational basics," asserted Ramon Cortines, former Chancellor, Board of Education, New York City Schools (comments at the Getty Center for Education in the Arts National Conference, Hanna 1995a). Dance became eligible, as one of the arts, to receive funding through the 1994 Improving America's Schools Act (U.S. 1994b). Congress has continued to authorize dollars for states and local school districts to develop and implement plans to improve student learning and offer long-term professional development for all teachers.

The target of dance education goes beyond exposure and access for a few to offer a many-faceted sequential curriculum for all students. There are about 113,000 public schools. Dance education has typically been directed toward youngsters talented in dance or students in physical education classes who are taught several social dances. Ballet, for example, has been for the few who could afford lessons at dance studios or schools for the arts. Kaufman (1995) remarks, "Dance educations don't come cheap (intensive daily classes at the preprofessional high school level can run $3,000 for the academic year; in that time a student can wear out seven to ten pairs of toe shoes, at $50 to $60 each)." The budding virtuosos who cannot afford dance classes often receive scholarships. If the goals of the Educate America Act are achieved, dance education will now be for everyone, from the budding virtuoso to the uniquely expressive person, for boys as well as for girls.

Toward Civilization: A Report on Arts Education (the National Endowment for the Arts, 1988) laid the groundwork for dance as a core subject. The report offered a compelling rationale and legitimacy for K-12 Discipline-based Arts Education (DBAE) (Brandt 1987-1988; Dobbs 1998). The arts disciplines included in DBAE involve creating art; understanding its place in culture, society, and history; critically perceiving, responding to and judging the elements of art and their connections (criticism); and realizing the qualities of art that contribute to the aesthetic response (aesthetics).

In DBAE, dance study becomes more than just dancing, becoming physically fit, developing technical skill, expressing oneself, or therapeutically escaping the intellectual demands of other subjects and stressful life experiences. Using this comprehensive approach, dance also provides an understanding of civilization, develops creativity, provides tools of communication, and develops judgment about images. Moreover, revamping instruction in other subjects includes the possible integration of dance.

Sequential K-12 curricula that introduce students to various aspects of dance, its history, culture, criticism, and aesthetics are still rare. Candidly assessing the successes and failures of how art education practice and theory have evolved in six regional consortia, Professor Brent Wilson (1997) offers guidelines for developing a sound DBAE approach.

DBAE, however, is not universally popular within the arts community. Critics fault DBAE as a "cookbook approach" to education, separating parts of a whole. They worry that the experiential creation of art will be slighted. Critics claim, furthermore, that DBAE requires rigorous grading, whereas withholding judgment of a child's art work encourages creativity. Emphasizing the unique, humanizing aspects of art, one critic of DBAE explains, "For children, the valuable contribution of art lies in developing their ability to confront their own thoughts and to organize and put these . . . [together] in a logical manner, all important aspects of the educational process" (Brittain 1988:55).

Although it only proposes options, the new Goals 2000 law still carries weight. It is supported by the possibility of future federal funding, a spur to state and district efforts to include or improve arts education in their schools. All instructional fields compete for scarce resources. Consequently, dance educators need to explain to parents and the community what dance education is and how it benefits youth and community. Without this support, less resources are available to train teachers and students.

If all students are to be served by comprehensive and substantive programs in dance education, of what should their instruction consist? Creating and performing dances is one critical component. Most students, however, will not go on to earn a living in dance. A broad approach to instruction allows students who do not feel good about their own dancing to feel better about seeing dance or writing about it. These students can become enthusiastic and knowledgeable audience members and avocational dancers.

VOLUNTARY WORLD-CLASS NATIONAL STANDARDS

At least 47 states and the District of Columbia have adopted voluntary national standards in the arts as outlined in the Educate America Act. For the first time, dance has voluntary world-class national standards (Howe and Kimball 1994). Indeed, this is the first time American education has had national standards for core subjects. Although the national standards have the stature that the word "national" implies, states and local school districts can choose to use, ignore, or adjust these standards to their curricula and other needs. Education, it is important to keep in mind, is a state responsibility and a local function.

Applying standards with objective measures of student accomplishment in dance education is controversial among dance educators. Some feel the standards were imposed and do not include the input of all kinds of dance educators. There is concern about the quality of those who set the standards. Some dance teachers have their own standards, syllabi, and certification, such as the Royal Academy of Dancing, Dance Masters of America, Cecchetti Society, and Dance Educators of America. Teachers fear that standards might stifle the flexibility and responsiveness upon which good teaching and substantive learning depend.

Standards speak for content, quality, and accountability. Moreover, arts education, and especially dance, must shed its image as a "soft" subject and take its place in the curriculum along with mathematics, science, and languages.

The National Association of Schools of Dance, designated by the Commission on Recognition of Postsecondary Accreditation and the U.S. Department of Education to accredit dance curricula, has had standards for curricula, teaching, facilities, and administration.

The National Dance Education Standards are the result of the most important nationwide effort to define the character of dance education K-12. State education frameworks, standards from other nations, and national forums for comment and testimony have contributed to an emerging consensus. As a guide that informs professionals and the public about an exemplary model of dance education, standards can help to lift the dance discipline into a more prominent position in school life. In addition, standards can be used in teacher and school self-analysis in raising the quality of dance education.

The National Dance Education Standards address the question, what should be taught in dance education? Focuses are movement-centered and audience-centered dance activities for every youngster. The standards spell out an ideal for what every young American should know and be able to do in dance education and an expectation that all students will have similar experiences. Suggested competencies are developmentally appropriate, sequential learning in a cumulative dynamic of exploration. For example, when a student meets a standard, a door is opened; the student can use the "achievement as a point of departure for other destinations" (National Arts Education Association 1994:12). Thus, a child who learns basic movements can then learn to use them to create and vary a movement theme (see appendix 2).

Anticipating the federal legislation to include student accomplishment in arts education, the Consortium of Arts Education Associations wrote the voluntary national standards. The National Dance Education Standards have been endorsed by the U.S. Department of Education and numerous other professional organizations. Publication of the standards for all the arts under one cover gives a sense of parity of esteem and equity among the arts. Using the same format, each discipline addresses content standards for grades 4, 8, and 12. For grades 9 through 12, the standards provide "proficient" and "advanced" achievement levels.

The National Dance Education Standards serve as a template without stifling local creativity. Deborah Brzoska, Visual and Performing Arts Coordinator for the Vancouver, Washington, school system, and Principal of Vancouver School of Arts and Academics, says, "the standards are like buckets—ways of organizing." Many states have frameworks or essential "learnings" for dance education that may link to the voluntary national standards.

Moreover, the National Dance Education Standards are malleable and subject to periodic reconsideration. Reasons for revamping them include new cultural trends, educational advances, problems in implementation, and technological developments.

ASSESSMENT

Accountability is integral to educational reform. Once we have standards for dance education, how do we know how well they are being implemented? How successful is the dance program? How well are students achieving? Here is where assessment enters in to the picture (see Ross 1994). Dance teachers have typically used their own criteria to evaluate student competency in the discipline of dance. The Vancouver School District of Washington has useful scoring guides for dance learning assessment. The arts coordinator for the district gives valuable workshops on their use. More standardized assessment instruments continue to be developed.

The National Assessment Governing Board intends to conduct a comprehensive assessment in 2007. In anticipation of the federally funded National Assessment for Educational Progress (NAEP) and related state NAEPs, the council of Chief State School Officers (CSSO) conducted the National Arts Assessment Consensus Project. It was designed to guide the development of examinations in various arts to assess creating, performing, and responding to the arts. The project conducted workshops, collected over a hundred exemplary assessment prototypes from sites and districts, and field tested assessment exercises.

The NAEP assessment requires a sample of students that reflects a true representation of the country in grades 4, 8, and 12 in public and private schools. Preliminary national assessment in dance education projected for 1997 was postponed, however, due to an insufficient number of dance programs from which to draw a proper sample. NAEP found that *fewer than 4 percent* of the schools taught dance. Two thousand students studying "dance" in course curriculum could not be identified.

Still, assessment sends powerful messages about what matters and creates positive change in the teaching and learning process. The subject of dance tends to gain security in a school because it is being evaluated and therefore taught better. Public schools are reluctant to teach what cannot be tested, both for teachers and students.

Because accountability in education is a key public concern, it is important for dance teachers to document, evaluate, and communicate student learning outcomes. Forms of assessing learning include evaluation of portfolios (collections of work such as performance videotapes and journals that document the learner's progress over time). Performance assessments (evaluating structured tasks using predetermined criteria) are another approach. Other methods are judging student responses to interview queries or questionnaires, teacher examination of learners' self-evaluation, and written exams. A combination of measures provides the fullest assessment of educational processes and outcomes. When assessment is part of the ongoing teaching and learning process, instruction can improve (see Wiggins 1993).

The ArtsConnection Talent Beyond Words project developed over seven years a new assessment instrument to identify ten qualities to look for to discover dance talent in students attending the New York City public schools who have had no prior dance training. In particular, this project is geared toward students who are economically disadvantaged, bilingual, or disabled. These qualities are used in assessment of achievement (see chapter 6; Oreck 1997).

The Chicago Moving Company has members working in two schools, one day a week each, throughout the school year. A multifaceted assessment draws on videotapes, student journals, outside evaluators, and group discussions. Students monitor their own progress and develop self-evaluation skills using videotapes.

Assessment is controversial (see Delandshere and Petrosky 1998). Some critics doubt if assessing dance artistry can be objective. Opponents claim that some things, such as art, sentiment, and expression, cannot be measured. They claim further that pencil and paper work requiring student reflection could make youngsters unduly self-conscious and work against imaginative achievements. Surely, experimentation with assessment can address these concerns.

OPPORTUNITY-TO-LEARN STANDARDS

The environment and resources for dance education (dance curriculum, staffing, equipment and materials, and facilities) make a difference in student achievement. Consequently, practicing teachers and administrators familiar with the day-to-day realities of classrooms and resources, coordinated by the National Dance Association, prepared voluntary opportunity-to-learn (OTL) standards (NAEA 1995). Part of the Goals 2000: Educate America Act, OTL standards refer to

> the sufficiency or quality of the resources, practices, and conditions necessary at each level of the education system (schools, local educational agencies, and states) to provide all students with an opportunity to learn the material in the voluntary national content standards or state content standards. (Conference Report 1994:H1626)

The OTL standards are intended to be an antidote to the potentially negative effects of testing on students, who, through no fault of their own, attend schools that provide an inferior dance education. States must have OTL standards to be eligible to receive Goals 2000 funding.

IMPROVING TEACHING METHODS

Educational reform calls for better ways of teaching students in all academic subjects. One way, an engaging, constructive, and active "hands-on" approach to meet world-class standards effectively, is dance. Cortines (Hanna 1995:57) said that, often the best road or prism to learning other subjects, the arts help kids connect what they learn in different subjects. "Images are at the core of education; [they] evoke modes of thought and activate capacities of mind; they optimize what students can learn," said Elliot Eisner, professor of education and art at Stanford University (quoted in Hanna 1995a). Dance teaching can improve through integration with other arts and academic subjects and the requirement of teaching certification in dance.

INTERDISCIPLINARY LEARNING

Teachers can use dance as a unique vehicle for integrating teaching and learning across curricula (see chapter 5). Dance teachers can work with their colleagues in other arts and other subjects when a concept or theme can be well taught through dance. Connecting dance to life makes teaching and learning dance and other core curricula more compelling. Indeed, more and more nondance teachers are finding

Children learn about architectural structures through dance.

Jim Kirby

that dance education enhances learning when it is integrated with their subjects. Dr. Charles Fowler, long-time author of arts education materials, makes the case that meaning is at the heart of arts education—not art for art's sake but for humanity (1988, 1996). Interdisciplinary learning need not jeopardize the integrity of the dance discipline. Former New York City Ballet principal, Jacques d'Amboise, links his dance instruction to social studies and English.

TEACHER CERTIFICATION IN DANCE

The total number of students, according to demographic projections, will increase dramatically in the 21st century from nearly 52 million enrolled in K-12 in 1996 to an additional three million over the next decade. Obviously this requires an expansion of the teaching force.

Dance is a candidate for inclusion in the new teacher certification of advanced competency program of the National Board for Professional Teaching Standards (NBPTS; see "What Teachers Should Know and Be Able To Do" 1994; National Commission on Teaching and America's Future 1996). Board certification goes beyond minimum accomplishment required by states for licensing a teacher.

Why have this kind of certification? Professions that Americans hold in esteem, such as medicine and law, have examinations that qualify individuals to practice. The arts professions, many believe, can gain esteem by meeting high standards for knowledge and teaching.

BUSINESS CONCERNS

Businesses are strong advocates of educational reform to meet the needs of the workplace. The basic skills of high school seniors have risen slowly, but still half of the high school graduates in the United States cannot read or do math sufficiently to work in a modern auto plant. At the same time, the skills required for a decent job have increased radically (Murnane and Levy 1997).

Increasingly businesses are recognizing that the arts contribute to educational improvement. They help students acquire workplace skills that meet the criteria in the U.S. Department of Labor's report by the Secretary's Commission on Achieving Necessary Skills (or SCANS). In recognition of the value of arts education for business, *Business Week* magazine had a centerfold special called "Educating for the Workplace Through the Arts" (Boston 1996).

Taught as a substantive discipline, dance can develop creativity, discipline, perception, critical thinking, problem solving, communication, and teamwork skills prized by employers today (see Hanna

1994b.) "Arts education taught me more than dancing," said entertainer Ben Vereen. "It helped develop the self-discipline, ability to communicate, and the creativity essential to find opportunities beyond Brooklyn and succeed in my career" (comments, Getty Conference, Hanna 1995a:58). Experience as interns, volunteers, or paid employees in dance organizations can help prepare students for an increasingly unpredictable world of work.

MEDIA AND CYBERSPACE

The education reform movement's emphasis on technology can benefit dance education. The media and the new electronic information superhighway are expanding across the country and the world (Ensman 1995). Having taken advantage of television for their classes, teachers can further harness television to enhance dance education. Television and videotape recordings can bring dance to populations that lack access to live performance. These media offer information on dancers, their lives, and the society in which they live.

The developing information superhighway includes the internet, a huge network of databases and communication resources accessible through a computer. The internet can serve as a vital means for the dissemination of verbal, visual, and auditory information about dance.

ArtsEdge is a continually evolving computer-interactive database funded through a cooperative agreement between the John F. Kennedy Center for the Performing Arts and the National Endowment for the Arts in partnership with the U.S. Department of Education. ArtsEdge is a venue for sharing knowledge and experience among people who make and support the arts. This database carries up-to-date information on promising and effective programs and links people to research libraries and other databases (see appendix 3).

RESEARCH AGENDA

The education reform movement calls for a strong knowledge base in dance education. At the national level, the *Arts Education Research Agenda for the Future* (National Endowment for the Arts 1994) and the recommendations of the Goals 2000 Arts Partnership (1997) provide guidance. Participants in dance education often know the benefits for students. Research will give others legitimating knowledge. It is expected that public and private resources will support further research on dance.

ENCORE

The last art discipline to gain recognition as a degree program and enter the public schools, dance has been a "stepchild" in K-12 and high education (Hanna 1989c). This is notwithstanding the exceptional performing arts, magnet schools, and elementary schools that have offered dance along with other subjects. Given the potential benefits of dance education and the demands of educational reform, might dance be the Cinderella of education?

The legacy of dance and education pioneers can go hand-in-glove with continually updating our knowledge. Surely this will make dance education viable in the 21st century. A newcomer to academe struggling to survive, dance now has a window of opportunity in which to grow and develop in a climate of support. Dance has received a national imprimatur as a core subject in the schools with national standards and assessment, improved teaching methods, and research. Unresolved is whether entrenched curricula will make room for dance education and the question of available resources on a long-term basis. Although obstacles still stand in the way of understanding, interest, and economics, the early and current steps in dance education are sound preparation for dance education in the future.

Chapter 4

Who Should Teach Dance?

[Teachers need] to learn to think critically rather than reverentially about their art and their chosen profession. They need to learn how dance is like other human ventures in that it can contribute to either freedom or oppression, personal meaning or alienation, community or isolation—and how different pedagogies offer them a choice of which of these they will promote.

— Susan Stinson, Professor of Dance,
University of North Carolina at Greensboro (1991:29)

*A*key issue in dance is the question of who should teach it. Who should teach K-12? What competencies are needed? What training develops these competencies?

Cross-cutting the many types of dance education are the background characteristics of the teachers. Teachers may be

- professional dance artists,
- educators with professional dance artist experience,
- educators with dance training,
- educators certified by states to be dance specialists (criteria vary), and
- classroom teachers with minimal or even zero dance training.

Dance artists sometimes ask, can educators without grounding in the rigors of professional dance pass on the essential aspects of this performing art? Can students be educated about dance without direct contact with compelling performances? And dance educators sometimes raise these questions: Are the artists primarily in education to develop an audience and professional dancers? Do they have a steadfast commitment to understanding and helping youngsters? Do they know how to teach different kinds of students at different levels of maturation and ability?

Because there are several models of dance education, competencies for teaching may vary. Focuses differ for the educational model and the professional model (Smith-Autard 1994), for example, the emphasis on process in the former versus product in the latter; development of creativity, imagination, and individuality versus knowledge of dance technique; feelings and subjective experience versus serious professional training; a set of principles versus stylistically defined dance techniques; and student problem solving versus directed teaching. It is possible, however, to combine both the educational and the professional models.

We know dancing and professional work are building blocks for dance education. I will now discuss the role of professional dance in this construction.

HOW DO PROFESSIONAL DANCE COMPANIES PROMOTE DANCE EDUCATION?

Dance education K-12 for all children has not been a priority for the professional dance world. Nor has teaching been considered prestigious. This low status within the professional dance world, however, is slowly improving.

A NEW VISION

Professional dance is awakening to the importance of widespread dance education. This is essential for the vitality and very survival of a performing art that requires dancers and audience members. Several studies have shown that dance attracts its following at an early age—dance education is the best predictor for dance performance attendance. The 1992 Survey of Public Participation in the Arts, conducted by the U.S. Census Bureau, found that "Those who had more arts education were more likely to attend arts performances, access the arts through video media, read more about the arts, and create art" (Bergonzi and Smith 1996:4).

Yet American culture and education have, for the most part, neglected dance education. Today many people in our culturally diverse society do not have the tradition or the resources to send youngsters to private dance schools.

Widening the Circle: Towards a New Vision for Dance Education (Levine 1994) is a National Task Force on Dance Education report. Launched by Dance/USA, a service organization for major professional dance companies, the task force engaged numerous dance artists, administrators, company board members, and presenters of dance to face the challenge of dance education. The report underscored that not all dance artists should be educators; education may be beyond many dance artists' artistic mission and resources.

The professional dance community—as one of many players in dance education—provides numerous paths to dance education. Certainly, academic schools can reap rich rewards as the professional dance world responds to the task force's call for action:

- ⅋ Become educated about the needs of learners (students and teachers).

- ⅋ Recognize the validity of different forms of dance (one aesthetic only values ballet).

- ⅋ Engage in professional development to clarify your own areas of expertise as you acquire current knowledge about dance and the educational terrain (e.g., dance as cognition, interdisciplinary learning, higher-order critical thinking skills, outcome-based education, national standards, performance-based assessment of student learning, cooperative learning, multicultural education).

- ⅋ Build collaborative arrangements with schools.

PERFORMANCE AS EDUCATION

Dance artists' performances are educational. A compelling performance communicates thoughts, feelings, and style, demonstrating how such a performance may galvanize a student's dance study and appreciation. Televised performances broadcast in places without easy access to live performances and in homes where people would not attend them are also educational. Dance organizations have mobilized to document and preserve the legacy of dance in images and words, another educational tool.

ARTISTS IN THE SCHOOLS

Many dance professionals teach. Beyond this, many dance companies also run dance schools. Some professional dancers have developed styles and techniques that are part of the curriculum in academic settings.

Since the 1960s, dance artists have taught in universities, academic schools K-12, and community settings, as well as in private dance schools. The National Task Force on Dance Education found diversity in these education activities.

The routes to dance artists teaching K-12 in the schools are shaped by local circumstances. Typically, they include everything from full dance programs to occasional classes to dance artists collaborating with classroom teachers in dance or other subjects. Professional dancers may encourage all classroom teachers to take advantage of their students seeing a performance by linking it to their particular subject matter lessons (e.g., a performance by Merce Cunningham's company could be linked to the study of music by John Cage; a performance by a local dance improvisation group could be linked to a writing class requiring students to be spontaneous with their ideas and to work collaboratively).

The "Artists in School Program," funded by the National Endowment for the Arts and initiated in 1969, spurred broader dance education. The John D. Rockefeller, 3rd, (JDR 3rd) Fund Arts in Education program (which ran from 1967 to 1979) did the same. It supported professional dancers in strengthening dance education, interdisciplinary teaching and learning, and effective use of community and cultural resources. These short-term programs were often students' first and only exposure to dance; many students were eager for more. In the context of these programs, numerous professional dancers "forged their initial commitment to education" (Levine 1994:13).

The requirement to offer educational programs in exchange for a professional dance tour subsidy, mostly provided by the National

Endowment for the Arts and state and regional arts organizations, abetted education. Dancers interacted with students during their residencies. Because of limited funding, however, teaching depended on the company's, or the individual dancer's, interest and availability, given their rehearsal and performance schedule. In 1987 the National Endowment for the Arts renamed its education program "Arts in Education." This change heralded a shift toward supporting school-based, curriculum-related dance teaching.

Chapter 2 mentioned the Alvin Ailey American Dance Theater and Dance Theatre of Harlem dance education programs. There are many others. For example, at BalletMet, in Columbus, Ohio, Liz Lerman, as an artist-in-residence, developed a dance that explored Sherman's march to the sea (he grew up in the region). Featured as part of the company's Morning at the Ballet Program for grades K-12, public school teachers were invited to tie the performance to history and social studies lessons about the civil war and slavery.

Faculty or guest artists of the Hartford Ballet in Connecticut have offered a master class for public school teachers in a dance that illustrated an interdisciplinary multicultural social studies curriculum for grades four through six. The School of the Hartford Ballet prepared audiotapes and teacher guides, and Hartford Ballet students taught the dance in pairs to the public school students.

The Boston Dance Umbrella, in collaboration with the Lesley College Teacher Training Program, has created a multicultural guide that uses dance to explore issues of diversity and acceptance for Boston's public schools. The multiphase project includes teacher training and workshops with students.

Black Choreographers Moving Toward the 21st Century in California has developed instructional units for teachers. Packets for students and videos for interested schools are part of the approach.

Ballet Hispanico of New York works with public schools to offer teacher orientation sessions, lecture–demonstration performances, instruction in Hispanic dance forms interwoven with historical contexts, and a final student performance. The company's curriculum materials help teachers integrate dance studies into their ongoing classroom activities.

The Pittsburgh Dance Council has worked with the Frick International Studies Academy to bring dancers to the school. The Adopt-a-School program is for grades K-12. Dance artists have offered movement classes for all sixth- and seventh-grade students.

Pacific Northwest Ballet has an in-house full-time education director to help develop and sustain programs in collaboration with schools. The program, "Bravo! Ballet," for example, served about 6,000 fourth and fifth graders and middle school children. Featured were specially designed 50-minute performances at the Opera House, teacher workshops, study resources, in-school residencies, and field trips to the company's studios to take a ballet class and watch student dancers at work.

The Ririe-Woodbury Dance Company in Salt Lake City, Utah, has offered a training institute for public school teachers (elementary general education teachers and secondary school dance specialists), professional artists, dance specialists working in the State Artist in Education Program, graduate dance majors, and university dance faculty. First, the artistic directors and senior members of the company gave a week-long workshop in creative movement prior to the school year. They used their video–workbook program, "Teaching Beginning Dance Improvisation," which has two 1-hour videotapes and an 80-page workbook. A second package for "Teaching Advanced Dance Improvisation" has four videotapes and a workbook. During this phase, a dance artist, school teacher, and university-based artist–educator formed teams. Then mentors worked with public school teachers in their classrooms collaborating in program development and providing feedback. Workshop participants met once a month for weekend workshops to share information. At the final meeting, participants compiled ideas and strategies for improving instruction. The next year, the company offered the same teachers mini-workshops to augment and solidify their knowledge.

The National Task Force on Dance Education noted other dance company curriculum resources. A single dance is the subject of The Pittsburgh Ballet Theatre's handbook on the "Nutcracker." The manual, *Africa & the Americas*, by Art of Black Dance and Music, Inc., explores a specific tradition. Aman Folk Ensemble's *Dance and Music Residency Handbook* gives teachers information about 40 folk dances worldwide, including information on history and practice, teaching suggestions, descriptions of the steps, suggested student activities, and reading and writing exercises.

An excellent example of dance as a means of interdisciplinary learning is the traveling show, "2 Guys Dancing about Math," featuring "Dr. Schaffer and Mr. Stern," who give performances in schools. Karl Schaffer, whose Ph.D. is in mathematics, breaks down common fears about his subject through dance.

Some dance companies, such as Dance Theatre of Harlem and Boston Ballet have hired curriculum experts. They train company teachers to work in schools for grades K-12. David Alexander, advisor to The Boston Ballet Center for Dancer Education, developed an enrichment curriculum for teachers and students in the Boston public schools who attend matinee performances throughout the year. "Informances" are part of the performance. Alexander pulled together enrichment curriculum models with experiences for upper-level ballet students to complement and inform their ballet training. Moving from service provider to academic school partner, dance companies want their artists to understand the goals, concerns, content, and pedagogy of teaching and learning in this academic ecology.

WHO SHOULD TEACH DANCE IN K-12 AND HIGHER EDUCATION?

The determination of who should teach dance in K-12 and higher education is a contentious issue. Ballet traditions have their syllabi, graded curricula, teaching methods, and examination procedures for the progressive education of dancers. Examples include the Cecchetti Method of Classical Ballet Training, the Royal Academy of Dancing, the August Bournonville School, the Vaganova Ballet Academy, and the School of American Ballet. Modern dance, too, has its pedagogies (e.g., the technique taught at the Martha Graham Conservatory of Contemporary Dance). Conceptualizations of dance and practices of dance education are continually evolving. Pioneers, such as Margaret H'Doubler, have laid the groundwork for new knowledge about dance and about education.

COMPETENCIES NEEDED

Institutions of higher education vary in their requirements for dance educators. Dancers with professional training are on faculties. However, the trend is for instructors and professors to have master's and doctoral degrees in dance, performance studies, or theater, in addition to dance training and performance. Dance teachers interested in updating their knowledge of dance, general education, and dance teaching practices must do more than simply echo popular buzzwords for what is being funded. K-12 preservice and in-service teacher training is beginning to confront the education reform demands that will permit dance education to fulfill its potential.

What is the current trend? Teachers are being challenged to create a kind and quality of education in K-12 schools never before attempted for all of our nation's youth. The box below presents The National Board for Professional Teaching Standards' (1994) five core ideals for teacher competency applied in terms of dance.

Five Core Ideals for Teacher Competency in Dance

1. *Show commitment to students and their learning.*

   - ❧ Based dance teaching on observation and knowledge of students' interests, abilities, skills, knowledge, family circumstances, and peer relationships. The experience from the first AileyCamp summer dance program showed the importance of teacher responsiveness to the needs of the students. Dance teachers from dance schools where students take direction without challenging or defying a teacher often have difficulty working with some children from inner-city, low-income areas (Hanna 1990b).

   - ❧ Foster respect for learning and individual cultural, religious, and racial differences. Promote self-esteem, motivation, character, creative expression, and civic responsibility.

2. *Know the subject of dance in all its aspects and how to teach it to students.*

   - ❧ Use knowledge about how students develop and learn (e.g., individual and social learning theory, child and adolescent development theory). Incorporate prevailing theories and knowledge of cognition and intelligence in teaching.

   - ❧ Develop an instructional repertoire to create multiple paths to dance, such as teacher-given knowledge and student discovery.

   - ❧ Teach students how to pose and solve their own problems.

   - ❧ Teach students to think analytically about dance content and how knowledge in dance is created, organized, and linked to other disciplines.

   - ❧ Draw upon curricular resources such as print and audiovisual material as well as other technological tools.

   - ❧ Use dance on video or film as a focus for interdisciplinary instruction; and connect students to other works of art, literature, music, and drama as well as language arts, social studies, science, geography, and math.

   - ❧ Attend performances by local dance companies and visiting groups and soloists that offer workshops and performances with pre- or postconcert discussions with performers, students, and teachers.

   - ❧ Use local public television channels that can broadcast exemplary dance student classroom activity.

» Access electronic networks for curriculum resources, units of study, grant opportunities, and research publications and preservice, institute, and other training, such as that offered at the John F. Kennedy Center for the Performing Arts (Hanna 1994c, 1995a).

3. *Manage and monitor student learning.*

» Articulate goals for students and plan instruction.

» Engage students using multiple instructional methods, such as modeling, lecture, Socratic dialogue, and cooperative learning groups. Good teaching recognizes that some students learn dance movements by watching a demonstration and then emulating it. Other students need to see the movements broken down into segments. Still others need verbal analysis of the movement segments.

» Engage colleagues and other adults to assist in teaching various aspects of dance.

» Motivate student learning and maintain their interest in the face of temporary failure.

» Employ multiple methods to assess student learning and use information about students' work as a guide to evaluating instructional methods.

4. *Think systematically about your teaching and assessment practices and learn from your experiences.*

» Seek others' advice and draw upon education research and scholarship.

» Adapt teaching to new findings, ideas, and theories.

5. *Participate in learning communities.*

» Contribute to the school by collaborating with other school personnel on instructional policy, curriculum development, and staff development (Hanna 1995a, 1996a).

» Question structures and practices; pursue change.

Adapted from the National Board for Professional Teaching Standards (1994).

Encompassing these ideals, renowned dance educators have their own priorities. Robin Collen (1997) explores a series of questions that provide a process for uncovering a personal pedagogy. For example, how do we come to know? What is there to know? Professor Susan Stinson directs the largest teacher preparation program in dance in North Carolina, the only state where the demand for certified dance education teachers in public schools exceeded the supply. Her experience led her to propose the strategy of being aware in order to understand movement from inside the body and look at dance more holistically, rather than as divided into so many separate courses. Public school dance teachers must find ways to integrate dance technique, choreography, history, criticism, and body science because they do not have the luxury of separate courses. (1993c:47)

Stinson emphasizes "paying attention to what one is doing," having sensory awareness, "and then reflecting on what one notices" (1994:1). Teachers "need to learn to problematize what they see, to question 'What if...?', to go beyond the taken-for-granted" (1994:1). Furthermore, Stinson asserts, dance educators must know how to write curriculum. In states where dance is a new subject, first-year teachers often have to write the first curriculum for their district. Advocacy skills are yet another competency needed "to try to ensure that existing dance programs continue to receive funding and support" (1993c:46).

Dance professor Luke Kahlich (1993) calls for teachers to be facilitators, catalysts for change, and caring individuals. Indeed, high school students told Stinson that a relationship with a caring teacher was the most significant factor in their successful learning (1993b:46).

PREPARING TO TEACH

Teacher training for dance education K-12 varies (see Durr 1993). Colleges offer undergraduate dance education courses, graduate programs with dance education courses, and undergraduate and graduate general education courses. The University of Washington has a program designed for retiring dancers that recognizes what 30-year-old and older dance professionals already know (Wiley 1990).

Teachers in all subjects may wish to learn about dance so that they can use it in their classrooms. A Minnesota statewide survey indicated many teachers believed dance and movement should be more widely included in student learning, but few felt qualified to teach it. In response to its survey, the Minnesota Center for Arts Education developed the Dance Education Initiative. This program has a pilot school, regional dance workshops, a dance resource collection, and a K-12 dance curriculum guide. Teachers learn how to integrate dance studies into their ongoing curriculum. The Minnesota Center for Arts Education High School (see chapter 5) is in one sense a laboratory for schools throughout the state. As of 1996, teams of teachers from 26 schools throughout the state have participated in developing pilot dance curriculum units. A curriculum guide outlines the program framework and includes a four-fold model of learning: dance movement vocabulary, dance making, dance sharing, and dance inquiry.

Teachers plan their lessons and assess student progress with a grid system that lists the four categories just mentioned on one axis and "know, do, value, create" on the other.

The Kennedy Center for the Performing Arts in Washington, D.C., has a Professional Development Opportunities for Teachers program based on the premise that all teachers can use the arts in their teaching. More than 1,600 teachers from approximately 14 public school systems and private schools in the metropolitan area attend workshops.

Although the Kennedy Center is in the nation's capital, its education program also offers resources for educators nationwide (Hanna 1994c). Building on local programs for teachers developed over the past 21 years, the Kennedy Center's Performing Arts Centers and Schools partnership program, inaugurated in 1991, has three components: (1) an institute that brings together partnerships of arts presenting organizations and their neighboring school systems to create new learning opportunities for teachers and students, (2) follow-up consultation to assist in program development, and (3) annual meetings to continue with work initiated through the institute.

Professor of dance, Sarah Hilsendager (1992:3), noted four factors that affect the preparation (or lack thereof) of dance specialists:

1. Most states do not require teacher certification (only 16 require certification in dance for teaching K-12). So university degree programs forfeit responsibility for adequate teacher preparation, curriculum development, and implementation.

2. Some dance teachers reject (often without understanding) the DBAE model widely accepted in arts education.

3. "Highly specialized dance training and research programs [are] housed in dance departments totally separate from [and often hostile to] the field of physical education, wherein the majority of dance teaching in public and private education, K-12, resides."

4. The majority of university dance programs emphasize ballet and modern genres, "which are Eurocentric in both content and teaching approach." Dance forms with origins other than in Europe are often slighted, causing future teachers to be unprepared for working with diverse student populations.

Hilsendager elaborates on the conflict between dance housed in dance programs and dance housed in physical education. In many states, she remarks, at the K-12 level, dance educators have no alternative but to work with and, as necessary, through the department of physical education. The dance specialists currently being prepared frequently do not have the necessary course work to qualify for teacher certification in physical education, a credential needed for public school teaching in many states that do not have dance certification. Thus, insufficient numbers of trained dance specialists are qualified for the dance positions within physical education. Because many university physical education and dance education departments choose not to accept responsibility to work together to prepare dance specialists who are employable, thousands of children are not introduced to the magic of dance. Hilsendager seeks to remedy this situation by calling for in-service training to begin immediately to prepare tenured faculty to incorporate new knowledge into previously developed courses.

STATE DEPARTMENT OF EDUCATION CERTIFICATION

State department of education certification attempts to place qualified teachers in the schools. Implicit in this is the desire to raise standards. Teacher certification in dance raises the respectability of dance in education for grades K-12. Education courses outside of dance are usually required (see Schwartz 1992).

Many schools require state certification to teach dance in the schools. Other states may require teachers to be certified in another subject to be able to teach dance. Individuals without any certification may teach under special provisions. For example, with insufficient certified dance educators to fill all positions in North Carolina, a number of teachers obtained positions under so-called "lateral entry" provisions. Namely, teachers with college degrees can teach for up to five years without certification as long as they accumulate at least six credits per year toward the certificate.

Some states have limited certification for dancers who lack academic credentials. In other states, noncertified dancers and dance teachers are permitted to teach dance in the schools. Sometimes these individuals work with classroom teachers to promote dance by itself or to use dance to enhance learning in another subject.

Preservice dance education teacher training toward state certification occurs in colleges and dance studios. Teacher training programs often collaborate with schools; school districts; and other state and community arts, dance, and education organizations.

What is the focus of dance teacher training for state certification? It usually focuses on the following:

* Use of the elements of dance (i.e., body, space, time, and effort)

» Different forms of dance: (and their culture, society, dancers, time, place, purpose)
» Ideational dimensions (i.e., symbols, themes, subject matter)
» Interpretation
» Movement analysis
» Theory and philosophy
» Knowledge of the body
» Participation in dance
» Exposure to live performance
» Exposure to dance through film and video
» Choreography
» Contribution to dance education frameworks and curricula
» Development of lesson plans
» Knowledge of developmental learner ability

University dance programs usually ground their students in performance, choreography, and some understanding of dance history and physical health. Generally neglected is teaching students to understand dance as a medium for integrating learning across elementary, middle, or high school curricula. Dance education faculty often lack familiarity with teaching other arts and other core curricula such as math, English, science, and social studies. Faculty in these disciplines, for the most part, lack training in dance and dance pedagogy. Consequently, preservice and in-service teachers need professional development in effective collaboration for interdisciplinary teaching and learning.

Dance artists have commented on the "fortress mentality," which isolates the university dance department from other departments and the community (Levine 1994:98). In North Carolina schools with site-based management, those dance educators who worked successfully with teachers in other subjects were likely to fare better when there were cutbacks in staff and resources. The dance educators had their colleagues' support.

State certification is considered irrelevant by some dance educators. They point to the certification offered by Dance Masters of America (DMA), a nonprofit international organization of dance teachers certified by test to teach in dance studios, as being equal to state certification. DMA includes as part of its mission statement the elevation of the art of teaching dance. It has been holding a professional Teacher's Training School at Kent State University for one week during the summer since

1976 (Chase 1995); its new home in 1997 is at the University of Buffalo ("Dance Masters Move Forward" 1997). The program provides basic techniques for new and prospective dance teachers, continuing education for working teachers, and "brush-up" classes for former teachers. On completing the program, teachers receive certification of proficiency.

The school now offers a three-year program in intensive training in technique and pedagogy. The curriculum consists of classes in ballet, jazz, tap, acrobatics, gymnastics, modern, pointe, lyrical, preschool movement, body alignment, liturgical dance, anatomy and injuries, choreography, kinesiology, theater dance, hip hop, folk dancing, and audition techniques.

Based on the DMA syllabus, four levels of classes are taught. Grade III-level class includes examinations for certification in dance forms of the third-year student teacher's choice. The examination includes written and oral tests in addition to demonstrated teaching skills with children with intermediate-level dance skills.

CONTINUING EDUCATION

K-12 in-service dance education institutes and workshops are held during the summer, on weekends, or after school. They help dance specialists, classroom teachers (including some who have not been introduced to dance or have little experience in it), and other interested persons to learn about various aspects of dance education. (See Carr and Silverstein 1994 for guidelines on leading an effective workshop for teachers.) Teachers can learn how to translate current dance knowledge into classroom practice and also contribute insights from their own experiences. In-service education is an effective and efficient means with which to try to overcome the neglect of dance education in colleges.

INDEPENDENT DANCE SCHOOLS
AND THE PUBLIC SECTOR

Independent dance schools and dance contractors benefit from recent reforms in education at the national and state levels. These education reforms encourage independent teachers to work out collaborative arrangements with public schools as compatriots rather than competitors to enhance teaching and learning.

Although some dance educators herald the promotion of dance as a core subject in the public schools, some members of the independent dance school community view dance in the schools as being in direct competition. Their fear, however, of losing their livelihood if the public schools offer dance education is unwarranted.

FEAR OF COMPETITION

State government-supported dance education creates a beneficial multiplication effect. In fact, dance in the schools actually increases growth in independent dance schools; student enrollment; dance performances; audiences; patrons; and dance literature, film, and video. Children exposed to dance often continue studying dance as adults. Maryland Youth Ballet in Montgomery County, founded in 1965, now has enrolled about 400 children and 600 adults.

A task force appointed by the Montgomery County Council of Maryland examined the relationship between public and private sector dance class offerings. The county council wanted to resolve complaints by some independent dance schools that government-supported dance classes were hurting their businesses. Appointed representatives from arts organizations in the private sector, county government, consumer groups, businesses, and universities found that with an increase in public-sponsored dance classes, the number of private studios grew and more dance teachers got a start toward owning their own studios. The reason is that dance education in academic schools often attracts otherwise uninterested youngsters and whets young people's appetites for more dance classes, that is, beyond what is offered in academic schools. Also, academic school dance instructors usually take private studio classes or workshops to refresh themselves and get inspiration for their teaching (Hanna 1982b).

Private teachers fear that public school dance teachers will exert their advantage of compulsory education. They will build a following and "steal" those students already attending some other independent dance schools when they open their own schools. Competition among independent dance schools already exists in most communities. Students often hear about other dance instructors from their friends and may choose to study with them. Most public school dance teachers are not interested in the capitalist enterprise of setting up their own school, or they lack the money and motivation to do so. And students rarely like all their teachers. It is true, however, that in some cases public school teachers do encourage talented students to study at independent dance schools where they may also teach.

Another fear of independent dance schools is that students in the public schools will receive poor dance training that is nearly impossible to correct once a child is 12 years old. Public school dance teachers, however, are expected to meet standards that support quality instruction.

Eduardo Patino

Jacques d'Amboise teaches in public schools and studios.

Independent Dance School Opportunities

Dance performers and teachers who lack formal academic training can take advantage of "limited certification." Nationwide there is a dearth of dance educators who can do interdisciplinary work, which presents an opportunity to offer training workshops.

Independent dance schools can include in their brochures and other advertising materials a description of how their programs contribute to the nation's education goals (Hanna 1996a). These schools can provide various kinds of programs to fill gaps if no dance programs exist in K-12 and higher education. In addition, independent dance schools can provide teachers and students with extended opportunities for study and professional training. Independent schools can request that senior students obtain release time from the K-12 schools to take dance classes. (Maryland Youth Ballet has worked out this cooperative arrangement with Montgomery County Public Schools.) Independent dance teachers can get involved at the local school district and state levels to help decide how the goals can best be met (the curricula, standards, and resources).

Independent dance schools can also encourage the K-12 schools to provide students with a list of private dance studios for further study. Periodic continuing education classes for all dance teachers in a local area with instruction by outside experts can promote excellence in dance instruction.

Most independent dance schools focus on only one of the DBAE disciplines, namely, creating dance. They teach the techniques of ballet, jazz, or tap, for example, and their students usually perform a dance, choreographed by the teacher, in an end-of-the-year recital. In modern dance classes, teachers may encourage students to create their own dance phrases or even entire dances. Independent dance schools could introduce an understanding of the dance form they teach in its context of culture, society, and history. They can teach their students how to critique the dance and to understand what qualities of the dance affect the audience. This type of analysis is especially valuable for students who have little or no dance education in their academic schools.

Many K-12 dance programs, colleges, independent dance schools, and other teachers have, of their own accord, always focused on portions of the National Dance Education Standards content. As noted earlier, the independent dance school world has had standards for some time (e.g., those set by Dance Masters of America and the National Association of Schools of Dance). Some dance schools spell out the particular standards that they follow in their teaching and standards they expect their students to achieve. Dance teachers everywhere can examine the National Dance Education Standards and local standards closely and share their views based on everyday experience with dance education with groups working on revamping the standards. Dance teachers can use the national standards to assess and enhance their own programs and students.

Independent dance schools can communicate their views on how best to assess student achievement. They can assess their own students' progress and share their evaluations with students, parents, and public schools in an effort to improve teaching, learning, and assessment.

NATIONAL REGISTRY OF DANCE EDUCATORS

As part of the effort toward improving dance education in both the public and independent sector, the National Registry of Dance Educators grew out of a need to recognize exemplary dance teachers, some of whom do not have academic degrees. The registry has criteria designed to maintain high professional, philosophical, ethical, and safety standards (including the National Standards for Dance Education, Opportunity-to-Learn Standards, and teaching practices). The application process to receive the Registry of Dance Educators (RDE) certification, includes a review of a teacher's education and professional experience and the teacher's pledge to adhere to the criteria and make them known to the public.

ENCORE

Dance education is indeed multipronged. Yet, professional dancers; independent dance school teachers; and academic school teachers, including certified dance specialists, have a common cause: cultivating both dancers and dance audiences. The bottom line is that it behooves independent dance school teachers and other dance organizations to join in the academic education effort for mutual gain to serve our youth.

The dance community is grappling with the issues of the role of professional dance companies in dance education and who should teach dance in academic institutions. At the crux of the matter is the purpose of dance education. Professional dancers provide models and offer unique training to preprofessional students who wish to learn demanding skills. Dance education for student appreciation and general participation has different requirements. Performing artists may be well-grounded in teaching the dance disciplines of choreography; understanding dance in terms of culture, society, and history; critically perceiving, responding to, and judging the elements of dance and their connections; realizing the qualities of dance that contribute to the aesthetic response; and understanding the developmental needs of youngsters. K-12 certified dance teachers can complement their instruction by working with professional dance artists and K-12 certified dance teachers in academia could collaborate on providing all students with a broadened view of dance in its essentials.

Dance educators and educators in other fields need each other, for themselves and for the students they serve. The next chapter elaborates on dance as a means of interdisciplinary learning.

Part II

Learning In, About, and Through Dance

Chapter 5

Teaching Academic, Citizenship, and Workplace Skills Through Dance

AileyCamp showed you how to work with others and help one another. . . . When we started . . . I was ready to give up without even trying. The instructors started encouraging us. After that I never gave up.

— ANDREW (AGE 13)

*I*n dance schools, for the most part, students learn dance technique and how to perform in a recital. The voluntary National Dance Education Standards, however, broaden our ideas about what students should know about dance, including its relation to other domains of knowledge and skill. This chapter discusses why dance can be more than it has been and suggests how. Many dance educators take issue with connecting dance to other subjects because they are concerned about compromising the integrity of dance. The integrity of dance, however, can be strengthened through such connections.

WHY CONNECT DANCE TO OTHER KNOWLEDGE AND SKILLS?

Dance education can prepare students with knowledge and skills applicable to academic and lifelong learning, quality of life, and success in the world of work—especially, if teachers help students make the transfer of learning. Beyond this potential, many businesses and schools believe that schools can bridge the gap between academic focus and career training. The idea is to prepare students for an increasingly unpredictable world of work (O'Harrow, Jr. 1995). Experience with dance (or other arts) organizations as dance interns, volunteers, or paid employees is one venue. Students can share what they learn with their peers and teachers.

In learning dance, students also learn about other subjects through dance. And in learning about another subject through dance, students learn about dance. Linkage to different domains of knowing fuels artistic creativity. The process is reciprocal and synergistic. Dance intelligence is multifaceted (Hanna 1992c).

How do students get into dance in the first place? Frequently, a mere taste whets the appetite. Cases abound of an introductory dance experience inspiring further dance involvement. Lee Williams, a dance teacher at Asheville High School in North Carolina, is among the many who have been successful in introducing students to dance through other subjects with dance productions that illuminate curricular themes. Her success led to mushrooming faculty requests for her to work in history and English classrooms, as well as to give dance classes for the school's athletes. Teachers in nondance disciplines at Asheville became advocates for dance education.

What Can We Teach Through Dance?

» Cognitive development

» Social skills

» Personal development

» Citizenship responsibility

» Aesthetic appreciation

» Business creativity

WHAT ARE SOME TYPES OF DANCE CONNECTIONS?

In the following sections I suggest illustrative ways of promoting cognitive learning through dance, teaching dance as a social art, fostering personal development through dance, developing citizenship responsibility through dance, encouraging aesthetic appreciation through dance, and catalyzing business creativity through dance. The following connections refer mostly to creating dance as in modern dance choreography or improvisation.

PROMOTING COGNITIVE LEARNING THROUGH DANCE

Included in the area of cognitive learning are dance education practices designed to stimulate mental alertness, modeling, sequencing, attention to detail, and memorization skills; to teach an understanding of symbols; to develop critical thinking; to extend reasoning; to foster analysis of images; to organize knowledge; and to promote learning in core curricula.

MENTAL ALERTNESS SKILLS

Dance educators stimulate students' mental alertness skills, such as modeling, sequencing, attention to detail, and memorization by teaching the dance elements of time, space, effort, technique, and choreography (how to make dances). In the AileyCamp program (see next chapter), students discover that success requires concentration on observing, listening to directions, following complicated instructions, and executing specific movements. Students actively learn first one step, then a second step, followed by a combination of steps in a phrase, and then yet another similar combination until they can perform 30 minutes of dance.

Teachers in various programs tell students that a professional dancer masters and remembers a repertory of 20 to 100 dances. This mastery is a dramatic accomplishment of cognitive processing and physical memory.

In Gloria Unti's Performing Arts Workshops, teachers in 28 San Francisco public schools (serving more than 14,000 students) used modeling exercises. Teachers instructed children to watch them perform a movement activity and then asked for volunteers to duplicate the action. Subsequently, teachers asked the students what they had observed and the ways in which the teacher's action was not duplicated by the student volunteers (Kramer 1991).

SYMBOLISM

To foster cognitive development by learning symbols, tools for thinking, teachers help students move from a concrete nonverbal action to its abstract verbal symbol and vice versa. Symbols are intrinsic to verbal language and a range of images in dance and other media. As linguists and psychologists have long reported, a child moves forward, backward, and around before knowing the symbols for these actions, that is, the words, "forward," "backward," and "around." When students create shapes with their bodies in different directions, they experientially comprehend the associated words for the directions. In the Learning to Read through the Arts programs, and in elementary schools throughout North Carolina, the interest-piquing dance movement experience helps students move from doing and looking to conceptualizing (see chapter 6). Creating symbolic dance phrases or complete compositions is the next challenge after students learn basic concepts of movement and dimensions of meaning in dance (see pp. 20-24).

Dance can also be used as a means of teaching students the symbols of geometry. At the Minnesota Center for Arts Education High School, teachers show students how dance movement enlivens abstract symbols in geometry through spatial designs in choreography with points, lines, angles, surfaces, solids, and transformations.

CRITICAL THINKING

Dance educators promote students' critical thinking skills by asking students to reflect and comment on different aspects of dance. Students consider dance instruction; choreography; and the knowledge, reasoning, or problem-solving processes that were involved in selecting and performing dance movements. Such reflection is an essential part of the Minnesota Center for Arts Education High School program.

In the history, criticism, and aesthetic inquiry of dance, teachers ask students to pose questions, test hypotheses, and examine evidence.

Some dance teachers require students to write in their journals descriptive and analytical paragraphs about each project. Video recording helps students to review what was actually performed. Instructors promote student commentary and discussion with peers and teachers to deepen students' thinking abilities.

One teacher gave students this problem to consider (Fratzke 1990:2-3):

> Begin with three dancers moving passively and one dancer in isolated space showing sporadic repeated patterns. Progress to a group of two dancers against the other two dancers showing level change and tempo change. The piece must end with all members of the group in a diagonal using distal movements repeated in canon. The performance must be between four to six minutes.

Eight groups of dancers in this class had eight different and unique problems to solve. Students learned how to define the problem in terms of all its parts. Then each group developed a dancer's statement to define what the group's goals were in performance and how the group would know it had achieved them. The students determined the criteria for choosing movement, music, costumes, and the intent of the performance. Once the criteria were selected, each group used a testing process within each area to make final choices for the piece. Before the rehearsals began, each group prepared a statement of their solution to the problem. Each new piece was performed before the student body. Following the performance, students evaluated their performance orally based on the criteria established by their group. Finally, students drew upon the information recorded in their learning logs and wrote a paper explaining the entire experience. To conclude the process, each group of dance students gave an oral presentation to the class evaluating the process and sharing personal observations about what had happened.

REASONING

To extend reasoning skills (a kind of critical thinking that is expressed verbally as well as visually, kinetically, tactilely, and aurally) educators give students exercises in creating their own dances. These exercises require students to form judgments and bases for action as well as to persuade or dissuade.

Conceptual decision making lies behind the procedure of putting everyday movement into dance to convey thoughts, feelings, or patterns in a visual form. As students experience, understand, and articulate the process of selecting specific elements of dance externally to transform their inner reality by giving expression to it, they broaden and deepen their reasoning ability. A teacher asking for new answers to a problem in making dances prompts the development of these reasoning skills.

IMAGES

Creating images is another means of critical thinking and communicating. Teachers lead students through a process to teach them how to analyze images. An illustrative progression is first the sequential mastery of a specific dance technique (such as ballet, Martha Graham modern, jazz, or tap). Next, students make dances in the style of this technique; dissect the process of choreography; describe the physical dimensions of dance; and, finally, interpret the kinetic images.

In advanced classes, teachers introduce students to methods of movement analysis, such as Laban analysis (Dell 1970; Hutchinson 1970), the most popular movement analysis in the United States. The semantic grid is a useful tool to discover and create meaning in dance (see figure 1.1 on p. 21). The ability to analyze images is essential in this era in which much learning involves television, video games, interactive computer software, and videocassette recordings.

KNOWLEDGE STRUCTURE

To develop a "knowledge structure" (Glaser 1987), or the organization of knowledge, dance teachers direct students to explore the basic elements of dance. Knowledge of how parts of the body can move in time, space, and with effort and embody meaning through content or style forms the structure for learning and understanding different kinds of dance.

INTERDISCIPLINARY LEARNING

Dance instructors often work with the teacher of a particular curriculum to connect dance to other core curricula. To promote learning in social studies (history, geography, government, anthropology, economics, sociology), teachers show by means of discussion, reading, and videotapes the place of dance in history, society, and culture. Without this knowledge, dancers would lack understanding of the dances they learn and whether their own choreography is relevant or irrelevant, innovative or imitative. Aesthetic canons in the United

States recognize innovation, reconstructions, and interpretations of different cultures' dances.

Many subjects, including architecture, are the focus of interdisciplinary learning with dance (Taylor, Vlastos, and Marshall 1991).

In Lincoln County schools in North Carolina, dance teachers fostered learning of geography by asking students to visualize a classroom as a map. Youngsters planned a trip to four cities and danced from one place to another using different kinds of movement for different modes of transportation such as car and rail.

Teachers also use dance to dramatize literature and understand vocabulary. At Duxbury Park Impact School for grades K-5 in Columbus, Ohio, kindergartners listen to Ezra Jack Keats's poem, "A Snowy Day," and then dance pathways through the snow and in the shapes of snowflakes. In the Vancouver, Washington, public schools, dance teachers encourage students K-12 to learn language using movement categories and their elements. First graders enliven words that signify movement through space (for example, *leap*) and those that move in place (*spin*). Knowing the steps and phrases of ballet requires the development of an extensive vocabulary in French and English.

Teachers promote the understanding of mathematical concepts through kinetic visualization of lines, angles, and other shapes, symmetry transformations, and the combination of movements in various measures of time. At Duxbury, fifth graders plotted graphs on the dance floor and choreographed a dance using these points. Students also explored the value of musical notes in relation to their knowledge of fractions (e.g., 3/4 time).

Science learning is another form of knowledge that benefits through creative use of dance. At Duxbury School students explored the molecular structure of water. Drawing inspiration from Augusta Goldin's book, *The Shape of Water*, students created dances about water molecules heating up as they zoom, spin, boomerang, and evaporate.

At Hall-Kent Elementary School fifth graders studied the earth's changing crust as reported in "A Moment of Science," an interactive software program (see Ferguson 1992). The dance instructor looked for movement words for the earth's surface, described in the software as comprising "several jostling, separating, and colliding plates, each about 75 miles thick, which float like ships on a sea of liquid rock." She divided the class into groups representing the earth's core, mantle, and crust and directed students to create a dance sequence using information from a science book.

At Minnesota Center for Arts Education High School, the first level of science explores the physics of dance. Rik Svien (1989:2) reports on the process of "de-exclusifying science" through dance. For example, in a unit on motion, students focus on the contributions of Galileo. The Brecht play, "Galileo Gailei," helps students become aware of Galileo's unique role in the history of science. Students investigate Isaac Newton's laws and note the largely adverse reaction they raised among the antireductionist poets of his time. Next students learn about conservation of momentum and energy, the raw material of theater/dance compositions. They learn enough about rotational mechanics to analyze pirouettes and other dance movements in terms of moments of inertia, torques, and center of gravity (see Laws and Harvey 1994).

The unit progresses with students next examining sound, its wavelength, frequency, amplitude, interference patterns (beats), and so on. Student groups research a selected musical instrument, and they analyze light as a wave phenomenon and color in terms of the modern quantum model of the atom (i.e., photon transmission from "excited" atoms). The effects of mixing different pigments and/or colored light are studied, as well as the physics of lenses and the physiology of the eye. Then students examine Einstein's Special and General Theories of Relativity. They construct "light cones" and space–time graphs and grapple with the modern physicist's view of the very small (quantum mechanics) and the very large (Big Bang cosmology). Students read and write some short fiction stories based on these scientific concepts. Along with traditional problem sets, demonstrations, and lab write-ups, students undertake writing assignments related to dance during each unit.

Dance teachers explain that dance depends on good nutrition, hygiene, exercise, and knowledge of principles of kinesiology and physics. This knowledge contributes to moving correctly, preventing injury, energizing oneself, and releasing tension. Based on research in the health sciences, teachers point out that dance has long recognized healing powers; and many hospitals, clinics, and mental health practitioners use dance as a method of healing (Bernstein 1981; Hanna 1988a, 1995b).

TEACHING DANCE AS A SOCIAL ART

Teaching dance as a social art involves dance education activities intended to develop interpersonal management and teamwork skills, foster the understanding of competition, and promote the appreciation of cultural diversity. I discuss the aspects involved in this domain of learning next.

INTERPERSONAL MANAGEMENT AND TEAMWORK SKILLS

Teachers at the Duke Ellington School of the Arts in Washington, D.C., help students develop interpersonal management and teamwork skills by encouraging students to assume the role of choreographer and make dances for their classmates. For a dance to reach the level of stage performance, time- and people-management and teamwork skills in an effort to achieve a mutual goal are essential. Collaboration is critical among the choreographer, the dancers, and the production crew to perform an ensemble work.

Choreographing a group dance with peers requires cooperation, attentive listening, clear communication of directions and corrections, scheduling of rehearsals, and beginning and ending on time. Teachers foster students' creative collaboration to let ideas spiral and ricochet, as well as to negotiate differing perspectives. Partner or group set dances also require interpersonal harmony.

COMPETITION

To understand the dynamics of competition, classroom exercises at North Carolina School of the Arts include a contest for key roles in a performance. Rasta Thomas, who has won over 100 competitions, described to me how his school experience had prepared him to achieve this goal (Hanna 1997d,e).

> Competitions motivated hard work, especially the two nationals. . . . Competing helps bring out the character inside you. It gives good stage presence. Judges are there to help you, give criticism. Some important people come to you, and they introduce you to others. It's one continuing process.

Dance competitions give students a chance to see and be seen. Competitions also help foster an esprit de corps and generate lifelong friendships and professional associations, sometimes even marriage.

CULTURAL DIVERSITY

To teach appreciation of cultural diversity, teachers expose students to the dances of various cultures. This helps students to broaden their perspectives, reduce prejudices, and celebrate ethnic identity in a positive way. The act of teaching students about different cultures enriches the individual and the society. An assumption is that experiencing similarities and differences with other cultures through the dances helps an individual become more skillful and comfortable interacting with members of diverse groups at work and at play. (See further discussion in chapter 8.)

Community Programs in the Arts (COMPAS) arts education programs place professional artists of diverse cultures in classrooms throughout Minnesota. COMPAS staff work with classroom teachers before and after a residency to develop a continuing relationship between existing school curricula in the arts and other content areas. COMPAS prepares study guides with such information as historical overviews, maps, greetings in indigenous languages, rhythmic charts, and discussion of the role of dance in religion.

FOSTERING PERSONAL DEVELOPMENT

Fostering personal development involves dance education classroom exercises designed to promote values, self-expression, and self-esteem. Education practices also provide a family substitute, supportive sanctuary, and sense of community for youngsters from poorly functioning homes and neighborhoods.

VALUES

Students' sense of values surfaces when educators encourage students to view dances and reflect on the principles they identify in the work (see Hodes 1995). Many aspects of dance are transmitted from

Highland Park High School Fine Arts Department

Students from Highland Park High School in Illinois in a production of "Anything Goes."

one generation to the next. Consequently, dance is a repository of values and a telling imprint of civilization.

Students in the ArtsConnection Young Talent Dance Program take field trips to see professional dance concerts. Afterward they discuss what values they think the performers conveyed and how they affect the individual creator and observer. According to Thomas Pilecki, former principal of St. Augustine School of the Arts, located in the Bronx, teachers promote an awareness of the communication of such values to help students cultivate inner strength with which to withstand outer negative peer group pressures.

Many students in New York City have seen the Urban Bush Women's performances of "I Don't Know But I Been Told." The dance is about struggle in society, the inequality of African-Americans and women, women as sexual stereotypes, the power of women's friendships, and conflict resolution. Students were asked the following: What are some of the values that the choreographer, Jawole Willa Jo Zollar, is concerned with? What in your own life are you reminded of as you look at this? What might the values presented here mean to society? (See *Window on the Work* 1996 for further discussion.)

SELF-EXPRESSION

To promote self-expression and thereby gain insight, educators ask students to communicate feelings, thoughts, and ideas through dance. By projecting their problems in dance, children may work through some difficulties in their lives that impede their success in school. Distancing oneself or holding up a conflict to scrutiny through artistic self-expression allows the dance maker to evaluate the problem and work toward its resolution (see chapter 10, "Dance Education and Stress").

At the AileyCamp dance program, teachers asked youngsters to make dances about their greatest concerns. The students danced about drugs and death in their communities. This opened both nonverbal and verbal communication among the students and teachers about the students' deepest concerns (see chapters 6 and 10).

SELF-ESTEEM

Youngsters can improve their self-esteem through dance by working on acceptance and appreciation of their bodies, feeling the kinesthetic joy of movement, making physical fitness a part of their lives, and feeling a sense of self-empowerment and the satisfaction that comes with achievement. (See Bandura 1997; Baumeister 1996; and Smelser 1989 on misconceptions about self-esteem.) The achievement comes through the mind-body integration of dance—making the body respond to the mind's dictate while being aware of bodily messages, as teachers can point out.

Improved student self-esteem through success in dance studies in the school setting makes school a positive place. The past principal of an arts high school in the Bronx put it simply: Students realize through the arts that "something can happen in places like the South Bronx where people think nothing can happen."

Teachers work toward promoting self-esteem by focusing on the whole person, not just the "dance" student. In addition, teachers try to involve the youngsters' families in assisting with and attending performances and exhibits. Parents' and guardians' praise of their youngsters' achievement further enhances students' self-esteem.

SUPPORTIVE SANCTUARY

To provide a family substitute and supportive sanctuary for youngsters whose home lives are troubled, teachers promote cooperative learning in dance. Teachers and peers fulfill some parental and sibling roles when they work intensively for a long time on a group project such as a performance.

DEVELOPING CITIZENSHIP RESPONSIBILITY

Dance can help prepare students for workplace and community life. Connections between dance education and citizenship develop through dance making and performing practices intended to promote creative problem solving, decision making, and risk taking. Teachers try to promote student understanding of organization, planning, and deferred gratification; to promote their independence; to expose students to dance-related occupations; and to help them understand the business of the dance profession.

PROBLEM SOLVING

To promote creative problem solving, decision making, and risk taking, dance educators ask students to make movement phrases within set parameters. This necessitates putting knowledge to use: choosing how to arrange elements of body, gesture, locomotion, time, space, and energy. Making dances requires this selection process many times over. In addition, it is germane to decide upon a theme, music, sets, props, lighting, and makeup; take initiative; get peers' and teachers' suggestions for new options; and realize that consequences follow from the decisions one has made. Most academic dance education programs include exercises in this kind of creative dance.

PLANNING

Dance educators promote an understanding of organization, planning, and deferred gratification by providing instruction in the acquisition of a dance technique that requires understanding how foundational skills gradually permit more advanced ones and eventually lead to a performance. In ballet, for example, the discomfort of physical exertion, regimentation, and anxiety in learning are often offset by dreams of success onstage. Endurance in dance develops the perseverance to master other domains.

Teachers encourage students' participation in a performance to demonstrate to them that they can take charge of their lives as responsible citizens. Participating in a performance promotes "knowing what one knows, planning ahead, efficiently apportioning one's time and attentional resources, and monitoring and editing one's efforts to solve a problem" (Glaser 1987:89).

INDEPENDENCE

Writers on the economy repeatedly call attention to the need for workers to make independent decisions in the service industry. Dance educators assist in the development of independent adults capable of productively participating in and contributing to society. To make and thus "own" a dance, for example, is a badge of independence. Presenting one's dance to others forces one to recognize something previously unrecognized. It demonstrates to the maker the result of motivation, hard work, perseverance, self-reliance, responsibility, and learning through errors. Such characteristics are likely to transfer to other kinds of work and endeavors.

Choreographing on one's peers displays authority, control, and power. North Carolina teachers Jody Sutliffe (Greensboro) and Noel Grady Smith (Winston-Salem) reported at a statewide staff development training session that student choreography appealed especially to their male students. The display of authority, control, and power are qualities that many male adolescents consider essential markers of their manhood.

CAREERS

Teachers expose students to dance-related occupational options, by suggesting career possibilities in dance in the public, nonprofit, and private sectors. Although the primary goal of dance education K-12 is for youngsters to learn knowledge, skills, and attitudes, it is important to also encourage students to explore careers that they may wish to pursue as adults.

Teachers explain to their students that many dance-related positions, such as manager, publicist, and health-service provider, require the same skills as many nonarts-related positions in the public, nonprofit, and private sectors. The confidence gained through performing is helpful to successful social interaction in the workplace.

Career Opportunities in Dance

- Dancer
- Choreographer
- Teacher
- Ballet master or mistress (the person responsible for setting and controlling a company's daily rehearsal schedule and making other preparations for a performance)
- Jobs in dance-related arts disciplines: musician, composer, artist, actor, script writer, costume designer, light designer, set designer
- Jobs in dance-related administration: stage manager, arts administrator, fund-raiser, publicist, grants manager
- Dance librarian
- Dance writer, editor, critic, anthropologist, historian
- Dance therapist
- Physical therapist
- Dance medicine
- Physical fitness trainer

BUSINESS

Dance education programs offer professional role models to teach students the business of the dance profession by providing full-time, part-time, or master-class instruction from professional dance artists and teacher–artists. St. Augustine School of the Arts is among the institutions that use practicing professional dancers as dance teachers. Dance artists discuss with students the realities of the professional dance world and what it takes to succeed: norms of commitment to a task; practice in pursuit of growth and development; on-the-job skills and attitudes, including such work habits as being on time, being groomed and dressed appropriately, and following the instructions of the choreographer and/

or director (the reality is that sometimes the directing style in the professional dance world is authoritarian). In addition, artists comment on developing coping skills for rejection or injury, networking for jobs and resources, and acquiring artistic humility.

Teachers, primarily in dance academies and arts high schools, discuss such facets in the dance world as the bid for dance talent; discrimination in salary by rank (e.g., from apprentice to principal dancer); union benefits; announcements for requests for proposals; government and private sector grant and contract proposal writing; contract negotiation; working with management; being an independent entrepreneur; and arranging for publicity. Such discussion often takes place during preparations for a public performance. Teachers explain that when a dancer creates a product, the social institutions of presenters and performing arts spaces are involved.

ENCOURAGING AESTHETIC APPRECIATION

Connections between dance and aesthetic appreciation lie in dance education activities designed to enhance perception and develop aesthetic appreciation. (See discussion of Lincoln Center Institute for the Arts in Education, chapter 2.)

ENHANCING PERCEPTION

Teachers enhance the skills of perception by giving students the various kinds of dance observational and participatory experiences described thus far. Teachers help students understand what is perceptually interesting and appealing in their transaction with such dance activities. Students explore different forms of dance communication, subjects, styles, and media. Teachers ask students to ponder the "big questions" of philosophers and art critics about the nature of dance: What are the differences between technique and creativity? How does dance relate to the beauty of nature? How does society value dance?

DEVELOPING BROAD AESTHETIC UNDERSTANDING

Students develop broad perspectives by considering how aesthetic appreciation extends beyond dance. For example, scientists often refer to formulas as "beautiful." They describe successful Cape Kennedy spacecraft lift-offs as beautiful. Scientists' artistic experiences enhance their scientific imagination and creativity, according to Robert Root-Bernstein, MacArthur Prize Fellow, who has completed a study of nearly 150 scientific biographies. He found that almost all great scientists and inventors are also active in the arts (cited in Zweig 1986).

Catalyzing Business Creativity

Several companies have asked artists to unleash employees' latent creativity to help find fresh solutions to old problems. The artists sometimes create the kind of exercises teachers give to students in dance education. For example, the General Electric Company's retraining program, WorkOut (to get mundane work out of the system), begins with military marches and calisthenics. The leader tells employees, "'You've just demonstrated what the work environment of the 1950s, 60s, and 70s, with their five-year plans and formal hierarchies, were like." Next a dancer leads employees through 10 minutes of aerobics to music. At this point, the leader likens aerobics' "energetic but disciplined approach to the heady buying, selling, and restructuring of the 80s." Then the leader explains how dancers strive for teamwork, self-expression, and skill development as the group experiences 10 minutes of freestyle modern dance. The leader likens this experience to the current business interest in worker empowerment, creativity, and continual improvement of skills (Deutsch 1991).

How Can Dance Be a Discipline and Be Interdisciplinary?

This section describes two different schools that offer suggestive approaches on how to offer dance as a sequential discipline unto itself and also as an aid to understanding other subject matter. One is a high school. The other is a middle school.

Minnesota Center for Arts Education High School

The Minnesota Center for Arts Education High School (ART HI), an innovative integrated arts and academics residential public high school for students throughout the state is an exemplar of dance education reform efforts. The state legislature created the school in 1989 in Golden Valley (a suburb of Minneapolis) after five years of planning. ART HI provides enhanced educational opportunities in the arts—dance, literary arts, media arts, music, theater, visual arts, and interdisciplinary studies—for 11th- and 12th-grade students who are highly motivated and committed to the arts. The school has five major goals: the acquisition of skills in learning, thinking, and problem solving; creativity and innovation; communication; organization, planning, and leadership; and social relations, economics, and self-regulation—all to be accomplished without losing the integrity of the individual art form being studied.

Admission requires an essay on what students hope to gain from and bring to the experience. Dance students complete a dance-oriented written assignment. They bring examples of dance to the review and perform a spontaneous group activity with other auditionees. Then they have an interview designed to assess their proficiency, motivation, commitment, creativity, imagination, and ability to acquire skills quickly. Evaluators seek students who have the greatest capacity for growth, irrespective of their prior training in dance. The school looks at students' transcripts to identify patterns that might indicate an attitudinal problem that would make their placement in the school inadvisable. The range of academic achievement in the student body ranges from National Merit finalists to students who have previously been considered low achievers.

By law the school must enroll students on an equal basis from each of the state's eight congressional districts. This results in a diverse student population. Students who do not reside within a reasonable commuting distance can live in a campus dormitory.

ART HI receives support for two reasons. First, it is an arts school that addresses the needs of an underserved population. And, second, the school has incorporated changes the legislature believes are needed in education. For example, ART HI incorporates the following:

- A learner outcome-based curriculum organized around what students need to know, to do, to value, and to create
- Individually based student learner plans, developed by the student in cooperation with faculty, which state learner goals, expected outcomes, and criteria to show mastery of learning experiences (the plans are reviewed every 6 to 8 weeks)
- Eight-hour days
- Separate blocks of instructional time that are arts specific, general studies specific, and interdisciplinary
- Individual instruction, small-group guided instruction, and whole-group instruction
- A continuous learning concept, allowing students to move beyond traditional course boundaries
- An expansion of teachers' roles in designing instructional experiences and advising students

✵ Flexible use of staff time and abilities

✵ Participation by students and staff from other school districts

Students work cooperatively both in and out of class. Furthermore, each student is required annually to complete a community service project that utilizes the student's acquired knowledge in both dance and general studies.

ART HI emphasizes both dance and the usual academic studies. In addition, interdisciplinary studies emphasize relationships among the arts and connect the arts and other subjects. "We especially wanted to show how art and academics connect to each other," said Barbara Martin, Deputy Director (quoted in *Articulars* 1989:1).

The Minnesota legislature mandated the dissemination of the innovative curriculum being piloted by ART HI: Indeed, the Minnesota Center for Arts Education identifies and works with at least one school district in each congressional district with the interest to offer magnet arts programs using the curriculum.

Descriptive "formative" research, which appraises a program as it takes place in order to improve its functioning, provides information to assist ART HI to modify its program over time.

ROGER WILLIAMS MIDDLE SCHOOL DANCE PROGRAM

The Roger Williams Middle School, located in Providence, Rhode Island, has a sequential dance curriculum for grades six through eight. It emphasizes the National Dance Education Standards with classes in a variety of dance styles, dance history, kinesiology for the dancer, the basics of choreography, business skills for the dancer, dance criticism, stagecraft, and even research methods. Students work on projects that integrate dance with other art forms and academic subjects. Classes in stage combat, tumbling, and pas de deux have boosted the number of boys participating in the program to 150.

This dance program for middle school students is far richer than many university dance programs! Susan McGreevy-Nichols founded the program in 1974. Originally an after-school club with only 12 students, the program grew to more than 400 students out of a school population of 900 by 1996. Three full-time and seven part-time teachers make up the dance faculty.

The sixth graders participate in the statewide "Chance to Dance" program developed by Dance Alliance, Inc., and the Rhode Island State Council for the Arts. This program prepares students for the

Susan McGreevy-Nichols

Students at Roger Williams Middle School in Providence, Rhode Island.

following grades' more intense dance study and the ability to perform in a school concert. The students develop physical skills, expand movement concepts, manipulate dance phrases and create new ones, perform dances that demonstrate learning in other subjects, and evaluate their own and others' work.

Seventh graders begin to learn dance styles such as ballet, jazz, and modern. They learn the basics of costume design, perform in two major concerts, and attend dance concerts locally. The students learn research methods for the Ethnic Dance Project. They interview members of their families and communities about their home culture's dances and then use this information to perform a dance demonstration. The students develop a fact sheet and bring in ethnic costumes, artifacts, and food.

Eighth-grade students reinforce what they learned in the earlier grades and go on to create scripts, costumes, lighting, and sets for full-scale dance projects. They also produce a quarterly dance newsletter.

Encore

Dance does not exist as an isolated entity, but it is embedded in our culture and society. Students can learn in, about, and through dance.

Dance can be an integral subject unto itself and also an academic, personal, interpersonal, citizenship, and workplace tutor. Beyond significant instruction in dance technique and creating dances is the goal of helping students make connections between and across subjects. Dance can taught through an interdisciplinary lens. Books plus dance make learning doubly inscribed.

Making connections through dance to other subjects and accomplishments can prepare students with knowledge and skills in dance that are applicable to other spheres of life. Dance education can promote cognitive learning, social relations, personal growth, citizenship responsibility, and aesthetic appreciation. Teachers use various practices to achieve these goals.

Connections among dance and the other arts or between dance and other subjects are of two types: correlation and integration. Correlation approaches show specific similarities or differences (e.g., how the nonverbal expression of dance and the verbal expression of poetry both use vocabulary and grammar). Instead of comparing or contrasting dance and another subject, integration approaches use dance and another discipline(s) so that they are mutually reinforcing. Classes in different disciplines can work on a common thematic interarts, interdisciplinary project. For example, students could study the solar system in science classes while dance students use the solar system as the subject of exploring movement and making dances. Students in the other arts would explore the solar system from their respective disciplines' perspectives. All would share their new knowledge and products.

For a common fifth-grade unit on the structure of atoms, the classroom teacher might set up this interactive experience: Students form groups of five. One represents protons, another neutrons, and another electrons. The teacher tells each of these "atomic particles" how to move. The students know from dance class what improvisatory dance is and how to do it. In a short time they combine science and dance to absorb the material.

Dance is a kind of intelligence and learning that can reinforce other kinds of intelligence, and dance is a means of acquiring knowledge. It is clear that dance education has great potential.

Chapter 6

Dance Education for At-Risk Youth

AileyCamp Rap
AileyCamp is the place to learn the steps.
Just ask a teacher if you need help.
The classes are fun, and you learn new things.
Don't take drugs or you might think you have wings.
Classes last for an hour and a half; hang on and you won't be lost.
The teachers are great, and they know what they do,
but don't come in their class doing the bugalu.
Because they'll send you out, and you might be mad,
but you'll get to come back. So don't feel sad.
Well, that's my rap about AileyCamp.
I'll see you later I'm about to vamp.
As for me, Antoinne, keep dancing AileyCamp.

— ANTOINNE JONES (AGE 13; QUOTED IN KANSAS CITY <u>FRIENDS OF ALVIN AILEY</u> 1990:27)

*T*his chapter looks at the special benefits of dance for youth at risk of not completing their high school education. I describe several dance programs. These successful programs illustrate how to harness the exciting potential of dance education as a catalyst for positive change.

WHY HAVE DANCE EDUCATION FOR AT-RISK YOUTH?

At a major gathering of artists and arts, the U. S. Secretary of Housing and Urban Development, Henry Cisneros, remarked,

> A discussion of expanding resources for the arts cannot occur without finding ways for the arts to touch unserved communities with new levels of imagination and resources. The arts can help fight violence, crime and gang problems in our inner cities. (quoted in Trescott 1994:C1)

Writer Thulani Davis appealed for the arts to become part of the social arsenal to solve our problems, noting, "a lot of the chaos in society has to do with the absence of art." She continued, "Let's give them [the despairing, endangered and unschooled youth] art as at least one tool with which to challenge their exile from us" (quoted in Trescott 1994:C1).

Coming Up Taller, a report by the President's Committee on the Arts and the Humanities (Weitz 1996), recognizes that "safe havens" of dance have proved "particularly potent" in stemming violence and drug abuse and in keeping students from dropping out of school (Blumenthal 1996). The committee spent 14 months reviewing 213 arts programs in 36 states and the District of Columbia.

In the United States, most people think that the overriding goal of education is, first, to prepare students to be productive economically and, second, to provide a liberal arts education. Many people predict that no money will be available to support "art for art's sake," as resources are being focused on problems of education, health care, and social services.

Yet dance can be a vehicle for at-risk youth to meet the National Education Goals. Students who are alienated from school often display oppositional behaviors that are commonly a misguided display of power and self-affirmation. In a sense, *all youth are at risk*, including the academically gifted and economically well off.

Is dance a form of therapy and an agent of personal and social change? Or, is dance an art form only? As discussed throughout this book, dance education is not a zero sum game. Dance can be an instrument of positive change and an art form at the same time, as illustrated by the following dancers' stories.

Dance education helped troubled student Rasta Thomas, who recalls fighting and bullying other children at a very young age. Rasta went on to become the youngest dancer, and the only American, to win a gold medal in the junior category at the International Ballet Competition in Varna, Bulgaria. His father recalls,

> I got involved in Rasta's education because of behavior prob-
> lems at the age of six and seven. Rasta was making a clown of
> himself. I was called in to his school three days a week for his
> misbehavior. Rasta only wanted a stage. He was happy onstage.
> He was asking to perform. The kid was auditioning. Some
> youngsters are thought to be hyperkinetic and given the
> medication ritalin. Many kids just want attention. I don't
> think we recognize this.

Ballet star Jacques d'Amboise's mother sent him to his sister's ballet school to keep him away from the rough streets of New York's Washington Heights, with its budding neighborhood gangs (Weinraub 1995). Carlos Acosta, featured dancer with the Houston Ballet, ended a career in delinquency at age nine when his father, angered at Carlos's school truancy and dismayed that his son was stealing neighbors' fruits to barter for movie tickets, sent him off to Cuba's National Ballet School (Verhovek 1997).

Success in dance education can engage students, release their imagination (Greene 1995), empower them through accomplishing artistic challenges of their own choosing, and make school a place where other successes occur. Students learn to take a task to comple-tion and find an identity as a dancer. Dance education can link students to the world beyond the studio. Without this connection between what goes on in the studio and in the outside world, dance can become more of a feel-good addiction that helps the dancer tune out the rest of the world instead of using dance as a path toward liberation (Stinson 1991:29).

Some parents of at-risk youth are concerned about dance educa-tion because they believe that their youngsters will not be able to focus on traditional academic subjects. They do not know the potential of dance education for their child's development. Some

African-American parents worry further about the stereotype that black students can be performers but not scholars.

A central question for dance educators is whether dance should serve as a handmaiden to other aspects of life. I reiterate that dance can be many things at the same time. The exciting potential of dance education is illustrated in the following sections. First, the spotlight is on the National Dance Institute. Second, I turn to the program, Learning to Read through the Arts. Third, I explore the ArtsConnection Young Talent Dance Program. Then, I describe the benefits of the AileyCamp program for troubled youth.

NATIONAL DANCE INSTITUTE (NDI)

In 1976, while he was still a principal dancer with the New York City Ballet, Jacques d'Amboise founded the National Dance Institute (NDI) (d'Amboise, Cooke, and George, 1983; A. Dionne 1997). He began working with children because he wanted to expose children to dance who would not otherwise be able to afford dance classes or performances on their own. d'Amboise never had to pay for his own dance classes as a child (he received scholarship support or worked for his classes). Although he is a high school dropout, d'Amboise urges youth to complete their education (Weinraub 1995). At first d'Amboise worked only with boys because he did not want them to think dance was "just for sissies or girls." The program now serves both boys and girls.

NDI'S MISSION

The NDI's goal is to bring dance to boys and girls, ages 8 to14, without the opportunity to experience it. Believing that the arts should be an integral part of every child's education, NDI conducts programs during the school day on school premises and incorporates multiple disciplines, both artistic and academic. NDI aims to instill in children a standard of excellence by giving them the opportunity to study with professional dancers and choreographers. This standard requires self-discipline, high self-esteem, and mutual support in teamwork, qualities that help children succeed in a variety of tasks. NDI enriches the public school environment and fosters international understanding through exchanges with children and artists from around the world.

STUDENTS SERVED

About 90 percent of the students enrolled in NDI come from under-privileged communities, and some have physical and emotional disabilities. Because of the ethnic (African-American, Latino, Asian, European) and economic cross-section of the children in the New York City metropolitan area participating in NDI, these young dancers learn to work with people of different backgrounds. NDI corresponds with parents in Chinese, Spanish, and English.

NDI began by offering weekly classes for 80 boys in four New York City schools; since then, the NDI program has swelled. Through in-school dance programs, workshops, performances, assemblies, and curriculum materials, each year NDI reaches more than 6,000 children throughout the New York metropolitan area and serves as a model for programs across the country.

ACTIVITIES

NDI employs professional dancers as teachers in a 30-week program and holds weekly dance classes for all fourth-, fifth-, or sixth-grade students in 20 schools throughout New York City and Jersey City, New Jersey. No auditions are held, and the classes take place during the regular school day to emphasize that the arts are as essential to schooling as reading and math.

The hour-long classes are in freestyle jazz and use live accompaniment. Children learn basic dance sequences and then progress to more complex choreography; creating characters and moods through dance; and, finally, polishing and refining their work in preparation for a performance. During the year, d'Amboise and NDI teachers choreograph original dances for each school. These are performed in the annual "Event of the Year" concert held each June, which has a special theme (Barboza 1990). NDI provides each partner school with curriculum guides to help teachers incorporate the NDI theme into their classroom work. Themes have included "Andrew Jackson and the Battle of New Orleans," "Paul Revere's Ride," "The Shooting of Dan McGrew," "Fat City," "The French Revolution," "Rosebud's Song," "Chakra: A Celebration of India," "Dance in the Life of Coney Island," and "Celebration of Literature."

Three performances are held for school audiences during the year to provide students with tangible goals and opportunities to demonstrate their newly developed excitement and accomplishment. Time is reserved for their peer audience to participate and try the dance techniques themselves. The assemblies gives the NDI dancers a chance to perform before an audience in preparation for the Event of the Year concert.

This spectacular performance at the end of the school year, about something historically significant, culminates the school program. Directed and choreographed by d'Amboise and the NDI teaching staff, the Event is an original musical featuring 2,000 children from the New York in-school program. NDI combines the dances from all the different schools. Children perform side by side with celebrated dancers, musicians, and film and television artists.

After the Event, NDI holds a special encore class to allow the children to react to the performance. This class helps NDI evaluate the program and inform children of opportunities to continue their involvement in dance.

During the in-school program, NDI teachers invite children who demonstrate special talent for dance to join the Saturday scholarship classes. Approximately 80 children join the SWAT Team (the label refers to dance specialists, like the police have specialists), which meets every Saturday morning for three to five hours throughout the school year. Many students who participate for a year and complete the Logan Summer Institute go on to join the Celebration Team. It also rehearses on Saturdays. Members of the SWAT and Celebration Teams have the challenging opportunity to study with d'Amboise and NDI senior choreographers as well as to become featured dancers in the Event of the Year. The Celebration Team performs "Celebration of Literature" throughout the year.

The SWAT and Celebration Teams have performed in "The Celebration Series," a children's subscription series at the Lincoln Center for the Performing Arts; in the Macy's Thanksgiving Day Parade; at the Academy Awards in Los Angeles; at Carnivale in Venice, Italy; and at the Kennedy Center for the Performing Arts. These students have also appeared in such films as *He Makes Me Feel Like Dancin'* (the 1984 academy award-winning documentary on the NDI), Walt Disney's *Offbeat*, and Children's Television Workshop's *Peanut Ballet*.

Scholarships are available for up to 75 of the most talented and motivated NDI students for the Logan Summer Institute. This intensive four-week program offers classes in ballet, jazz, ethnic dance, tap, and voice. The Institute culminates in a free outdoor performance, such as one given at the World Financial Center plaza in Battery Park City before an audience of 1,600 people. Many Institute graduates have gone on to study with the Alvin Ailey School, Ballet Hispanico, Dance Theatre of Harlem, LaGuardia High School for the Performing Arts, and the School of American Ballet.

STAFF

NDI artistic staff are professionals who audition for their jobs. They must like children; have an energetic and theatrical personality; an understanding of children and their developmental needs; familiarity with the teaching and learning process; and an attitude that exudes confidence, enthusiasm, responsibility, sincerity, and openness. Teachers and choreographers complete an internship at the Logan Summer Institute and participate in workshops on choreography and teaching techniques that are held at other times. During the school year, d'Amboise and his Co-Artistic Director, Ellen Weinstein, visit classes regularly to assist the teachers with new techniques and critique their choreography.

Training for NDI teachers and choreographers is highly structured and closely monitored. The NDI program materials include a detailed, step-by-step 38-page *NDI Teacher/Choreographer's Handbook* that explains NDI and its performance-oriented approach to the arts in education. A section on program philosophy spells out the relationship of dance training to other student personal and academic goals. The handbook describes further the roles of key NDI and school personnel and how NDI builds relationships with the principal, assistant principal, in-school coordinator, and classroom teachers. Issues to be discussed before the program starts are listed.

Instructions are given for teaching the NDI class that include tips for getting the children's attention, structuring the classroom daily warm-ups, teaching choreography, greeting the youngsters, and saying good-bye. Teaching objectives and techniques include how to correct mistakes, work with children with special needs, and maintain discipline. Performance guidelines provide the staff with a specific road map so that NDI can achieve its goals.

COLLABORATION WITH THE SCHOOLS

NDI works with principals, superintendents, teachers, and in-school coordinators to make sure everyone understands the program. Interested individuals from the schools may observe or participate in classes. Special classes are given for teachers who perform in the Event of the Year with all the school children.

The historically important theme of the Event and the related curriculum materials are designed to complement Board of Education requirements for English, social studies, science, and math. NDI curriculum materials include descriptions and analyses of the historical theme; its chronology; vignettes of the life of the people involved; recipes for their food; and illustrations of the music, art, and literature of the time. Study questions, a list of current exhibitions that students can attend, other resources, and a selected bibliography are included in the materials.

SPECIAL PROGRAMS

NDI also works with children who are physically challenged. Twice a week throughout the school year, NDI choreographer/teachers work with groups of children who are hearing impaired and/or visually impaired. After a few weeks of classes, children without disabilities are mainstreamed into these classes to work alongside dancers with disabilities. NDI works with children with emotional challenges as well. In addition, NDI has offered classes for children from city shelters and welfare hotels. These classes were held at schools after hours because children could not return to the shelters until evening.

In 1989 NDI began its expansion program based on a month-long residency model. A team of four to five NDI staff members travel to a community and create an original dance performance using children from two to three schools. With the help of the school principals, an age group or grade is targeted to participate in the dance classes. Concurrently, children from other grades in the chosen schools participate in visual arts projects to create the sets, costumes, properties, and publicity materials for the production. All of the schools in the participating districts can work with curriculum materials created at NDI. These are designed to help children relate their arts experience to their academic endeavors. Finally, students perform the production for one week during the day, and thousands of children ride buses from local schools to see their peers on stage. Within the greater New York City area, individual schools may have smaller scale two-week residencies.

From 1978 to 1988, NDI offered a dance class program for New York City police officers. This gave inner-city children and police officers a unique opportunity to work together toward a common goal: the police officers performed with the children in the Event of the Year. In addition, from 1987 to 1988, participants in NDI dance programs for senior citizens rehearsed and performed with the youngsters in the Event of the Year, creating bonds between generations.

SUCCESS

Jacques d'Amboise has received numerous awards for his work with the NDI. These awards include the New York Governor's Award in recognition of his extraordinary efforts to make the arts a vital part of children's education, the 1988 Actor's Equity Paul Robeson Award for Humanitarian Services, a MacArthur Fellowship for his accomplishments in arts education, and a 1995 Kennedy Center for the Performing Arts' National Honor Award.

Two principals of New York City schools testify to the outcomes NDI has generated. Principal David Fong of P.S. 2M, who has had the opportunity to partner with NDI since 1986, remarks,

> I have spoken to hundreds of students from P.S. 2 who feel that NDI was the high point in their elementary school education. . . . Most important is that ingredient which helps students succeed in school—persistence in trying to do your best. (1996)

Principal Tanya Kaufman (1996) of P.S. 183 elaborates further,

> The NDI program . . . provides our students with an excellent opportunity to explore their own creativity through dance. . . . The skills of observation, replication and repetition are also valuable in their academic lives. The program has served to increase students' self-confidence and self-esteem. It provides a model for kids to be disciplined, to set and achieve high standards and to celebrate each others' successes. . . . It helps young adolescents gain some control over their bodies at a time when both coordination and embarrassment can be problematic. And most importantly it provides teachers with an opportunity to see kids in a new light. . . . In short, NDI has made a difference in the lives of our students and our whole school community.

The encore class that allows students to react to the Event of the Year performance provides another component of the program's assessment.

Not surprisingly, NDI serves as a model for many school systems, and NDI has helped launch pilot programs in California; Illinois; New Hampshire; New Jersey; New Mexico; Maine; Massachusetts; Mississippi; Pennsylvania; Texas; Vermont; and Washington, D.C. In March 1997, NDI launched its first international residency in Israel for Israeli and Palestinian students and teachers. Based on a course that has been offered in the summer at SUNY-New Paltz since 1993, and at the University of Southern Mississippi in 1997, NDI began a semester-long class for Bank Street College students that combines participation in the NDI in-school program with readings, in-class discussion, and an independent project.

Learning to Read through the Arts (LTRTA)

Learning to Read through the Arts (LTRTA) uses the arts as a core for teaching reading and writing skills to underachieving youngsters in grades 2 through 7 (ages 9 to 14). Bernadette C. O'Brien, an arts teacher as well as a reading specialist, started LTRTA in New York City in 1971 (Zamdmer 1994).

In 1974 LRTRA was selected as one of 12 exemplary reading programs in the United States by the American Institute of Research for the National Right to Read Effort; this honor brought national recognition that continues to this day. In 1979, with funding through the U.S. Department of Education's National Diffusion Network, LTRTA became a demonstrator/developer project. This status enabled school systems throughout the country to replicate LTRTA's experiential, individualized arts and academic education program in their educational settings. At least 32 other states; 832 school districts; 2,850 schools; and 7,341 supervisors and teachers have implemented the remedial LTRTA program. Trainers for LTRTA have worked with more than 200,000 students.

In 1985 New York City's P.S. 9 Manhattan, became a demonstration school, implementing LTRTA methodology in general, special, gifted, and trilingual education classes for grades K-7. The program now serves general, special, gifted, and bilingual education classes for students of all socioeconomic backgrounds in grades K-12.

Dance and Remediation

LTRTA provides students with concrete arts experiences through reading-oriented arts workshops held twice a week and reading workshops given daily. Instruction is either school based or students ride buses from their regular schools to a central program site. Specially trained teachers work as individuals or in teams with classroom teachers on arts-centered academic learning to mesh LTRTA instruction with classroom core curricula.

In the dance classes, as well as in other performing and visual arts classes, students listen carefully to instructions; talk about what they are going to do; and record information, directions, and descriptive and analytical paragraphs about each project in their personal journals. The interest-piquing dance experience, with its emphasis on creativity and opportunity for self-expression, helps students move from the nonverbal experience to the verbal experience, from dancing to writing and reading. The dance workshop helps promote positive social interaction as students investigate and comment on each other's goals, process, and achievement. Students attend performances in the metropolitan area to build a reservoir of background knowledge. These field trips are also oriented to promote proficiency in language development by requiring listening, speaking, writing, and reading. Reading becomes a tool to learn more about dance.

The success and sense of achievement many students feel in creating dance often gives them the self-confidence and the motivation to master other school offerings. Because students read and write about dance, they find these activities purposeful, and they develop positive feelings about learning and academic achievement. Students perform for the public in an annual festival, which provides further validation of their accomplishments.

ACADEMIC ACHIEVEMENT

As evidenced by standardized test scores, academic achievement for most LTRTA program students eliminates their eligibility for special reading services to meet minimum standards. Since 1971 evaluations of past programs show that students improve an average of 1 to 2 months in reading for each month they participate in the program.

PROGRAM ADOPTION

Continually revised materials available for a range of LTRTA program adoption options include a staff training handbook, curriculum guides, workshop lesson plans, a dictionary, a newsletter, videos, and evaluation procedures and forms. Schools may request government monies for preservice training, site visits to exemplary projects, curriculum writing time, supplies, and special consultants. Admission fees to cultural institutions or educational resource centers may be necessary. Schools may choose to adopt LTRTA as a part of the school day or as an after-school or summer program.

Teachers who participate in the LTRTA program have at least 12 hours of preservice training and 1 period per week of in-service work to learn about new developments in theory and method as well as to discuss problems. Parent workshops are held to explain how children learn and how parents can help their children's learning. Ongoing evaluation of the project is a major feature.

ARTSCONNECTION YOUNG TALENT DANCE PROGRAM

The ArtsConnection Young Talent Dance Program (herein referred to as "YT") is a four-year sequential dance education program that began in 1978. The "pull-out" program (students are taken out of other classes) has optional tutoring for missed class time. Serving students in grades three through six in 10 New York City public schools, the program targets at-risk students and underserved inner-city school populations who are generally excluded from special activities. The program has been identifying and training talented students in the performing arts to work with some of the city's most respected performing arts organizations and teachers at school and in professional studios and theaters. Chapter 2 describes the positive results of this program.

Evan Kafka

Intelligence comes in different forms.

STUDENT SELECTION

ArtsConnection and a panel of professional dance educators audition students for YT. The auditions take the form of large master classes held within an academic school. Selection criteria include the skills of physical control, coordination and agility, spatial awareness, observation and recall; rhythm; motivation; ability to focus; perseverance;

and creativity in terms of expressiveness, movement qualities, and improvisation (Oreck 1997). In addition, participants must have the signed agreement of their principal and classroom teacher and the consent of a parent or guardian.

CONTENT AND EMPHASES

Youngsters in the YT program learn many kinds of dance, a different style each year, drawn from different countries, techniques, and traditions. Children learn modern dance, jazz, African, Spanish, Caribbean, and ballet; the development of each child's creativity and potential is the common thread. Through exploring new movement possibilities, students experience different ways of learning, acquire new concepts, and develop a connection with cultures whose dance forms they are studying.

During the first year, Level I, all third-grade students, along with their teachers, receive an introduction to the art of dance and the energy and concentration required in a serious dance class. The students attend a series of workshops titled, "Your Body Is Your Instrument," and take one class a week in the school gym on a designated day for 5 to 10 weeks. They learn dance basics such as good posture, anatomy, nutrition, listening skills, warm-up stretches, focusing techniques, dance vocabulary, and rhythmic structure. In addition, they use their imaginations to discover a wide variety of movement possibilities that are uniquely their own.

Following this introduction, YT staff audition students when they reach grade four to identify children with the ability and enthusiasm to benefit from extended training in Level II dance instruction. Teachers evaluate students in these major areas of performance:

- ❧ Skills/physical development (posture and alignment, body coordination, memory and recall, musicality/rhythmic awareness, and artistic sense)
- ❧ Classroom discipline and behavior (concentration and focus; class preparation, including uniform and homework; self-control; ability to understand and apply correction; and cooperation with teachers)
- ❧ Personal development (creativity, problem solving, expressiveness, teamwork skills, confidence, and leadership)

Level II students (about 25 at each school) take one in-school class per week for 25 weeks and attend three field trips in consecutive weeks for master classes at professional studios, such as the Martha

Graham School, Harbor Performing Arts Center, Harlem School for the Arts, and Ballet Hispanico, and at least one trip to a professional performance at a theater, such as the Brooklyn Academy of Music or Aaron Davis Hall. ArtsConnection, in association with the New York City Board of Education, Bureau of Pupil Transportation, provides bus transportation for all the program's out-of-school activities. School or parent chaperons and/or ArtsConnection supervisory personnel are present at all times during travel and at activities.

YT introduces second-year students to the elements of dance technique, increasing their movement vocabulary and knowledge of the body in the atmosphere of a professional studio environment. A structured class routine allows students to work on rhythmic and spatial awareness and perform exercises to improve strength, flexibility, and stamina. Students who successfully complete Level II can move up to Level III.

Level III students (years 3 and 4, for fifth and sixth graders) receive 25 workshops in their school gym or auditorium and 20 weekly classes at professional studios, such as the 92nd Street YMCA, Dance Theatre of Harlem, or Harlem School for the Arts. A focus on dance technique demands greater concentration and practice than is possible in the in-school class. Students learn and recall movement phrases and develop them into choreography. This work helps youngsters develop the attitudes and discipline necessary to succeed in the field of dance or any other serious endeavor.

DISCIPLINE

YT students have to follow standards of attendance, dress, and discipline. The program expects them to attend to all personal needs and be prepared to begin dance class at least five minutes before the class is scheduled to begin. YT drops students from the program who have more than three unexcused absences. First-year students come to dance class with clothing that permits them freedom of movement. The second-, third-, and fourth-year students receive a dance uniform to wear to each class. Students must keep their dance clothing clean. If they fail to bring clean dance clothes to class, they are excluded and counted as absent.

EVALUATION AND TUTORING

YT evaluates students at the end of each year and sends report cards to the parents. The YT Counseling and Tutoring Program helps dance students who miss time from the academic classroom to maintain academic performance and resolve personal or familial problems. Students in Levels II and III are eligible for individual or small-group tutoring once or twice a week before or after school. Tutors, selected by principals, consult with classroom teachers to develop individualized programs of study for each student. YT keeps parents informed of their youngsters' progress and counsels them on junior high schools and private studios where they can pursue dance training after graduation from the sixth grade. A parent liaison works with dance instructors, classroom teachers, and families to assist in resolving behavior problems.

SPECIAL SERVICES

Besides the four-year intensive movement training, YT offers services to the entire school. Three- to five-week dance resource workshops for classrooms and their teachers in grades K-6 link movement with areas of the academic curriculum such as language skills, social studies, and history. YT also holds workshops for special education students, bilingual classes, and other distinct groups within the school. Background information allows the classroom teachers to take advantage of the workshops. After-school classes are held for teachers, parents, and the community.

AILEYCAMP

A new thrust in forging the link between dance education and academic achievement was the Kansas City Friends of Alvin Ailey (KCFAA) AileyCamp programs. The urban Kansas City, Missouri, School District and 19 other community organizations collaborated in 1989 to offer this program. Originally funded by two competitive grant awards from the Gannett Foundation to use dance education to promote literacy, AileyCamp has drawn upon the experience of New York's Alvin Ailey American Dance Theater Company, its school, and the KCFAA. In turn, successive AileyCamps draw upon the knowledge gained from previous AileyCamps (Favors 1996). AileyCamps have been held in Kansas City, New York City, and Philadelphia.

Ailey's multiracial and internationally renowned company is "dedicated to the preservation and enrichment of the American modern dance heritage and the uniqueness of black cultural expression." Founded in 1958, the company reports it has performed before about 15,000,000 people in 48 states and in 45 countries on 6 continents. Alvin Ailey, the company's founder and choreographer, died a few months after launching the first AileyCamp. He wanted to reach the people who cannot afford to go to the theater and to excite children about dance. The company continues his legacy by conducting a broad array of outreach educational activities nationwide.

Founded in 1984, KCFAA is a biracial community arts partnership that has initiated 90 innovative, cultural, civic, corporate, and governmental collaborations, including 5 school districts, 8 dance studios, and 30 service organizations. Annual KCFAA residencies have split Ailey dancers into teams that target unserved and underserved communities.

Bill Foley

Young people participating in an AileyCamp program.

A CHILD'S NEEDS

KCFAA recognizes the multiple needs of a child at risk. Consequently, the unique AileyCamp program draws upon research on minority education and dance as well as experience teaching dance by itself and using dance to teach English and social studies. The four As—acceptance, attention, appreciation, and affection—are bywords for trusting relationships among students and teachers.

SELECTION OF AT-RISK YOUTH

In 1989, KCFAA designed and implemented an eight-week pilot summer dance program for 102 at-risk inner-city youth, grades six through eight, with 51 students in each session, which met five days a week for four weeks. A motivating factor was that summer learning can be exceedingly valuable in preventing the loss of gains made during the school year (Entwisle and Alexander 1992).

Students selected for the program met these criteria: (1) attending a Kansas City, Missouri, School District middle school; (2) living with a single parent or none; (3) eligible for the school lunch program; (4) having a sibling who has dropped out of school or become a school-age parent; (5) teacher recommendation as having difficulty within the traditional school structure; (6) interest in and aptitude for dance, athletics, and creativity; and (7) low self-esteem. Student recruitment began with dance movement demonstrations to more than 1,500 students by two black male dancers. Men demonstrated to motivate interested boys because boys are at greater risk of dropping out of school. Then 450 students submitted applications to school teachers and community centers signed by their parent or guardian. KCFAA board members, in teams of black and white partners, conducted face-to-face interviews with 350 students and telephone interviews with an additional 100. Next they rated students on the selection criteria using a scale of one to five. To achieve a gender and racial mix among the 129 students chosen, they accepted all eligible male and white applicants. All 10 middle schools in the Kansas City, Missouri, School District were represented. Of the 117 students who began the program, 102 completed it. The make up of that group was as follows: 83 percent female, 17 percent male; 51 percent seventh graders, 49 percent eighth graders; 84 percent black, 15 percent white, and 1 percent Hispanic.

ACTIVITIES

AileyCamp designed a curriculum and published a handbook of information for each student and his or her parent or guardian. The handbook included biographical information on the dance and other counselors and administrators, a description of each class's objectives and typical activities, definitions of dance vocabulary, rules of AileyCamp, and a schedule of classes and special events. The program had seven teenage volunteer AileyCamp assistants and a college volunteer supervisor. The staff collected parent or guardian permission slips for field trips and health reports.

The Superintendent of Schools secured the Middle School for the Arts as the campsite, Penn Valley Community College contributed personnel to make a documentary video, and Genesis (alternative) School provided expertise on the development of a creative writing curriculum. The dean of the department of education at the University of Missouri at Kansas City helped to assess the impact of the AileyCamp experience on academic achievement. (See Fineberg 1995 and Fineberg and Wilson 1996 for subsequent evaluations of AileyCamps.) Specific assessment methods are described in a later section.

AileyCamp students took classes in different dance techniques, including ballet, Lester Horton modern technique, Katherine Dunham African-Caribbean technique, and jazz. Students had improvisation and performance experiences and more. The program offered creative writing (poetry, fiction, and nonfiction) and counseling (on nutrition, drug and alcohol abuse, sex, decision making, and self-esteem; see Smelser 1989 on the problems with the concept and measure of self-esteem). Besides participating in these activities, students went on outings to swimming pools and the Wildwood Outdoor Education Camp teamwork training center. The Mattie Rhodes Arts Center brought a program to the campsite. AileyCamp included involvement with the students' families to increase and reinforce attendance; a picnic for campers and their parents to meet the staff was held each session to promote this relationship. The teachers and administrators provided role models for success. Through talks with the students, KCFAA corporate members and representatives from agencies dealing with health, nutrition, drug, and self-education were exemplars for career options.

Reinforcement followed AileyCamp teaching and learning experiences. Follow-up activities included having the students serve as teacher assistants for activities sponsored by the KCFAA during the school year. At a community college, students from both camps took a master class with a visiting choreographer/dancer. This was the first time that the boys from one session had danced in front of the girls from another, so the reunion was less disciplined than the second master class held two months later. By then, students were more comfortable with each other. Sixty students took a master class with the Alvin Ailey Repertory Ensemble; attended a self-esteem class; watched a rehearsal; and, after dinner, attended a performance. The Repertory Ensemble performed for schools during the fall months. AileyCamp students took master classes during the following year when Alvin Ailey teachers or dancers came to Kansas City for other outreach activities.

AileyCamp established a parent-support network to sustain the values and goals of the program, to assist in the long-term evaluation of student academic and interpersonal skills, and to supplement KCFAA activities. A group of about 10 parents from the KCFAA AileyCamp auxiliary organized a Christmas party for the youngsters.

The program made efforts to place former campers in year-round activities with opportunities for positive artistic, academic, and interpersonal growth. Several campers who displayed exceptional dance talent received scholarships from the Westport School of Ballet in Kansas City to continue their training during the school year. Ten of the 20 members cast in an all-city musical were AileyCampers. Exemplary AileyCampers had the opportunity to become second-year senior campers and to be entrusted with leadership through training both before and during camp.

ASSESSMENT METHODS

The program aimed to develop student self-esteem and interpersonal and cognitive skills. Reports from teacher and student evaluations and a Laban Effort/Shape analysis of motor behavior suggested the program was successful. Means of assessing academic achievement were the Degree of Reading Power test used by the Kansas City, Missouri, School District; grades; attendance records; and teacher, counselor, and parent comments following AileyCamp compared with the same at the end of the previous school year.

Subsequent AileyCamps have continued evaluation centered in the participants' growth and progress. Each camper has a folder with teacher notes, and teachers and staff receive feedback from campers, parents, and outside evaluators.

STUDENT EXPERIENCE

At the outset, some AileyCampers were so physically out of shape that they could not complete five minutes of physical activity. These students would quit in frustration, their patience and stamina depleted. "Too hard" was a common complaint. Two weeks later, however, these same students were actually energized by a one-hour, nonstop rehearsal. Andrew, a 13-year-old boy, explained,

> AileyCamp . . . showed you how to work with others and help one another. It made us work as a team. When we first started. . . . I was ready to give up without even trying. The instructors started encouraging each of us. After that, I never gave up (quoted in Kansas City Friends of Alvin Ailey 1990:21).

Perceptual and math skills were so deficient that campers initially could not perform five equal steps through space. They learned to create dances with counted steps and to improvise movement phrases to poems they had written. Empowering the campers with the necessary skills to create movement and express themselves in writing seemed, according to the camp staff and parents, to remarkably improve the youngsters' self-motivation, self-awareness, self-esteem, and self-confidence.

Youngsters initially reluctant to stand up and give their names clamored to perform just four weeks later. The campers produced so much material in the creative writing and improvisation classes that they wanted to put on their own talent show on the last day of camp. And they did! Without adult supervision they rehearsed on their own time, chose a narrator, and brought their own music and costumes.

The culmination of AileyCamp was the final performance for 700 friends and family, which was reviewed in *The Kansas City Call.* How many 12-year-olds can boast about being reviewed? Youngsters wrote material for what they choreographed, produced, and performed in the show. LaKeisha, age 12, loved performing: "The roar of the crowd and the long hours spent working on the performance . . . made me feel like I really accomplished something. I would jump at the chance to come and experience it all over again (quoted in Kansas City Friends of Alvin Ailey 1990:26)."

The first AileyCamp took place with little time for planning. The director commented, "The camp went from paper to it's over." Not only did this experience happen very quickly, but so much of what occurred was unexpected for students and staff alike. The diversity of the students was a surprise. Even the twins enrolled differed behaviorally from each other! Some youngsters feared special attention. They clung to the dance barre against the classroom wall and were reluctant to move into the center of the room. Other campers loved the limelight. One boy refused to do pelvic isolations in jazz class—he thought his mother would disapprove!

TEACHER EXPERIENCE

The dance teachers faced the challenge of cultivating an appreciation of dance as a theater art in inner-city youth with no previous exposure to its discipline. This challenged teachers to become involved in their students' lives, to teach them to respect themselves and their peers, and to share personal experiences about what it took to become successful. By doing this, the teachers became realistic role models.

Some teachers also needed a bit of preparation. The creative writing teacher, for example, lacked knowledge about dance; and some of the dance teachers lacked in-depth knowledge about the needs of students at risk. The camp director helped address this by assisting the camp counselor to disseminate information.

In the typical studio dance class, students do as the teacher says and does. Many at-risk youth are accustomed to relying on street survival skills, responding to peer pressure, and engaging in peer decision making. Consequently, they do their best behaviorally and academically when they have a say and a stake in determining the rules for activities governed by adults. This is especially the case for conflict resolution, daily routines, special events, and the themes for doing dance improvisations and other performances (cf. Crawford and Bodine 1996; Hanna 1988c; Vorrath and Brendtro 1985). At first the youngsters did not respond to writing assignments. However, when they chose what to write about in the camp newsletter, they had a lot to say, especially about drugs. Many students deal with substance abuse at home, in school, and on the streets.

Students felt more secure in moving from the known to the unknown. When the campers decided to have a talent show, they chose improvised street dance movements. The new creations began with familiar locomotor and gestural actions (the known) that led to insights about the concepts of time, space, and effort using improvisation to discover unfamiliar movement patterns (the unknown). The concepts of space, time, and effort apply to dance, academics, and life in general, as discussed earlier.

AileyCamp provided options for the few youngsters who thought they wanted to dance and then refused to participate in the final performance. They were allowed to observe and report about the camp activities or work backstage.

LESSONS LEARNED

The second KCFAA AileyCamp program, with some modification based on the experience of the first, took place in the summer of 1990. This time around the AileyCamp selection process took into account that some youngsters cannot benefit from the program. For example, staffers were not trained to deal with students with learning disabilities and/or behavioral problems. Students also need to be physically fit. Because the first group of AileyCampers had no idea of the energy and commitment that were necessary, the next camp recruitment showed AileyCamp pictures and videotapes to potential campers and their parents. Former campers were now able to describe to their peers what is involved. There was also more extensive and in-depth orientation for the staff.

Building on the Kansas City experience, AileyCamp had its premier season in New York City in 1991. The New York City AileyCamp was co-sponsored by the Alvin Ailey Dance Theater Foundation and the Children's Aid Society, which serves more than 100,000 of New York's neediest children and families each year. A new feature of the 1995 AileyCamp in Manhattan incorporated photography so that each youngster could take pictures of a partner camper over the course of the summer. This documented experience gave students evidence of their own and their friends' growth and development.

In the summer of 1997, AileyCamp Philadelphia implemented a pilot program in conjunction with NetworksArts Philadelphia, a consortium of community-based arts organizations. Additional AileyCamp locations are in the planning stage.

ENCORE

In most of our schools today, knowledge is cut into subjects pedagogically unrelated to each other— and, more important, to real life. This type of schooling turns off many youngsters, especially those at risk of dropping out of school because of poverty and boredom or absence of intellectual challenge. Many at-risk youth lack the psychological strengths and learned skills to succeed academically. The good news, however, is that attendance records, test scores, and graduation rates from about a dozen schools nationwide offering dance education attest to the fact that it can "grab" many such youngsters' attention through their immediacy and active involvement of both mind and body. Without attention, the most intimate power a person has, no learning occurs.

Once students are engaged in dance education, a hook and an anchor to school, other educational options present themselves. The palpable, enveloping excitement of dance, the discipline required, and the success achieved propel many students to academic achievement and productive citizenship.

I sketched four illustrative programs that serve unserved or underserved youngsters. The National Dance Institute is an example of a dance organization headed by a distinguished former dance star. NDI is performance oriented but links its theme to the school curriculum.

Its faculty of dancers work with schools to teach youngsters dance and relate the dance theme to other classroom activity. All students receive an introduction to dance, and those who are especially talented receive more training.

Learning to Read through the Arts uses dance and other arts to teach basic academic skills. Classroom teachers receive special training to use the arts. Dance is incidental but motivational.

ArtsConnection Young Talent Dance Program works with the schools. It targets at-risk students and underserved inner-city youngsters who are generally excluded from special activities. Those students who show accomplishment in dance education have opportunities for further study.

AileyCamp is often the centerpiece of other programs to help the individual youngster. This program involves a web of interrelated school and private and public health, social services, arts, recreational agency, and parent partnerships to help the whole child. The child is strengthened in the spheres of home, school, and community. Motivated dance students have opportunities to continue their dance education.

These four illustrative programs are just some of the ways that dance education can benefit our youth. They suggest alternative ways of teaching at-risk youth in, about, and through dance. Like the students they serve, the programs also grow over time. The programs learn valuable lessons as they unfold, and they transform to deal with lessons learned.

Chapter 7

Children's Dance at Play as a Teaching Tool

[The body] is at once the most intimate and inward and the most obvious and outward aspect of how we see ourselves, how we see others, and how others see us.

— HAROLD R. ISAACS (1975:47)

*T*his chapter discusses the meaning of dances children create apart from any adult teaching, using examples from a year-long study conducted at Hamilton Park Elementary School in Dallas. Outside the formal educational exchange between adult teacher and child, children can be found dancing as part of their play activities on playgrounds, in classrooms, and in halls. This spontaneous play has implications for teaching and learning. By observing a child's dance at play, teachers can learn how a child thinks, feels, and moves and adjust their teaching to better reach the student. Past experience and many kinds of knowledge, including the elements of dance and its historical, cultural, and social contexts, are building blocks for the education process.

The body in motion especially arrests attention, for it implies a change in environmental conditions that may require a reaction to ensure one's safety. Dancing readily attracts notice. Children's own dance creating and viewing contribute to their habits of thinking and moving, providing a sensory anchor against which they validate old and new ideas.

HOW DO CHILDREN'S OWN DANCES AT PLAY CONTRIBUTE TO SCHOOLING?

Dance education involves teaching and learning, sometimes most poignantly by student peers both inside and outside the classroom. Children often share tales about their lives, conveying beliefs and attitudes, during activities of their own choice (Goodwin 1991). For example, in Helmut Segler's documentary film presented at the 1982 International Conference on Dance and the Child, children's spontaneous and creative songs and dances were a means through which they commented on cinema, television, adult behavior, and children different from themselves.

Similarly, Kyra Gaunt's interviews with African-American women (ages 18 to 56) who grew up in urban communities, combined with descriptions of her own experience, show how girls' own dances are constantly shaped by interpretations of race, gender, and sexuality. The tradition of African-American girls' dances continues to thrive throughout the United States. Learned skills inform the performances and are passed down through the generations through observation, imitation, and practice (1997). Liese remembers that "dancing allowed her to explore sexuality while defining her blackness and femaleness in political ways" (quoted in Gaunt 1997:181).

USING DANCE AT PLAY AS A DIAGNOSTIC TOOL

Teachers can learn how their students represent knowledge through their dances and dance phrases at play. Students' kinesthetic voices can be a teacher's diagnostic tool for understanding the dancers' concerns and beliefs. Martha Graham reminded us that the body says what words cannot.

In *The Unschooled Mind: How Children Think, How Schools Should Teach*, Gardner (1991) argues that teachers need to identify and then build off students' preconceived ideas to help them understand new concepts. Psychologist Diane F. Halpern notes that we must incorporate into our teaching an understanding of the ways in which learners represent knowledge. In this way we can expose the misconceptions by presenting the facts and showing how they relate to students' initial understanding of them (Halpern 1996; see also Bean 1997).

USING DANCE AT PLAY AS A KNOWLEDGE BASELINE

Because fundamental learning occurs in the absence of teaching, and learners construct their own knowledge, the dances children perform at play display their natural movement competencies. Teachers can observe and then assess these in terms of specific dance education standards. The assessment of what children demonstrate through their play provides a baseline for classroom instruction in dance and other subjects.

WHAT DID I LEARN ABOUT DANCE AT PLAY IN AN ELEMENTARY SCHOOL?

My year-long study at Hamilton Park Elementary School (HPES) in Dallas, Texas, uncovered a dramatic connection between children's own dance and other aspects of life (Hanna, 1986, 1988c). As in Africa and many urban areas in the United States, African-American students commented on their concerns through dance, song, and mime. They spontaneously performed dances on the playground, in school classrooms, and in school halls.

HISTORICAL CONTEXT

Chuck Davis (quoted in Levine 1994) believes that dance can tell us about the performer's culture, and the culture can tell us about the dance.

In attempting to understand the dance play at HPES, it is useful to place the school and the community in their historical context. The school is located in a black community created in the 1950s as a consequence of white terrorism and fire bombing of black homes, which were purchased or being built in formerly all-white residential areas. (I use the terms "black" and "white" as they were used at the school). Desegregation took away the black community's control of the formerly segregated school. A five-year long U.S. Justice Department civil rights effort culminated in a court case that led to the creation of a magnet school that required white children to be bused to the school voluntarily.

White families who volunteered to send their children to the school were interested in interracial mixing. Yet little interracial mixing was evident as black children chose black partners or seats next to other black children for an activity. Black–white proximity had led to harassment of blacks in the past; consequently, the black community was not unanimously in favor of having a desegregated magnet school.

Because the residential territory occupied by blacks is historically small and precarious, it has been especially treasured. Thus the children's use of space, including their cutting of shapes in space through dance, became poignantly endowed with meaning.

Many low-income black youngsters do not value the pursuit of academic excellence, nor do they do what is necessary to earn high marks (Ogbu 1986). Indeed, at HPES some children devalued and belittled the ethics and activities of formal schooling. In spite of the low esteem they have for academic success, they are nonetheless sensitive to public revelation, such as in oral recitation, of their inadequate school work. This leads some of them to face-saving behavior, or what has been described as defensive structuring that occurs among groups under stress and with limited resources (Siegel 1970). They seek arenas in which they can dominate and gain recognition, and they attempt to establish a prideful group identity when they perceive external threats to that identity (as evidenced in the anecdote in the following section of a person-naming song and dance). This process involves the subordination of the individual to the group as it masters challenges cooperatively.

Dance or athletics, avenues for expressive symbolic behavior, are acceptable arenas for mastery that reinforce an individual's sense of being the kind of person that "significant others"—his or her peers— esteem. Through dance themes, participation criteria, and performances in a white-controlled school system, youngsters at HPES identified themselves as being distinct from the "shuffling black" stereotypes of earlier historical periods and from their white class-mates. Michael Moffat found, as I did, that a person's dance move-ments appear to be at the core of his or her personal and group identity and feeling of belonging or alienation (1989:150; Hanna 1992b). The dancers in the person-naming dance described below declared a wished-for privileged status and, in a sense, they attained it by rejecting the participation of their white peers.

Children and adults at HPES generally recognized black children's superior performance in certain realms. These included kinesthetic intelligence, such as dance and sports.

What are the fundamental bases of dance as a form for creativity, compensation, or defensive structuring? The primordial and most vital marker of identity consists of the ready-made set of endowments that each individual shares at birth with members of her or his group: the body itself. If one has few material possessions and little power, as is the case with oppressed minorities and with children, the body and its use are likely to become particularly important. The significance of the African-American "body in motion," has roots in Africa, the American slave auction block, and antebellum labor markets. Many African societies, from which African-Americans descend, view the body in motion, especially in dancing, as predictive of an individual's personality, work capability, creativity, and innovativeness.

DANCE AS A WAY TO EXPRESS IDENTITY
ON THE PLAYGROUND

At HPES during recess outdoors on a warm sunny day, groups of black girls spontaneously organized dances. Using a spatial form of children's dances that is probably British in origin and learned from white Americans, the girls moved in the African style with a loose, flexible torso; extension and flexion of the knees with an easy, breathing quality; shuffling steps; and pelvic swings and thrusts. They created syncretistic dances that combined both white and black styles of dance in a form that has been described elsewhere as "ring and line plays" (Jones and Hawes 1972:67-68). A leader either sang a phrase that the group answered, or the leader led the performers. Movements accompanied and accented the song text or illustrated it. Hand clapping or other body percussion punctuated the performance to create a syncopated rhythm within the song and dance.

Gaunt describes how dancing helps dancers to identify themselves within their culture, to learn "what it means socially to be a black girl." In cheers that incorporate "real" black girls' names, "the naming of ourselves" announces individual identity and permits self-expression through dance or dancelike gestures (Gaunt 1997:161).

In one instance at HPES, when a white girl wished to join the black girls in one of the dances, a black girl stepped back, put her hands on her hips, and looked the white girl up and down about the hips and feet. Then, with a quizzical look and scowl, she said loudly for all to hear: "Show me you can dance!" Everyone watched as the white girl withdrew to the sidelines.

Later a different white girl joined the "Check Me" ring play in which the name of each participant in the circle was singled out in turn, going to the right. One girl's name was called by the girl standing to her immediate left; she identified herself, sang a refrain while clapping her hands, and then called on the next girl to her right.

> Check [clap], check [clap], check [clap].
> My name is Tina,
> I am a Pisces.
> I want you to [clap]
> check, check, check,
> to check out Bridgette.
> Check [clap], check [clap], check [clap].
> My name is Bridgette. . . .

When it was the white girl's turn to be called, the black girl just passed her by and called to the next black girl. Rejected, the white girl called out, "I can do it, too!" No one paid attention.

Clearly, the dance activity placed the black girls in a dominant status. It was an arena in which they gained recognition. The exclusionary behavior of the girls in the dances protested the way society and school are structured. Perhaps the dances served as a means of catharsis. Dance can be viewed as the source of new cultural and social patterns. Black pride, identity, boundaries, and neighborhood loyalty seemed to coalesce in the dances groups of HPES girls performed. The dances asserted camaraderie, provided fun, and let the performers work through problems in a world in which they feel a lack of control. The dances appear to be a means of in-group bonding in an arena in which they can excel; they serve as a response to their awareness of past white oppression and exclusion of black people. Their dancing further recognizes a future of racial separation possibly carried on as in the past—or even a possible reversal of power relations. Gaunt explains, "Play is where we can imagine and reconstitute ourselves, those around us, and our view of the world" (1997:188).

DANCE AS A CHALLENGE TO CLASSROOM AUTHORITY

One day, during an unusual 40-minute second-grade classroom period, several black children yelled out remarks and walked about the room before the teacher could establish control. They played with furniture pretending it was gymnastic, musical, or military equipment. They pushed, pulled, or hit others. A black boy tried to cut a white girl's blond hair.

One black girl kept talking loudly. In response to the white teacher's question, "Would you like to go out?" the youngster got up from her chair and walked into the aisle, where she stood, feet apart and knees bent. She brought her knees together and apart four times while crossing her hands together and apart in unison with the knees in a recognizable Charleston step. Then she scurried back to her assigned seat and sat down. Moments later she skipped to the door, opened it, picked up a book lying outside, and ran back to her place. Next she stood up on the chair seat and performed what in ballet is called an arabesque. Standing on the ball of one foot, she lifted the other leg backward as high as she could, one arm held diagonally up and forward, the other diagonally down. From this position she laughed as she lost her balance and fell to the floor. The teacher picked her up and carried her out of the classroom. During the girl's performance, her peers gave her their undivided attention.

The girl's dance movements can be construed as dramatically defying the white teacher by acting inappropriately during a formal lesson. The child broke the rules of both the white-dominated school (which she later readily described to me) and of traditional ballet style. She mocked the teacher by leaving her assigned seat and walking into the aisle to perform a Charleston movement, part of the repertoire of several black African groups and part of her African-American ethnic identity. Then, again, out of the appropriate time and place, she performed an arabesque movement, part of the white ethnic ballet tradition. To add a further incongruity, she performed a dance movement that is usually done on a stage floor on the seat of a classroom chair. She placed her feet where the buttocks are supposed to be. Then she deliberately fell off the chair in a clumsy manner instead of moving from the body supported on one foot to both with elegant and graceful body control as the arabesque is finished in ballet. Breaking all these school and ballet rules, the child sassed the teacher in a display of insubordination.

This performance suggested the historical pattern of blacks parodying white behavior (Hansen 1967; Levine 1977); it appeared as a metaphor for the teacher's inability to control her classroom generally and the black children in particular. Note that radio and television coverage of African-American Arthur Mitchell teaching in Dallas made common knowledge the history of ballet as a European tradition formerly only studied, performed, and viewed by whites. Commentators repeatedly said that until Mitchell founded the Dance Theatre of Harlem, there were few black ballet dancers. HPES offered extracurricular ballet classes. In this way black children learned the ballet rules well enough not only to execute them but to also break them.

Many children disliked the teacher for yelling and fussing at them too much. The incident with the disruptive young girl appears similar to sympathetic magic in the sense of the student symbolically enacting, through body motion, wished-for behavior in another realm. The girl collapsed her arabesque pose in lieu of concluding it with the traditional ballet aplomb. Thus she seemed to symbolize, or with the compelling power of metaphor to effect, the white teacher's complete downfall from authority. Symbolic actions are often meant to bring about what they express.

DANCE AS SELF-EXPRESSION IN THE HALLS

At least once a week I saw one to six black children spontaneously dance a few steps in short sequences in a variety of situations both inside and outside the classrooms. The dancing did not disrupt formal teaching and learning. For example, as a second-grade class was being dismissed, one boy exited performing a Charleston step three times. This was the same step the girl described earlier had performed disruptively in the classroom. After the first boy exited, a second boy followed performing the same movement phrase. The sequences occurred repeatedly until six boys had left the classroom. In a fourth-grade music class, several black boys "be-bopped" (walked rhythmically) before the admiring eyes of their peers. One boy walked with exaggerated hip shifts, his upper and lower torso moving in opposition; another boy walked about while shimmying his shoulder blades. A third sat snapping his fingers and then got up and performed a step-kick walking dance sequence. A fourth boy shimmied his shoulders and rippled his torso. As a sixth-grade class was going through the halls to the cafeteria, several black boys and girls performed a variety of dance movement phrases.

It was uncertain to me what specifically triggered these children's dance movements in the classrooms and halls. The youngsters appeared to enjoy dancing to gain their peers' attention and admiration. Some children find structured classroom activities incompatible with their capabilities or moods; dancing may be a way for them to release pent-up energy after adhering to a formal academic regime. One elderly black dancer describes how she and her peers would "dance awhile to rest ourselves" (Jones and Hawes 1972:124).

ENCORE

Children at play dance about what interests them, what's on their minds. They move as they are moved. They educate each other about ideas, feelings, and dance. Minority youngsters who are aware of the history of white discrimination use individual and group dance to express their views on school and community life, proclaim their identity, and defy school authority. They draw upon dance movements that are part of their heritage.

Black girls at HPES asserted black power, in-group exclusivity and superiority, and the possibility of reversed black/white power relations through their own dance. It seems reasonable to conclude that the black children's dance movements, contexts, and participation criteria symbolized and mediated existing and preferred social relations. The children's social world embodied the image of possible adult life. Dancing at HPES emphasized respect and mutual recognition that positions of power and influence may be reversed or at least moderated. At HPES this behavior did not mirror the concepts necessary to legitimize a social system of structured inequality in which they would be unequal to whites.

Children's peer education through dance is a different, though no less valid, means of learning than through the transmission model where schools prepare the knowledge and students with skills the schools deem important. The transaction or constructivist model (following the ideas of Piaget and Vygotsky) prepares students to participate in the reconstruction of themselves and their society, acting intelligently in experience, and solving problems. To follow this model it is important for teachers to be aware of students' real-life experiences. Children's interests and developmental needs guide their own inquiries and provide a base for teacher planning.

Do teachers just dismiss students' own dances and dance movements as mere play and "fooling around"? Or do they pay attention to the messages students send? The movement skills their dancing reveals? Teachers can use dance diagnostically and as a scaffold for teaching and learning.

Dance reveals students' interests as well as their misconceptions. Who dances what, where, when, and how comment on self- and group identity as well as cooperation and conflict. Misconceptions can be corrected by teaching students about their history and helping students develop interpersonal skills through dance education (after all, much theater dance has explored social themes). Teachers can involve a class in discussing the issues raised by the children's own dances at play. The class can explore how the problems revealed can be addressed and why rules broken should be adhered to. The teacher can lead students into a discussion of the role of dance as emblematic and how and what dance communicates. What are the messages of popular dances? In addition, teachers can ask students to teach their dances to other students. This empowers students in the formal learning context. When students teach others, the process fosters their analytical skills as they explain or break dance into pieces for instruction. When they teach their dance to others, children widen their friendship circle and make the themes everyone's concerns.

Chapter 8

National Identity and Cultural Diversity in Dance Education

It appears that we are to have a national dance.
The discovery that we have none was made the other day. . . .
The new national American dance will have nothing to do with love or war,
since these are not American occupations. It will be distinctively a business
dance, with perhaps a suggestion of politics.

– A National Dance, a <u>New York Times</u> editorial, December 21, 1884.

*I*n the 1980s an ongoing debate concerned the question of a national dance to represent the United States. The American Square Dance Association lobbied Congress to name the square dance the national dance. But because of the thriving diversity of America's dances and cultures, testimony against such a designation halted Congressional action.

Individual groups are examining how to keep their group identity distinct but also identify themselves as full members of the nation in which they reside. The question of cultural diversity is also a concern for dance education (Hanna 1994a). Although the issue of cultural diversity affects many nations, I focus this discussion on the United States because the issue seems particularly relevant given our changing demography. I turn first to the issue of commonality and dances as a nation's emissaries. Next, I address the values and challenges of achieving cultural commonality and diversity in dance education and suggest ways of dealing with these challenges effectively.

HOW CAN DANCE REFLECT ONE'S NATIONAL IDENTITY?

How do we reconcile what it is to be an American and respect cultural diversity at the same time? Are there characteristics that distinguish American dance from the dance of other nations? Are there differences within a genre (e.g., ballet, modern, disco)? A dance, like flags and anthems (Cerulo 1995) or even one's clothes, conveys messages of self, generation, gender, ethnicity, social class, and nationality reflecting a collective conscience (Hanna 1992b). Dance, like the mini-skirt I once wore (a symbol of the youth culture of the time), may embody philosophy, style, thematic content, an environment for creativity and production, the consequences of performances, and government policy.

DANCE MIRRORS A NATION'S MOTTO

E pluribus unum, Latin for "out of many, one," is the national motto America adopted in 1777. Dance history in the United States reflects this motto. An American is a person born in the United States or, if born elsewhere, someone who has sworn to support and defend the Constitution and the laws of the United States. American citizenship rests on common legal standards, political ideas, and a system of freedom under the law.

Americans are open to different forms of dance. After all, America is the land of opportunity, and individuals can always move to new frontiers geographically and culturally. Americans have a taste for risk and adventure, and innovation is a reigning aesthetic. On our nation's shores we have accepted, rejected, or used in part, the resources of the world.

Many dances from around the world have become part of the U.S. heritage and have entered the repertoires of theatrical and social dance. These dances, however, may not maintain their original form. Dancers of one culture often turn to other cultures for their creative inspiration. Indeed, most Americans belong to multiple groups and cultures, some of which overlap.

"Authenticity," consequently, is an elusive concept at best. Dance changes! Traditional dance is the dance of a group that is considered by most members of the group to be their cultural heritage; current participants have not created or introduced it. Ritual dance is behavior that is predictable, stereotyped, and basic. Yet a copy of a dance is in itself original and worthy of consideration in its own cultural context. Moreover, a theatrical format calls for a transformation; innovation here means that a custom can be an inspiration for new forms.

America has broken through the limitations of the high-art ballet establishment spawned by the European royal court. Although the aristocratic ballet previously sought inspiration from the dances of European peasants and other countries, American ballet cast its net even wider to match the nation's many peoples. Ballet dancers in the United States first appeared in the opera. Initially the dancers in these operas were American, English, Hungarian, German, French, and Italian, many of whom spoke only their native tongue. So the ballet master often gave directions in pantomime.

The Russian choreographer George Balanchine transformed the genre through his work with the New York City Ballet. Speed, one of Balanchine's hallmarks, reflected the tenor of the heterogeneous city in which he had come to reside. Style and theme in his work further mirrored various cultural currents in the United States. Balanchine transformed and adapted the kinetic energy and rhythms of African-Americans and used this inspiration in some of his ballets (Gottschild 1996).

DANCES BECOME A NATION'S EMISSARIES

Drawing upon dances from around the world, two groups in the United States, women and African-Americans created unique forms that call attention to the nation. These dancers perform and teach abroad and visitors see and study with them in the United States. Now TV and film facilitate the representation of the country through its dance.

Some women choreographers created new kinds of dance in the modern dance tradition of innovation and creative independence. Each choreographer tends to break away from and rebel against a predecessor.

In catalyzing the transformation of the dance landscape, female modern dancers drew upon other cultures and influenced male choreographers. Isadora Duncan found inspiration in early Greece. Ruth St. Denis, mother of the most flourishing lineage of modern dance, borrowed from other cultures, especially Asian, for the visual beauty, spiritual message, and sexuality of the dancing. When St. Denis was choreographing and performing in the early 1900s, genteel women did not attend the ballet, which was similar in status to striptease dancing today (Hanna 1998b, 1999). She helped to elevate dance to an acceptable and respectable art form. Her partner, Ted Shawn, drew inspiration from the dances of Japan, India, Egypt, Mexico, and the Aztec and Hopi Indians.

Since St. Denis and Shawn founded Denishawn, the country's first dance company in 1915, American choreographers have been involved in an endless search for new material among different cultures and ancient traditions (Solomon and Solomon 1995). Helen Tamiris drew upon the African heritage of hip movements and bent knees in her dances to African-American spirituals (Hanna 1983). Martha Graham, the quintessential American, drew inspiration from her homeland, including the Penitente Indians of New Mexico and church-goers of the rustic Appalachian mountains in Pennsylvania. She also was interested in Hindu philosophy, Buddhism, Noh, and Balinese culture. Graham's work has suggestions in it of Egyptian profiles, Javanese flexed feet, and Cambodian knee walks.

Erick Hawkins, after earning a B.A. in classics from Harvard University, studying and performing ballet, and being a member of Graham's company, read F.S.C. Northrop's *The Meeting of East and West* and studied Zen in the 1950s. He came to believe that movement should happen sensually and naturally, in harmony with nature and convey an inner movement quality of enlightenment and spirituality. He was fascinated with the prominent role of men in southwest American Indian and Asian dance because ballet had come to favor the female. So he visited New Mexico and Arizona, explaining, "I had to see and feel whether a grown man could dance without being a fool" (quoted in Kisselgoff 1980:43).

Many other prolific American choreographers also found inspiration in other cultures. Jack Cole, father of jazz dance in the Broadway style, choreographed the musical "Kismet" with Indian influences. José Limón drew upon his Mexican and Spanish heritage with choreographic themes of jealousy and machismo. Seeking their roots, Katherine Dunham and Pearl Primus used movements from Caribbean and African dances. Kei Takei continued to choreograph new work using Japanese style movements and themes after moving to the United States.

The crucible of social dance creativity lies in our streets, homes, and clubs. New social dances provide grist for the choreographic mill and represent the United States abroad.

Rooted in African traditions, black Americans gave birth to jazz, which evolved fully fledged and triumphant in Harlem's emporium of dancing. Jazz was the source of dancing madness, and ragtime was riotous. Such dances as the turkey trot, fox trot, and jitterbug signaled the breakdown of the Victorian era. However, these new styles of American dancing were considered immoral by many in the United States and Europe at the time. For example, Swiss hotels in 1912 prohibited them. In 1913, a Prussian general was so infuriated by a colonel's criticism that he had allowed his daughter to dance the turkey trot with an officer at the garrison ball that he insisted on a duel to the death (Duel Over Turkey Trot 1913). African-Americans have continued to create new social dance styles that are soon appropriated by other groups (e.g., hip hop) (Spalding and Woodside 1995). Theatrical dance, too, has been enriched by black creativity in dance (Gottschild 1996).

American dance marathons were popular during the Depression, with participants performing 27-hour stretches of nonstop jazz-style dance. These marathons were a contest for survival: Control over the body might temporarily compensate for a sense of imminent loss. The endurance contests emerged from the American penchant for novelty and popular heroes, such as aviators Charles Lindbergh and Amelia Earhart, whose record-breaking feats (Calabria 1993; Martin 1994) were an inspiration for marathon dancing.

Theater and social dance in the United States have drawn upon the dances of many cultures. From this richness has emerged dances that reflect the nation.

WHAT ARE THE VALUES OF CULTURAL DIVERSITY IN DANCE EDUCATION?

The reasons for looking at other cultures' dances are multifold (see Banks 1997). Although dance is not a universal language, each individual has a body that moves; we can identify with other cultural groups through the shared experience of the human body in motion. Cross-cultural understanding depends on the interplay between skilled performance and an observer's sensitive perception in feeling movement and interpreting it.

To learn the dances of many peoples was, for Ted Shawn, to learn to love the people themselves. Diversity has created what is considered American dance and what is now part of the search for parity in this culture. U.S. society is becoming more diverse demographically than ever before. Moreover, as the world continues to shrink and homogenize with technological advances, exchanges among dance communities and peoples increase.

Going as far back as the 1893 World's Fair in Chicago, in which "belly dancers" served as emissaries for their Middle Eastern countries, other nations have had dances that showcase their national identity. Examples include the Morris dance in England, flamenco in Spain, and classical dances such as Bharata Natyam in India. The following sections discuss how dance helps us to understand other cultures as well as gain a better understanding of ourselves; by understanding other cultures through their dances, we can derive choreographic inspiration and other benefits.

UNDERSTANDING OTHERS

Dance is a particularly vibrant means through which to begin to understand a different culture; dance enables one to learn much about the dance's creators, producers, and audiences (Ijaz 1980). Dance, like language, is a window to a person's worldview, as we saw in chapter 7's discussion of children's dance at play. Exposure to various aesthetics and their sociocultural contexts and history allows a person to see and understand more than her or his own footsteps. Diverse cultures have unique and meaningful ways of expressing universal themes.

UNDERSTANDING ONE'S SELF

By looking at ourselves in our infinite human variety, we can better understand our own forms of dance and gain a deeper self-knowledge. Learning about one's own culture usually provides a sense of identity, roots, and self-understanding (Cunningham 1991; Hanna 1997d).

The path to self-understanding includes learning about our own culture-bound assumptions about dance (see Chalmers 1996:14-25). In the United States these assumptions have included the views that

Europeans have produced the best dance in the world, ballet is the most important dance form, and the most important choreographers are men.

CHOREOGRAPHIC INSPIRATION

Dance creations do not arise out of thin air. Choreography involves the intertwining of creative, independent invention with the borrowing of others' themes; styles; structures; and use of space, time, and effort. Knowledge of other cultures' dances provide grist for the choreographic mill and source material for dancer and audience interpretation (Hanna 1991a).

OTHER BENEFITS

Experiencing similarities and differences in dance modes of expression may help an individual to become more skillful and comfortable interacting with members of diverse groups at work and at play. Learning about other cultures can stretch the mind and help dissolve prejudice.

In addition, exposure to other cultures gets people out of their own frameworks, stimulates curiosity, and develops imagination. Awareness of alternatives and borrowing can stimulate cutting-edge critical thought, a key element in sound decision making in a competitive world economy.

ARE THERE PROBLEMS WITH CULTURAL DIVERSITY IN DANCE EDUCATION?

Culture is constructed, negotiated, and contested, anthropologist Jack Eller points out (1997). It is political and must be treated as such. Multiculturalism, he continues, is "a *social movement*. . . . The debates . . . are really about which groups and interests will hold power and shape the production and reproduction of society in such domains as education, government institutions, and art" (p. 251). The main thrust of multiculturalism "seeks an overall improvement in knowledge and awareness through the inclusion of multiple perspectives" (p. 254).

Supporting cultural diversity in the schools is a goal in education and even a mandate in some states. But although using dance to support cultural diversity is invaluable, the odyssey to achieve parity is troublesome.

An example of the problems of cross-cultural understanding comes from audience members at a Japanese Kabuki dance concert in one of my studies (Hanna 1983). An American opera singer said, "My comprehension was limited to certain body areas due to Western cultural blinders. I found myself focusing on facial expression which is probably typically Western." Another spectator said, "The dance form is too unknown to interpret." A teacher agreed, "It is difficult to know where you are in a dance and a dance form you are not familiar with." This kind of problem could be improved somewhat by instructing audience members about Kabuki dance prior to the performance. Other problems with supporting cultural diversity in dance education are not so easily solved.

SELECTING CULTURES OR DANCES TO EMPHASIZE

A key issue in using dance for culturally diverse education is whose culture? Whose dance? Intracultural variation exists within an individual culture; that is, diversity exists within diversity. Society often puts homogeneous labels on groups that differentiate themselves. A cultural designation, in this context, may thereby become a false and even damaging stereotype behind which an individual is submerged.

Members of a "group" may disagree on what aspects of a group's or subgroup's culture should be reflected in school and how. This group's disagreement may in turn create school–community friction. Given the richness and abundance of cultural diversity, along with limited time in school, putting priorities on what receives attention is unavoidable. When a group lacks a specific, easily identified form of dance, which other groups may have, who decides what is appropriate to create and designate as one's own dance and how this decision is to be made? Like the work of many African-American writers, film director Spike Lee's film "School Daze" shows that African-Americans often recognize divisions. These encompass social class, skin color, region or country of origin, amount of time lived in an area, gender, age, religion, and kind of racist oppression experienced. Yet, policy makers often regard African-Americans as a homogeneous, unified group because they are American citizens with African roots.

Some African-Americans even view emotionally expressive aspects of African-American culture, such as gospel music, feeling the spirit through motoric manifestation, and traditional dance genres as aesthetically inferior. In a Philadelphia school, officials banned children's spontaneous playground dancing, what the students called, "doin' steps," on the grounds that it was "lewd, fresh, inappropriate for school, disrespectful, and too sexual" (Gilmore 1983). Yet officials in a Dallas school had no objection to this kind of dancing (Hanna 1986; see also Hanna 1994d). Some people give attention to their African heritage through doing or viewing dance (Hazzard-Gordon 1983; Kerr-Berry 1994), whereas others have different interests. Such diversity within a single group of people is neverending.

The "Hispanic" and "Caribbean" communities of New York City, Miami, and Los Angeles include recent immigrants and established families of Cubans, Dominicans, Guatemalans, Haitians, Jamaicans, Mexicans, Nicaraguans, and Puerto Ricans. This diversity, compounded by generational and life-cycle divisions, reflects a plethora of diverse music and dance.

Note that some Christian religious groups do not permit dance. Other groups who participate in dance are suspicious about the morality of the dance movement, themes, music, and dress (Willis 1995a:50). Still other Christian religious groups view dance as a healthy and positive expression.

LACK OF EVIDENCE THAT MULTICULTURAL PROGRAMS WORK

A worthy panoply of rationales for multicultural education and multicultural arts education is apparent. Yet, little evaluation is done to determine if specific programs and approaches are doing what they are supposed to do. Rationales for supporting multicultural education are based on such transformations as helping at-risk students to succeed in school, improving social relations among groups, and assisting all individuals to reach their potential. Developing respect for diverse but equally valid forms of expression, avoiding the causes of oppression, and dispelling stereotypes are other purported reasons to support diversity. Even more basic, however, are the criticisms of untested and insupportable assumptions regarding goals, strategies, and outcomes of multiculturalism (Hoffman 1996).

At least one evaluation has demonstrated the gap between such program goals and outcomes. Raymond Giles (1972), who coordinated New York City's African-American Institute in-service courses on Africa, later interviewed 15 classes of predominantly African-American students in grades four, five, and six in Central Harlem. The students had undergone nine months of hourly study once or twice a week on African culture and history, with the goal of improving student self-image and engendering an appreciation of their African heritage. Most of the students, however, expressed the same hostile beliefs and negative stereotypes about Africa held by the uninformed or misinformed.

In contrast, Lorenzo Trujillo (1979) found that high school students who participated in a six-week Hispanic Ethnic Dance Curriculum benefited from the experience. A significant gain was observed in the students' self-concept and academic achievement.

It is possible that exposure to dances symbolic of a cultural group might evoke a new negativity toward that group. For example, if students dislike another group's dance, or previously held negative associations remain unchallenged, they could dislike the group the dance represents.

THREAT TO SOCIAL MOBILITY

A third problem in supporting diversity in the schools is the sometimes antithetical relationship between preserving symbols of a cultural group, such as the dance, and socioeconomic mobility. The dance can reflect what is as well as suggest what might be. For migrants or immigrants to a new place, holding on to a familiar cultural dance often provides an anchor in a sea of uncertainty and an emotional ballast for life's travails. Some parents, however, do not want their own cultural dances to be presented in schools because they want the schools to "Americanize" their children. If the dances are embedded in a low-status, culturally conservative group, the dances may ultimately hamper the performers' integration into a new social setting and limit their socioeconomic mobility. Some researchers, in fact, criticize multicultural education as a palliative to keep minorities from rebelling against oppressive systems (Modgil et al. 1986)!

At times, upwardly mobile groups eschew their own cultural dance aesthetic expression. In exchange, they take on the dance forms of the group they wish to emulate on the next rung of the socioeconomic ladder. In Texas, German and Polish farmers were better off economically than Mexicans. So Mexicans incorporated beats and patterns of the music and dance of the farmers into their own cross-pollinated Tex-Mex music and dance. It is often only when people have improved their socioeconomic situation that they rediscover their earlier cultural heritage.

APPROPRIATION OF ANOTHER'S CULTURE

Because dances often reflect a group identity and are viewed as property, a fourth problem needs to be considered in supporting diversity: An outsider's appropriation of a cultural group's dance may be resented, even considered a form of theft or offense. Some groups dance their dances as emblematic of their group. Consequently, they do not want outsiders dancing them. At times, voices call for African dance for African-Americans, Latino dances for Latinos, and so on.

Religious dances present another challenge. Often such dances are supposed to be only for the practitioners of a particular religion. The religious beliefs among some Native Americans, for example, preclude a secularization of sacred dance.

By today's "politically correct" standards, Western dance could be accused of vulgarizing, idealizing, and appropriating facets of non-Western cultures. Recall that ballet and modern dance incorporated Western visions of other people's dances and inspired interest in ethnic styles through their interpretations.

EMBARRASSMENT

A fifth issue in supporting diversity in the schools is that good intentions in the use of dance in multicultural education may go astray. People may not be sufficiently aware of each other's point of view. Sometimes a dance form may be romanticized unrealistically, symbolize a low-status group, or have a ritual status. Because people may feel uncomfortable discussing cultural differences, they may inadvertently offend or hurt one another.

Recognition of ethnic-related dance diversity itself may cause problems. Some children do not want to be singled out for the background from which they come. Recognition for any reason, be it cultural group aesthetic expression or academic achievement, may subject children to ridicule and humiliation. Fear of humiliation ranks high among children's concerns (Yamamoto 1987).

HOW CAN WE SOLVE PROBLEMS OF CULTURAL DIVERSITY IN DANCE EDUCATION?

Although cultural diversity is invaluable, its promotion can also have negative consequences as just discussed. The three approaches discussed next are useful for dealing with these challenges.

Investigate Sensitivities and Complexities

It is critical for educators to recognize that cultures are not only internally diverse but also in a constant state of change. Besides receiving multicultural training, educators can benefit from learning how to discover the views and problems of the groups they serve. Moreover, schools should encourage parents, teachers, and students to speak forthrightly in settings free from incrimination and penalty.

Listening to children's voices is necessary to educate them well. Teachers need to listen to and learn about students' views about their social world, their peer group priorities and pressures, their family and community life, and their culture's dance.

Balance Assimilation with Diversity

It may be wise to provide all individuals with the opportunity for choice. Instructors can teach the skills, knowledge, and dance culture that allow a person access to socioeconomic mobility with the possibility of code switching (being able to operate in one or another dance culture at will). In addition, recognizing the cultural ethos that defines what it means to be an American helps to avoid enforced divisiveness.

Students can compare their own creative dances with the dances of other cultures. They can explore the similarities among dances that provide unity as well as the differences that provide variety. In looking at the dances of other cultures students can compare the use of the human body, staging, time, space, effort, dancer training, and public presentation. Who does what? What are the emphases in movement? What are the themes? Do the dances function as cultural transmitters or catalysts for change? (See appendix 1 for discussion questions about diversity and similarities and Chalmers 1996 for further issues to explore with students.)

Evaluate

It is important to discover whether dance education programs intended to support diversity in schools validate their goals. It is also critical to assess the many surprisingly unintended effects caused by well-meaning programs. Cultural expressions, such as dances, are symbols; as such they are a form of cultural shorthand and susceptible to distortion. Moreover, symbols and their meanings change over time

SOLVING PROBLEMS OF CULTURAL DIVERSITY

Problems	Possible Solutions
Misunderstanding dance	Dance instruction
Selecting a culture or dance to emphasize	Investigate sensitivities
No evidence about program	Evaluate programs
Emphasizing the dance of a culture can hinder the performer's integration into a new social setting	Offer choice of dances, balancing assimilation with diversity
A culture resenting outsiders dancing their dances	Discover diverse cultures' views
Singling out a child representative of a culture may cause embarrassment	Explore sensitivities and similarities

in response to environmental forces. Research can reveal students' felt and reflective experiences in response to exposure to different cultures' dances.

ENCORE

U.S. culture is integrative, cross-pollinating, and part of globalization. Americans have many identities: personal and group identities along with common cultural identities. Recognizing people's differences could create divisiveness in American society. Yet it need not become an immutable stone wall to our country's strength. Eleanor Holmes Norton, the District of Columbia's representative to Congress, said that "racial and ethnic pride are almost always wonderful, and they are almost always dangerous." The challenge for America, now as always, is to 'strike a balance' between legitimate group pride and aspiration on the one side and an embrace of an

Susan McGreevy-Nichols

An African dance class. Listening to children's voices is necessary to educate them well.

American identity rooted in pluralism on the other" (quoted in E.J. Dionne 1997).

We look at other cultures' dances to learn about them, to show respect and parity, and to gain choreographic inspiration. Given the limited time for dance in K-12 education and given cultural sensitivities, however, teachers must tread carefully in selecting dances of different cultures. These diverse dances have contributed to what is considered American dance and what is now part of the search for parity in American culture. The United States has become demographically more diverse than ever before. Moreover, as the world continues to shrink and homogenize with technological advances, exchanges among dance communities and peoples increase, and the dances themselves are subject to change.

Chapter 9

Dance Education and Gender

*Holding up a mirror, dance
says to us: Look at yourself or
at how you might be. The
image we see may be
pleasing, awkward,
or even terrifying.*

— JUDITH LYNNE HANNA
(1988B:XIII)

Sex roles, or gender, do not just happen. Beyond biological determinants, culture and society create and perpetuate notions of what is considered to be appropriate behavior for males and females. This chapter explores what dance images convey in this regard and what are the implications of different gender behavior in dance education (see Arkin 1994, Bond 1994, Ferdun 1994, Meglin 1994).

DO WE LEARN GENDER THROUGH DANCE?

An individual tends to reproduce attitudes, acts, and emotion exhibited by an observed live or symbolic (film or videotape) model, according to psychologist Albert Bandura's (1986) social learning theory. So we learn what it is to be male and female through the images we see and make. Children learn gender patterns through observing in dance who does what, when, where, how, along with or to whom. Dancing, both realistically and symbolically, may be about a range of social relations. One may see and create visions of courtship, climax, male chauvinism, feminist thought, interpersonal exchanges, group interaction, casual relations, and stable associations. Moreover, dance is a medium through which choreographers manipulate, interpret, legitimate, and reproduce the patterns of gender cooperation and conflict that order society. Teaching and learning of sex roles are implicated in the dance studio, classroom, theater, and social setting.

The potency of dance images to "show and tell" gender continuity and change in contemporary Western society reflects its numerous dance students. It also reflects the accessibility of dance in popular films, television, and publications. No longer the province of elite, ticket-paying theatergoers primarily in large cities, dance performances can reach nearly an entire nation through television. Visual imagery is especially important in a generation of television watching and computer viewing.

As a youngster I had not given any thought to differences between male and female dancing or the relationship of dance to society. I noticed, however, that far more girls were in my dance classes than boys and that males led females in social dancing. Years later I was invited to join Ewe dancers in Accra, Ghana, during field research. As I danced the women gently corrected me: I was not supposed to imitate the males' energetic movements but instead the females' more subdued style.

Among Nigeria's Ubakala people, I learned that when the biological and gender roles of men and women are most diverse (men as the warrior life-takers and women as the childbearing life-givers), their dance movements differ most markedly in the use of time, space, and effort. Men use angles, rapid rhythm, and large, forceful gestures and movements, whereas women use circles, slow rhythm, and sustained small gestures and movements. However, young people of both sexes have relatively similar dance movements and often perform the same dances. Elderly men and women have the same pattern (Hanna 1987, 1988b; see Kerr-Berry 1994).

After returning home I became more aware that over the nearly half century that I had been watching dance, the images of gender behavior had changed. And what I observed both on and off the stage in a variety of different dance forms coincided with dramatic changes in the United States. Dance was mirroring, refracting, and even prefiguring what was taking place in the women's and gay liberation movements and what the reactions were to these changes. Innovative thrusts in new directions also evoked nostalgia for the past.

But still behind the scenes and at the helm were mostly male artistic directors and choreographers. They made the decisions and most dancers were women obediently taking orders.

DO WE TEACH SEX ROLES IN EDUCATION?

So how do gender changes in society and dance relate to dance education? The literature on education reveals that schools generally reproduce the status quo. Unfortunately, if you happen to be female, this means your subordination to males. Women continue to challenge this pattern as schools are being required to create gender equitable programs (Nilges 1996).

Prior to the 1970s, girls in U.S. society were engaged in the sex-typed activities of sewing and cooking, while boys were sawing and building. Then in the 1970s some schools began to institute programs in which all youngsters participate in home economics as well as shop training. Physical education had been markedly different for each sex as well. Now in many schools the same movement activities in sports and dance are becoming available for boys and girls. In some respects, attire has become unisex. And women increasingly take on leadership positions formerly held by men in all fields. The Prohibition of Sex Discrimination Act (Title 9 of the

Education Amendments of 1972, 20 USC Section 1681 et seq.) mandated equal opportunities for males and females.

What Does History Tell Us About Gender in Dance?

History reveals remarkable changes in male and female kinetic images in different dance genres. Sometimes the dance imagery prefigures future directions in social life.

Changing Gender Images in Dance

Whereas in the 400-year-old European classical ballet men lifted and supported women, in the 20th century, modern dance permitted women to dance on their own. Women became free from the restraints of male-dictated movement, training, body image, narrative, costumes, management, and strictures on sexuality.

Since the 1960s we have seen not only unisex patterns but also role reversals. Men lift and support men as women do likewise. Like their male counterparts, women now also use weight, identify with masculine traits, and project their own vigor. In Jiri Kylian's "Symphony in D," which premiered in 1976, women caught an airborne man. In 1981 in his work, "Shared Distance," Bill T. Jones, a large and muscular man, lifted Amy Pivar, a small and petite woman—then she lifted him.

Ballet danseur Igor Youskevitch believes the classical pas de deux overstates a life situation: the man, as a gallant gentleman, helps the woman and voluntarily endures hardship for the sake of her comfort. Yet partner roles often mirror patronage by the stronger sex of the weaker sex. The woman "looks up" to the man, rising en pointe to meet him. Rising en pointe in some positions renders the dancer helpless and requiring assistance.

For Yousekevitch (1969), the male dancer reflects his masculine inclinations to lead, achieve, and be a hero. Reflecting gender stereotypes, he alleges that the female does not need a meaningful motive to dance, whereas a male dancer must justify the action! Ballerina Gelsey Kirkland complained that choreographer George Balanchine, and other Russian men she has known, did not think women are capable of thinking and engaging in ideas (1986).

Traditional forms rarely survive unscathed over time. Ballet has incorporated gender patterns from other countries and aspects of other dance forms, including modern, postmodern, and jazz. For example, ballet danseur Bruce Marks (quoted in Newman 1982:206) pointed out that it had been inappropriate in the United States, but not in France, for a man to lift his leg higher than hip level for extensions and stretching. Change came about in the 1980s, and today one sees men's legs extend easily in a stretch.

Tap dance, incorporating African and Irish style movements, was limited to an all-male street corner competition in the early 20th century. It moved into theater and film and bottomed out in the 1950s. A renaissance began with the 1980s trend among professional white women dancers to return to the roots of tap. They are learning from older black male performers and tapping in concert.

RESPECTABILITY OF DANCE AS A CAREER

The historical status of dance as a career for men and women varies. Although Louis XIV and his courtly followers danced, after the French Revolution and Industrial Revolution along with the prevailing view of a mind–body split, mental activities took pride of place over the physical. Prestigious men eschewed dancing. For males, dancing was primarily thought of as emasculating, an activity for homosexuals. Besides, as a profession, it paid poorly. Dancing, but not dance management, became feminized.

As noted in chapter 6, Jacques d'Amboise at first worked only with boys because he did not want them to think dance was "just for sissies or girls." Some contemporary males did not become dancers or choreographers until they were in college.

Rudolf Nureyev, a Russian defector to the United States, brought male respectability in dance to the fore once again. He possessed outstanding technical and dramatic prowess; international recognition; and, of significance, a stature that accrues to a person with a six-digit income!

The recognition of a mind–body integration, liberation movements, potential male earning, and new educational efforts have all helped to make dance for males more acceptable. The media compared the six-digit income for danseur Rudolph Nureyev with the earnings of athletes. Mikhail Baryshnikov, a very masculine and athletic dancer, has also been a big earner and media publicist for dance. Arthur Mitchell's Dance Theatre of Harlem is a source of inspiration for black male ballet dancers. Dancers Fred Astaire and Gene Kelly, on film, and Ted Shawn, José Limón, Paul Taylor, Alwin Nikolais, Merce Cunningham, Donald McKayle, and Alvin Ailey, in theater, are also among those who have inspired male dancers. When professional and collegiate sports teams take ballet as part of their training, dance gains respect for its physical demands.

Female dancing onstage was not respectable either until the mid-20th century. My father, a musician for the Ballet Russe de Monte Carlo, told me as an aspiring dancer, "Dancers aren't treated nicely." He did not elaborate. I later learned that female dancers were thought to be part of the demimonde, or echelons of prostitution. More attractive than working in sweatshops or as a domestic, dancing was an avenue for poor women with pretty faces and bodies and talent to attract the attention of wealthy patrons.

By the 1920s, however, due largely to the efforts of modern dance pioneers from well-educated, middle-class families, theatrical dance for women was gaining respectability. Martha Graham, whose father was a medical doctor, boosted the respectability of women dancers on onstage.

The 1960s heralded a general freeing of sexual mores and occupational choices. Still, dance education was primarily thought of as a girl's activity. Bucknell University dance director Danna Frangione explains that higher education dance professors have worked over the years against the prejudice that their role was merely to train young women in "poise, posture, and deportment" (1988).

In 1997 there were still fewer male than female dancers. A dancer survey conducted in that year shows that, "men seem to have fewer problems finding a job. More men have worked full-time in dance . . . and they are also more likely to achieve principal status as professionals. . . . Even when women achieve a leading position, full-time jobs are significantly more common for men than for women. . . . Male dancers perform longer, on average, and retire eight years later than female dancers. . . ." (Hamilton 1997:64; 1998). Perhaps men do better and hold a greater number of positions of leadership in the dance world than do women because society has expected women to be more passive and obedient (see Stinson 1987).

WHAT ARE THE IMPLICATIONS OF GENDER ROLES IN THE DANCE CLASSROOM?

In many forms of dance, different patterns of movement exist for each gender; we must become sensitive to these patterns and how they constrain the individual dancer's potential and the art of dance. Paying attention to these issues will help educators to make dance

Paolo Galli/The Kirov Academy

Do we teach the same or different movements to boys and girls?

more relevant and accessible to the young. Students have their own unique historical time and place (see Meglin 1994); educators need to recognize this to make dance more meaningful to their students.

NATURE'S CONTRIBUTION TO GENDER IN DANCE

Granted that kinetic imagery is a way of knowing, a relevant question must be addressed: Are there biological bases for different movements for males and females? The human species is sexually dimorphic; distinctions exist between the male and female body shape and composition, physiology, and functioning. These differences become noticeably apparent with maturation during adolescence. Men are generally heavier, taller, and more muscular than women, which gives men superior speed and strength. Because women sweat less profusely and are able to conserve body fluids more easily than men, women do well in endurance activities and compete successfully with men. Women have less upper body strength and a lower center of gravity concentrated in the hips and legs. Their pelvic structure forces them to take smaller steps than men whose legs might be the same length. They have smaller hearts and lungs and run slower and shorter distances. Despite these inherent differences, training prior to a person's maturation and afterward can make a difference in what an individual, nearly irrespective of sex, can do.

TEACHERS' CONTRIBUTIONS TO GENDER IN DANCE

Gender is learned through what people do and what they see as well as what they are told verbally. Why can't girls be "girls" and boys be "boys"? Do we want both sexes to feel comfortable in our dance classes? Do we show more pictures of one or the other sex? What does the dancer do? What movements do we teach boys and girls? Do we teach them the same steps, phrases, and styles; the same pace, space, and effort? Are girls encouraged to jump high and leap broadly? Do we encourage young girls to be leaders? Are boys urged to increase the extensions of their legs? These are some of the questions we must ask ourselves in our classrooms and studios as we seek to achieve equality in dance.

Some dance forms and stories have distinct gender roles. Others are unisex in that the movements are done by both sexes in the same way. Assuming that movement is a marker of a person's identity, are there times when we want specific movement for males and females? If we want to preserve traditions and distinct gender, says Hortensia Fonseca, Maryland Academy of Youth Ballet director and teacher for 40 years, the answer is "yes." Fonseca has trained such luminaries as her son, Peter Fonseca; Susan Jaffe; and other American Ballet Theatre principals. Because homosexual males are disproportionately represented in ballet and harassed in society, she confines boys' dancing to male folk dance-derived steps, such as the leap and gallop, and emphasizes elevation and strength. She also prefers masculine-style clothing. When a youth becomes 15 or 16 and wants to work on more lyrical movements, she incorporates these into the boy's training.

Professor John R. Crawford offers this view:

> The challenge is to structure movement experiences that create a sense of gender identity without enforcing rigid stereotypes. Speed, power, and scale of movement should be chosen to reflect boys' interests as well as girls'. All participants should be encouraged to explore movement outside their usual range. (1994:42)

An argument for teaching boys apart from girls in the early stages of professional classical ballet training (10 to 12 years of age) is based on physical growth distinctions (Lawson 1989). Boys do not change physical shape until late in puberty and must therefore adopt a correct stance at the beginning of their training, whereas girls must continually adjust their stance to accommodate the development of bust and buttocks.

There are other questions for dance teachers to ponder when thinking of the part they play in deliberately and inadvertently teaching gender roles to students. What are the themes and stories of the ballets and other dances taught in class and staged for performance? Ballets based on fairly tales and myths, such as "Cinderella" and "The Nutcracker" tell us how to behave. Many situate women in the home, subordinate them to a male prince or father figure, and give them no alternative future but marriage. Passivity, dependence, and self-sacrifice are celebrated as the heroine's cardinal virtues. Does the female dancer exist only for Prince Charming or is she assertively accomplishing things? Is the man only a prince, father figure, or country bumpkin? What about an ordinary male?

Who sews the costumes and builds the sets? Are dance activities reinforcing patriarchal unequal norms? Do the dance activities encourage boys and girls to think and make choices among possibilities? Do they have a say in creating or selecting specific dances, interpreting character roles, and designing and developing the dance production?

What dance teachers say and do, and how they look and respond to students' reactions, convey gender notions. Teachers also need to respond thoughtfully to a student's evaluation of another dancer's movement as belonging to a member of the opposite sex. Verbal comments, movement demonstrations, and adjustment of students' bodies are telling. Despite a teacher's good intentions, the issue is what the students perceive.

BALANCING NOSTALGIA WITH RELEVANCE

A distinction lies between tradition, nostalgia for the past, and relevance to the contemporary era. Dance allows us to escape reality, to gain respite from stresses beyond a dance activity, and to release tension; in addition, dance helps us to confront our dilemmas and perhaps go on to solve them. I am not arguing for or against tradition, its preservation, revision, or elimination. What I am urging is awareness of how what we do in dance fits in with the rest of our lives. We need to share this awareness with our students and their audiences by placing tradition in its historical context and comparing tradition with contemporary values.

ENCORE

We learn what it is to be male or female from the dance images we see. Many dance teachers give students only dance movement technique. Instruction is primarily based on a visual–kinetic tradition along with commentary passed down through an oral tradition. Teachers often teach as they have been taught. In many dance forms they convey traditional gender roles as well as promote students' physical and mental discipline, coordination, gracefulness, physical fitness, and dance appreciation.

Yet in the course of studio and classroom physical activity, teachers can also convey an awareness of gender in dance and the changes in male and female roles in culture, society, and history. A career as a dancer now holds more prestige, and the binary division in gender has blurred with unisex and role reversal movements on stage. With your students, you can analyze gender in a historical context and debate how different dance forms relate to sex roles in society (Daly 1994). And in the regular school classroom, teachers can teach a range of social studies subjects through focusing on dance and its transformations to show what it is be male and female in different times and places.

Chapter 10

Dance Education and Stress

I was scared to death. And my parents were there!

— HELEN TAYLOR, DANCE TEACHER, ADMITTING HER FEARS ABOUT PERFORMING

*D*ance, as a performing art, is affected by the dancer's state of being. The dancer's gender, academic grades, ethnicity, and sexuality can be factors in causing stress as well as the pressures often felt in class and onstage.

Sometimes the signs of excessive stress are obvious: icy hands in a hot room; blushing, trembling extremities, shortness of breath, furtive eyes; tears and other emotional outbursts; nervousness, increased perspiration; extra trips to the bathroom; a cry of pain due to a muscle tear. At other times a stressed dancer alone is aware of the symptoms: a palpitating heart, muscular tension, faintness, back strain, depression, anxiety, difficulty in swallowing, headaches, loss of appetite, intestinal and eating disorders, insomnia, bruised psyche, feelings of frustration and resentment, and a knotted stomach.

This chapter begins by examining stress. I consider how to cope with stress through dance and avoid stress in dance and dance education (Hanna, 1990a, 1995b; Hamilton 1998).

WHAT IS STRESS?

A moderate amount of stress spurs a dance student or professional to rise to a challenge. Dance teacher and former member of New York City Ballet, Tomi Short, told me in conversation, "Nothing succeeds like success, and when you've pushed yourself to your limit and then achieve, there is a wonderful fulfilling sense of accomplishment that transcends all stress."

Dance teachers, students, parents, and performers alike are both victims and beneficiaries of stress. Stress, the "spice of life" or the "kiss of death," has been part of human existence dating back to our earliest written records. Today, stress is ever present in the media, medical literature, and psychological self-help industry.

Stress is not just "all in your head." Stress is the result of *any* demand on the body, whether it is a mental or physical press for survival or for the achievement of one's goals (see figure 10.1). Stress is a response process that takes place when individuals have to cope with pressures that are beyond that for which they are ready. Stress results when people feel strained, pushed to the outer limits of a particular capacity. An emergency or disaster, mounting everyday worries and pressures, or extraordinary excitement may trigger the response.

In the stress response, brain cells fire electrical signals stimulated by seeing, hearing, or smelling and associated thoughts. As the body mobilizes to cope with harsh conditions or excitement, it produces inflammatory hormones that give it increased speed and strength. The heart rate increases to pump blood rapidly to the muscles, blood pressure goes up, and digestive activity is inhibited. In preparation for possible injury, the immune system partially shuts down so that the body does not overreact and attack itself (Cooper 1996).

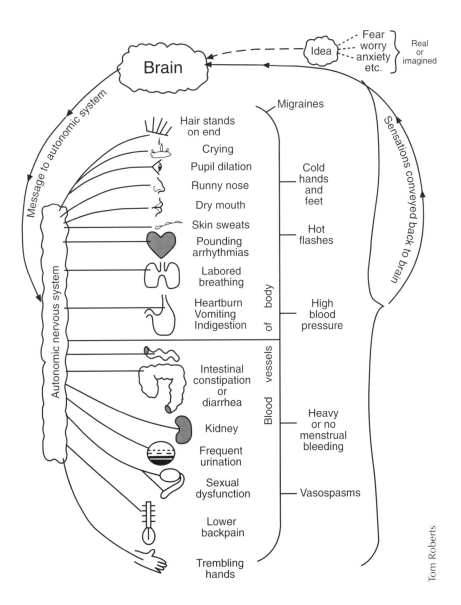

Figure 10.1 How the body can react to stress.

The so-called "fight or flight" response to stress is a critical survival tactic developed in our early ancestors. Following the stress response, the body produces anti-inflammatory hormones that conserve energy, rest the body, and return corporeal processes to normal.

If a person experiences unceasing stress, however, the body's immune system changes, and the heart and blood vessels carry extra burdens. When the body's defenses against the harmful effects of stress become overworked and exhausted, damage to the organism can be long-lasting or even permanent. Inability to use the body's mobilization effects—that fight or flight response—can leave the individual in grave peril.

Note that stress is a complex, textured phenomenon with mediating factors between stress and distress (Avison and Gotlib 1994). A stressor for one person may not cause stress for another. Although this selectivity is not entirely understood, an individual's personality, cultural attitudes toward potential stressors, and prior experience dealing with pressure all make a difference.

How Do We Cope With Stress Through Dance?

Stress is a demand to adapt and to change; it is a basic part of life itself. Since early history dance has been one means of coping with stress. Dancing buffers the negative impact of some kinds of psychological stress in many ways. Other stress reduction techniques include body movement, role playing, meditation, relaxation, and drugs.

Dance may be a means of dealing with the symptoms of stress but not the actual causes. Some problems are best dealt with by confronting them head-on. But coping with stress through dance may relax the dancer sufficiently to allow him or her to focus on resolving the stressors themselves. Some individuals develop a healthy passion for dance early in their lives. The downside of a life of dance is possible stress when one cannot dance regularly for whatever reason and has not developed nondance coping strategies.

Dance as a Stress Inoculation

Dancing may be a kind of stress inoculation. The physical exercise conditions an individual to be able to moderate, avoid, or even eliminate chronic (persistent) fatigue or lessen the impact of acute (short-term) fatigue, which are symptoms of stress.

ESCAPE

The well-known ballerina Gelsey Kirkland grew up in a stressful home, with a father who had fallen upon difficult times and had turned to abuse of alcohol and his family. The glamorous and secluded world of ballet offered Kirkland a means of escape from her unhappy home life (Kirkland 1986). Later, the ballet world also caused her stress.

As an activity in itself, dancing may cause a performer to experience emotional changes and altered states of consciousness. Because dance is different in some ways from other aspects of daily life, dancing permits a person to escape from self-consciousness, academic rigor, and work or personal problems.

The moving body, the instrument of dance, increases the circulation of oxygen-carrying blood to the muscles and the brain. Dance also alters the level of certain brain chemicals, in much the same way as the body returns to normal following the stress response pattern. In this way dancing can dissipate muscular and emotional tension and induce a sense of well-being and release.

Vigorous dancing induces the release of endorphins thought to produce analgesia (painlessness) and euphoria (a great high). Some dance teachers, such as Joe Orlando (former dance department chairperson of the Interlochen Arts Academy) and Bonnie Slawson (choreographer–director of Motion Mania), build an infectious, euphoric spirit in the studio's communal setting by exuding electric energy levels in their own classroom demonstrations and often dancing with the students. They do this carefully without sacrificing the development of students' strength, flexibility, and technique. Many dancers become ecstatic on a dance high that is similar to a drug-induced high but without the dysphoric downer effects. This sensation generated the terms "jazzed" and "on the jazz"—and keeps dancers coming back for more.

Dance also allows individuals to escape stress by moving into a fantasy world onstage or using mental imagery as they dance in class. A dancer can be a prince or princess, an animal, a ladies' man, or a siren. Sequined and tutued or dressed in form-revealing shiny unitards, a dancer onstage is far from the oversized sweats, Levi jeans, or business suits typifying everyday life.

MASTERY

Mastery of exercises and movement sequences in dance education increases one's sense of control over one's life. This mastery provides confidence and a respite from stressful situations. Of even greater importance, feeling this sense of control gives one the feeling of being able to cope with what was previously an excessive demand, that is, a stressor. As a young girl, dance was a creative arena in which Gelsey Kirkland could vent her fears and rage; unable to control her social world, she could nevertheless begin to coordinate the movements of her own body. Certainly dance provides an arena for young people, who have yet to possess the control of adults, to be self-empowered.

In chapter 6 I noted that accepting and appreciating the body and what it can do promotes a student's self-esteem and sense of self-empowerment. Mindfully controlling the dancing body gives students pride in the results of their efforts. In turn, mastery of this mind–body integration gives dancers the courage to tackle other difficult subjects.

Academic subjects, shop class, home economics class, or sports are also valid means for building mastery and self-esteem. But dance should at least be offered as another opportunity for mastery for those who are unable to achieve proficiency in other endeavors. Moreover, some communities need to overcome a history of athletics being associated with poor academic achievement, athletes who do not graduate from college, and universities that graduate illiterate athletes. Professor John Hoberman points out that the success and fame of black athletes has led to values exalting athletics at the expense of more intellectual pursuits (1997).

In addition, dance has distinct features as indicated in chapter 1. These include the intertwined multisensory, creative imagination; feeling; physical action; and languagelike communication through historical time and across geographical space. Mastery in dance has made some students realize that they can achieve in areas where people do not expect it of them.

CONFRONTING STRESSORS IN A SAFE ENVIRONMENT

Because of its languagelike quality, dance can represent events, ideas, and feelings; in turn, these can evoke anxiety or fear. Yet, fearsome representations through dance are "pretend" and do not hold the impact of real-life stressors. Consequently, fears and anxieties can be played with at a distance and thereby made less threatening.

Promoting self-expression through dance education encourages students to gain insight into themselves and others. This helps them prepare for the positive and negative domains of life. Moreover, by projecting their problems in dance form, students work through difficulties in their lives that create stress and impede their overall success. Distancing oneself or holding up a conflict to scrutiny through artistic self-expression allows a dance maker to evaluate a problem and work toward its resolution. Recall that at AileyCamp for at-risk youth in Kansas City, teachers asked students to make dances about what was disturbing them most. The students responded by making dances about drugs and death in their communities. Making, doing, or watching dances about real-life stressors are a means of coping with them. In addition to the loss of a beloved family member, many students today face the hazards of the drug and gang cultures with their violence and homicide; and youth suicide has increased. Students can work through these and other issues, such as sexuality, gender roles, and discrimination, by using dance as a springboard for communicating their concerns.

Classmates in dance education, furthermore, can provide a support group for coping with stress. Dance students share exercise; aesthetic enjoyment; and a sense of separate and collective energy, grace, accomplishment, mutual goals, concerns, and fellowship. Dancers may share their hopes and anxieties before and after classes as well as in class or during rehearsals. Children from dysfunctional homes may find a family substitute when teachers promote cooperative learning in dance. Teachers and students fulfill some parental roles when they work intensively for a long time on a group project such as a concert.

I have talked about how dance can be a medium through which students deal with stress. The flip side is next on the agenda.

CAN DANCE INDUCE STRESS?

Yes, dance does sometimes induce stress; however, as teachers know, dance stress may at times be beneficial. Moderate amounts of discomfiture, alerting and invigorating, make us function better. Stress goads productivity and sparks peak performances, the ability to "go that extra mile." Stress may stimulate a dancer to work harder to master multiple turns. Short told me, "Students are physically stressed in a classroom if they have a good teacher. The teacher works them to their ultimate limit." Stress can heighten a performer's awareness, sensitivity, and drive to succeed in the pursuit of excellence.

Some people seek out stress in the challenges of a dance career. Stress motivates aspiring stars as they passionately pursue the glory of success with its potential euphoria.

Gold medal winner in the junior division of the International Ballet Competition in Varna, Bulgaria, Rasta Thomas reported a problem that can be stressful for students who want exposure to a variety of dance styles: possessive dance teachers who want exclusivity. "They want you under their wing."

Dancers become what my orthopedist called "titrated," or accustomed to a certain level of physical activity. So it can be painful, frustrating, and very stressful for a dancer to become ill or injured and then have to work at regaining their prior level of fitness and technique. Each day of inactivity requires about 2 days of activity to regain the level of fitness experienced before the illness or injury, according to Dr. Harvey B. Simon of the Harvard Medical School. Those who attempt too rapid a comeback run the risk of excessive fatigue and injury.

TEACHING PRACTICES

Some students are easily intimidated and fear making fools of themselves before a teacher or classmates. They recoil from having to, for example, wear form-fitting dance outfits, critique themselves or others, or be critiqued by their teacher and peers. Many are concerned with their weight. Children may be developmentally and experientially unable to handle routines that are too challenging or complex. Youngsters who succeed early in their dance classes, however, usually develop the confidence to compete, audition, and pursue a dance career if they so choose.

A health survey conducted by Hamilton (1997:5) of dance students, professionals, and ex-dancers found,

> first, and perhaps most important, abusive training (from a dance teacher who verbally humiliates students, for example, or asks that an injured dancer perform full-out) results in much higher levels of stress and injury and can shorten a dancer's career (Hamilton 1997:5).

It is stressful for dancers to try to please the authority figures whom they view as holding their careers in their hands.

Is there a clear-cut balance between eustress (good stress) and distress (bad stress)? "No," answered Lani Rutter Hill, a dance instructor, who explained to me that

> dance is a most useful tool in the search for balance because it helps increase one's awareness of the body's natural responses. As with learning style, each individual's reaction to stress tells us something about his or her mode of operating, which can be worked with and expanded upon to promote healthy growth.

To find the delicate balance between eustress and distress, dance professionals, teachers, and students must discover how stress affects them and the people with whom they work. One tactic is to ask students and performers about teaching techniques, rehearsal procedures, and performance situations. Are they too stressful? Short (date?) was surprised to learn from her former students, Jodie Pattee of the Chicago Opera Ballet and Natalie Mofett of the Minnesota Ballet Company, that they were "scared to death" of her when they were about seven years old. The sometimes military-like discipline and exposure of one's body in form-revealing clothes in front of others can be stressful for novice dance students.

Giving public praise or correction, singling out an individual to perform, using competition, dividing students into ability and achievement performance groups, speaking with sarcasm, shouting, or even mildly slapping a misplaced body part in class may induce eustress *or* distress in a given individual. Factors that determine how an individual will react are an individual's age; upbringing; culture; social class; ethnic group; prior experience; and reason for dancing, be it preprofessional training, pleasure, dance appreciation, or physical fitness.

TEACHER STRESS

Teachers may burn out, or experience so much stress that it causes physical and emotional exhaustion. Dance teachers often compete for student enrollment, especially for those students with the potential to become professionals or at least to star in the end-of-the-year concert. The pressures of running a program, budgets, staffing, and interdisciplinary relations leave some teachers feeling overwhelmed.

Short reported that she and her colleagues, who have had dynamic professional dance performing careers, often feel the effects of the physical stress their bodies have undergone. Arthritis and knee and hip problems, for example, are above and beyond what the nondancer suffers. Moreover, ex-professional dancers often have to teach and execute steps without being sufficiently warmed up themselves.

PARENT-, SELF-, AND
COMPETITION-INDUCED STRESS

Students, like their teachers, can burn out, turn off to dance, and become prone to injury. Children may be asked by parents, coaches or teachers to accomplish more than that for which they are physically and emotionally ready, resulting in stress. Age, development, and multicultural expectations affect readiness; although some youngsters are simply naturally precocious. Juggling such things as academic requirements and dance classes or being unable to go to friends' parties because of class or rehearsal commitments can also be stressful.

Some parents unhealthily attempt to realize their own romantic theatrical ambitions through their offspring. Hortensia Fonseca, a dance instructor who is closely involved in the lives of her students, said to me that

> very often parents begin to realize their youngsters have talent; they see them perform. But the parents push these children a lot. They take them to auditions and urge them to take part in school and other local shows. Sometimes the floors [at these performances] are not right for dance. The children suffer tendinitis, shin splints, and knee and back injuries. They are taken to doctors, chiropractors, and physical therapists. They drop out if there are insufficient resources for treatment. The parents don't realize their children are too young to be doing so much. I tell the parents they are not helping the children.

Youngsters, however, may also impose unrealistic demands upon themselves. Because there are now numerous sources of information, students read about dance, the competitions, prizes, and scholarships—and they push themselves to obtain them. Impatient, they believe their bodies are indestructible. "I try to calm them," says Fonseca. Furthermore, those students who attend boarding schools of dance education often feel homesick.

Competitions are controversial and stressful (Hanna 1997f). Students with fragile egos and shaky self-esteem may take the competitions personally and suffer when they lose. A second-place winner in one competition threw his trophy in the garbage can!

Yet competitions also have benefits (Sims 1996). Rasta Thomas, who has won over 100 competitions, described to me how they had helped him.

> Competitions motivated hard work. . . . Competing helps bring out the character inside you. It gives you good stage presence. Judges are there to help you, give criticism. Some important people come to you, and they introduce you to others. It's one continuing process. Besides, I like traveling and seeing the world.

Dance competitions have also been praised for giving students a realistic perspective about their capability in relation to their peers. Competitions usually include master classes that expose young contestants to different forms and styles of dance. Competitions can raise personal standards and give "sheltered" students some sense of what the real dance world is like—highly competitive.

Furthermore, competitions give dance students the opportunity to win trophies, cash, and scholarships. Dance company directors often sit in the audience scouting for future performers. In a competitive society, dance competitions provide students with tangible goals.

Some parents judge a dance school by how many trophies are in the window, hoping their youngster's wins will help pay for her or his dance education and related expenses. Many major performing and choreography competitions held worldwide every year are, in a sense, high-level auditions for places at prestigious dance schools, in first-rate dance companies, and with fine coaches.

STAGE FRIGHT

Some students, and, indeed, many professionals, suffer the performance stress called stage fright. Helen Taylor, a dance instructor, surprised her adult students, myself included, by admitting to this problem. But she believes that "if you can identify and confront fear and nervousness, you can use the energy constructively to enhance the strength and joy of your performance." Prior to going onstage to perform a dance she tells herself she is the best person to dance.

Forty percent of dancers in a *Dance Magazine* survey of students, professionals, and ex-dancers report suffering from performance anxiety. "Dancers who are unjustly humiliated by their teachers in class—in contrast to those who were not—report significantly more symptoms of stage fright" (Hamilton 1997:62). Onstage anxiety may be a "symptom rather than a cause." This stage fright can come from a build-up of pressures a dancer is currently experiencing, with the stage performance being the "last and most difficult stressor in the sequence of life events" (Hipple 1996:2).

SEXUAL HARASSMENT AND PARITY

Sexual harassment, unwanted verbal or physical sexual attention, is stressful. Dancers may be sexually harassed by either gender (heterosexual, bisexual, or homosexual). Awareness of unequal employment opportunities for women and men may also be stressful. As noted in chapter 9, men have an easier time finding employment than women, have longer careers, and are much more secure financially.

CAN WE AVOID STRESS IN DANCE AND DANCE EDUCATION?

Some of the mechanisms for coping with stress through dance can be harnessed for prevention. Knowledge of matter and mind can help us reduce or avoid stress in dance and dance education. Reducing or avoiding stress is often difficult, however, and specific solutions depend on the individual and the particular situation. The following sections provide some general guidelines for dealing with stress in dance.

PHYSICAL FACTORS

Fortunately, research on motor learning, kinesiology for dancers, and dance medicine helps us know how to prevent undue physical stress; this can improve and lengthen the performing time a dancer has and make dance training more efficient. Dancing on concrete floors is definitely disastrous.

Dance and Stress

Ways Dance Alleviates Stress	Ways Dance Induces Stress
A stress inoculation	Incorrect teaching
Escape	Inappropriate expectations
Mastery	Stage fright
Confront stressors	Gender inequality

So too is overuse of one part of the body over an extended period of time, says Glenna Batson, former dancer and currently a physical therapist in North Carolina. Repetitive steps and/or rehearsals, typically when one is very fatigued, are harmful. Other stressors to avoid are incorrect preparations and landings in jumps; misalignment of the feet, knees, hips, spine, and shoulders; hyperextended knees and swayback; inward rotation of legs and feet or "toeing in"; driving, weighted bounces in a grand plié (deep squat); and pushing from a maximal stretch. These practices increase the likelihood of physical injury over a person's lifetime. Batson explained to me that dance teachers often neglect to include enough release work in their technique classes. Teaching the art of letting go of muscular tension gives dancers increased longevity in both the short and the long term. You see, for example, ballerinas vigorously executing a combination at the barre, all lifted and beautiful, and then when the combination is over, slumping like rags. You may wonder why. They are recuperating. They are letting their muscles rest before being called upon to work again.

Deep breathing before dancing helps calm a dancer by oxygenating tissues and reaffirming a sense of control.

Dance publications and newspapers regularly report the results of new studies challenging accepted practices. These studies can guide dance educators. Numerous conferences are also held on the correct use of the body in dance.

PSYCHOLOGICAL AND GENETIC FACTORS

Before going onstage, dancers often psyche themselves up with pep talks ("You are going to be great!"). When onstage anxiety is a symptom rather than a cause, the young performer can, with the help of an adult, identify the ongoing problem. This process alone may help the individual because "the situation is no longer so mysterious" (Hipple 1996:4). Other steps such as professional counseling may be necessary.

Teachers can learn and convey notions of child development to students and parents alike so they can have realistic expectations about professional dance. Richard B. Reff, an orthopedic surgeon formerly on staff with the Children's Hospital, National Medical Center, Washington, D.C., who treats young dancers, urges dance teachers to understand kinesiology and to discuss frankly the goals of training with students and parents. "The trinity of professionalism," he explains, "is motivation, training, and genetics." Reff distinguishes between goals, which have a reasonable probability of achievement, and dreams:

> Genetics limit individuals in effectively performing some movements. I see many dance students who are born with ante-verted (turned-in) hips and have knee pain related to doing plié movements. Those individuals with retro-verted hips have natural turnout. The statistics for the population is ante-verted two to one.

> The youngsters suffer not just physical but emotional stress. They strive to do what they are asked, and quitting is not

something they've been programmed to do. Sometimes girls between 7 and 11 have flexibility (soft tissues, ligaments, and tendons) and can overcome anatomy until they are about 15 to 16. If a youngster cannot realistically become a professional, a realistic goal is to develop a proficiency for a lifelong activity that enhances one's self-image and sense of accomplishment. Of course, there are many forms of dance, other than ballet, that have less stringent demands in terms of turnout and flexibility or preferred body type. These forms offer professional career opportunities.

BEING PREPARED

Being knowledgeable about dance helps prepare a dancer for survival as a professional or amateur. To preclude stress, teachers should encourage students to keep up with current news about care of the body. Students should know the closest location of a dance medicine center and the names of doctors who specialize in dancers' health needs. Acquiring relaxation techniques such as deep breathing, visualization, and talking and writing about one's concerns help prevent distress. Developing outlets for self-expression and learning to organize and plan while still remaining flexible are yet other strategies. Likening class to a performance accustoms students to being onstage and helps to lessen performance anxiety.

Some teachers mention these issues during class; put relevant articles on bulletin boards; and give students responsibility for dance production, from designing costumes to preparing programs. This enables students to discover new interests in the event that they cannot or choose not to dance. Most people today go into professional dance due to a passion for the art form rather than the reward of financial security and stability of conventional occupations. Therefore, they can at least be forewarned of the pitfalls and pathways to alleviate some of the anxieties of the unknown. For themselves, teachers often take classes from other teachers in different dance forms to help prevent and relieve stress.

ENCORE

Stress factors differ from person to person; what is stressful to one person may be invigorating to another. Stress refers to a process in which an individual is pushed beyond a particular capacity. A disaster, mounting everyday worries and pressures, or extraordinary excitement may trigger the physical stress response. Life, including dance and dance education, is often stressful.

Dance can help a person cope with stress in her or his life in several ways. Dancing may help one become resistant to stress by building stamina through physical and psychological training. This conditions an individual to avoid or reduce the fatigue symptoms of stress. Dance may be a means of escape from the stressor by finding a refuge in dance participation, being in a fantasy scene, or dissipating muscular and emotional tension. Mastery of the elements of dance increases one's sense of control over one's life and thereby one's ability to cope with stress. By expressing worrisome themes in dance, a person can confront stressors and figure out what to do with them.

Dance itself may cause stress. Good stress motivates success. Bad stress may create physical and psychological harm. Professional dancers, teachers, and students may be overworked or work in inadequate performance facilities. Stage fright, or performance stress, is common for young and old, amateur and professional dancer alike. Some teaching practices cause student stress. Parents often create stress for students and teachers alike when they expect their offspring to do that for which they are not sufficiently developed in terms of age, maturity, and training. Students may also impose unrealistic demands on themselves.

Stress, however, can be lessened and avoided in dance and dance education. Educating students about mind–body integration enables them to sidestep many potential problems.

Finale: Overcoming Obstacles and Moving Forward

> Meritorious in itself, dance is a form of kinesthetic intelligence, pleasurable as an end, and needing no outside excuse or pretext. It warrants in-depth attention apart from any relationship to other disciplines.
>
> Dance can also mesh with other subjects through curriculum integration. Not only can students learn the discipline of dance, but this kinesthetic intelligence can also enhance learning about academic disciplines and personal and public concerns about ethnic and American identities, gender, and stress.

Following many pages of a textual constellation about dance and dance education, it is time to reflect on what this book has presented. Thoughtful reflection readies us for taking the next steps in pursuit of successful learning in, about, and through dance. Permit me to what I have discussed in this book and move one step further. To do so, it is necessary to examine the obstacles currently confronting dance education and address some ways to overcome these obstacles.

KEY ISSUES IN DANCE EDUCATION

I asked why we should have dance education in our schools (K-12) and colleges. The answer is complex. In brief, the importance of the subject matter of dance is being increasingly recognized, as seen in these mid-1990s milestones: inclusion of the expectation of dance education for all students in the National Education Goals, development of National Standards for Dance Education, inclusion of dance in projected national assessments, opportunity-to-learn standards and teacher certification. Dance education is a manifold tapestry that can meet many of the needs of our nation's diverse youth. Moreover, dance can help meet most of the nation's education goals. Without dance education, out of which flow dancers and dance audiences, the field of dance is in jeopardy.

HOW DO POWER AND IDEOLOGY AFFECT DANCE EDUCATION?

Dance education today is in a paradoxical situation. It exists within a largely supportive climate of the education reform movement and of localities and states where economies are doing well. Yet there are moral assaults against the arts and demands for fiscal austerity (Loyacono 1992). In addition, dance education may be viewed as being primarily for females. Similar to the arts in general, support for dance education has it ups and downs; simultaneously, we can find oases and deserts of support in different school districts, regions, and states.

The views of the general public and the educational and political decision makers about dance and dance education in public and private schools contribute to the ecology of dance education. The public has a primary concern with educational objectives, not dance objectives, so it is important for the public to know how dance education meets their goals for education (review chapters 1 and 2).

MONEY

Dance education is generally given short shrift in times of fiscal austerity and economic restructuring. The United States is reexamining its institutions in light of dramatic international change and threats to its comparative economic advantage.

In 1995 the arts took a big hit with declining federal funding, the elimination of 89 employees at the National Endowment for the Arts and elimination of its Dance Program, the collapse of some dance programs in universities and public schools, and shrinking coverage of dance in the newspapers. When economic indicators such as the stock market, employment rates, balance of payments, and national debt indicate a healthy economy recovery of fiscal support for the arts is possible.

CENSORSHIP

The ongoing "culture wars" are partially about what does and does not qualify as educational content and, therefore, for economic support. Some religious groups campaign to establish their own rendition of suitable cultural material for everyone.

People's concerns over the appropriateness of some art should not keep us from teaching dance in the schools. The arts have been used through the years to express every type of belief, even the beliefs of those who might oppose some pieces of art. And, if dance is valuable in itself as well as a means with which to support achievement in other academic areas, we certainly do not want to limit the opportunity to teach dance in the schools.

Some legislators have attempted to silence dissent through massive attacks on the arts. The People for the American Way (1994) reported 204 challenges during 1992 and 1993 to paintings, sculpture, films, plays, and performance art. These attacks reflect sharp divisions in the United States on politics, race, religion, gender, and sexuality. The report points out that while the new congressional leadership couched the debate over the arts in economic terms,

> this attack was really the final escalation of the Religious Right's
> "culture war." Because it reflects the complexity of our society

today, art has become the scapegoat for ideological and social divisions. Our work to stem the erosion of artistic freedom is about more than art, of course; it is about liberty as well. No freedom is more central to the American way than speech. It is the engine of our democratic form of government and the catalyst for our rich culture. Still there are those who would curtail that freedom (1994: 23).

Fear of dance is not new (Hanna 1983, 1987, 1999). But arguments for dance as protected "speech" under the First Amendment is of more recent vintage (Hanna 1998b). Teaching dance is important for many reasons noted earlier. Drama professor Beeb Salzer (1995: B1) adds another.

[The arts] are a potent weapon in the battle to preserve a free society. . . . Artists are almost always dissidents, which makes them an essential ingredient in a democracy that claims to tolerate difference. Artists' approach to life is the opposite of that of politicians. Politicians are required to provide answers; artists ask questions. Politicians must always appear to be certain; artists steep themselves in ambiguity, in the unknown.

Dance both reflects and influences culture and society. It is noteworthy that the court dance spectacles of Catherine de Medici were not only expressions, reflections, and symbols but also the medium for political negotiations. The ballets "Swan Lake" and "The Sleeping Beauty" provided ethical instruction for court behavior. Isadora Duncan's dances heralded progress for women's liberation, and Elvis Presley's African-American derived hip swivel dance ushered in a new era of freer attitudes about the body.

Educators are supposed to encourage critical thinking. This means asking questions and considering alternatives (Daly 1994). Organizations such as the American Civil Liberties Union, with branches throughout the United States, and the National Campaign for Freedom of Expression, aid dancers who are harmed because of attempts to suppress their expression.

IMAGE

In difficult times *outdated conceptions about dance* and the relevance of dance education are especially harmful. Impediments to successfully building dance education programs are its image, belief about dance, and reality. Dance has a nonessential image that educators reinforce when they advocate dance only for arts' sake (see Kaagan 1990). Buttressing this image is dance education teacher training that fails to incorporate current thinking about dance in light of developments in other fields of knowledge. Similarly, professional dancers themselves may pass on outdated cumulative wisdom about their own art form.

The bald reality is that many universities and colleges have no program of dance education or have had cutbacks to existing programs. Without adapting to the demands for education reform and incorporating up-to-date findings that correct and add nuance to existing bodies of knowledge about dance, the survival of dance education is at stake. Alas, the rhetoric and funding of political

Table 1

Percentage of Public Elementary Schools Offering Dance

Subject	Percentage
No dance	57%
Dance as part of physical education and taught by a PE teacher	36%
Dance as part of physical education and taught by a dance teacher	3%
Dance as a separate program taught by a dance teacher	4%

From the National Center for Education Statistics (1995).

Table 2

Percentage of Public Secondary Schools Offering Separate Instruction in the Arts

Subject	Percentage
Music	94%
Visual arts	89%
Drama/theater	54%
Creative writing	47%
Dance	13%

From the National Center for Education Statistics (1995).

support given to arts education in general is incomparable to the support given to, for example, science and mathematics education. Furthermore, support for these subjects is not left to the local communities as it is for dance education!

The National Center for Education Statistics (1995) points to the magnitude of the problem facing dance education. Only 43% of public elementary schools offer dance instruction. The breakdown for secondary schools is far worse: Only 13% offer dance. By comparison, 94% offer music, 89% offer visual arts, and 54% offer drama or theater (see tables 1 and 2).

CAN WE SURMOUNT HURDLES TO SUCCESSFUL DANCE EDUCATION?

About the dance industry Bonnie Brooks, as director of Dance/USA, writes "We are learning that making and sustaining audience relationships is very much about evangelism, about making new converts to dance as well as encouraging the enthusiasm and appreciation of the already-converted" (1998).

Education policy makers face competing demands for scarce resources and financial and moral triage. Consequently, they need education about the academic values of students learning in, about, and through dance education how dance education helps to prepare youth for the workplace, thereby contributing to economic growth. Gaining support of policy makers who back art education is critical (see *Principal* 77(4) 1998).

As mentioned throughout this book, the case for a utilitarian rationale for dance education *supplements, rather than diminishes,* other rationales for dance education. Policy makers support dance education if they understand how it helps youth in academics and in preparation for the workplace. I have heard policy makers say they need to believe in dance education and to convince their constituents who blithely dismiss it.

Widespread suspicion and anger often develops among individuals and groups affected by school change. The dance community is not exempt. Dialogue among teachers in the disciplines of dance and other subjects, including those in physical education, the professional dance world, and private studio teachers, is necessary. Together they can adapt to changing times for dance and dance education and find ways of addressing common concerns and problems. Ideas out of such a dialogue can sustain *dance education in all kinds of schools.*

Dynamic advocacy, curricular legitimization, teacher certification, and financial support for dance and dance education leave much

Promising Pathways for Promoting Dance Education

» Place what is known about dance within the current state of knowledge in the arts, humanities, social and behavioral sciences, and multidisciplinary pedagogy.

» Help update dancers' and educators' knowledge through publications, workshops, and preservice and in-service training.

» Document the career paths of students over time and the apparent impact of dance education on their lives.

» Involve parents in joint child–parent activities. The month before students return to school is a good time to explain dance education to parents.

» Publicize students' dance performances (Willis 1995).

» Encourage television stations to air and promote programs on dance, and the arts in general, which contribute to dance education. Enlist the help of renown dancers.

» Express outrage against negativity toward the arts. When local, state, and federal governments threaten to cut resources for the arts, an outcry of protest calls public attention to the value citizens attribute to the arts, including dance.

» Write one-page letters to legislators and school boards that show critical knowledge in support of dance.

» Develop partnerships with arts and dance organizations (see Cordiero 1997).

» Continually assess vital signs of dance education to adapt accordingly.

work ahead. It is my hope that this book will help inform students, teachers, dancers, parents, and policy makers. For dance education to reach its potential, dissemination of knowledge about the benefits of dance education and what is necessary to realize them is essential. See the "Promising Pathways for Promoting Dance Education" above.

FUNDING AND PARTNERSHIPS

Resources for dance education programs usually come from the school district, state, and federal government as well as from private sources. Educators can apply for funding to develop programs that integrate dance and academic education under categories of programs for core curricula, disadvantaged youngsters, gifted and talented, drug and violence prevention, Indian education, and magnet schools assistance. (See Peterson and Howes 1997; Schiffman 1993 for pointers on proposal writing and NALA 1995 on how partnerships between local arts agencies, schools, businesses, and community organizations can have a positive impact on arts education and community development.)

The National Endowment for the Arts' (NEA's) Education & Access program has funded such projects as

» curriculum-based arts instruction for students in grades pre-K through 12 that provides substantive and sequential learning (such projects involve the combined efforts of arts organizations, artists, and schools, as appropriate);

» instruction (not for academic credit) offered by arts organizations or artists that provides sequential learning in the arts over an extended period of time;

» activities, such as the distribution of publications, that provide access to underexposed art forms;

» master classes, workshops, and apprenticeship programs;

» curriculum development, including interdisciplinary (between disciplines in the arts) or integrated (between the arts and other academic subjects) instructional programs;

» training and development of artists and/or teachers that enhance arts education skills; and

» program evaluation and/or assessment of student learning.

The NEA's Heritage & Preservation program has funded projects that pass on dance repertoire, techniques, aesthetic principles, and oral traditions to future generations. This can be through apprenticeships or other forms of instruction.

Private foundations often underwrite dance education. For example, the Rockefeller Foundation supported the District of Columbia Public Schools Superintendent's Academy for Humanities and Arts teaching to revitalize and revamp curricula for 15 junior high schools and 3 senior high schools. The goal was to motivate students and reduce the school system's 42.4 percent dropout rate. The Gannett Foundation funded the initiation of the Kansas City Friends of Alvin Ailey AileyCamp described in chapter 6.

Because the priorities of governments and private foundations often change, a potential applicant for dance education support must obtain current guidelines. The Foundation Center publications, the *Federal Register*, and *Commerce Business Daily*, along with electronic arts networks, provide useful information in this regard.

Once informed about dance education and its needs, the business community can assist, especially with in-kind services. The numerous dance service organizations also can join the web of support for dance education that the National Dance Education Association, founded in 1998, has begun to establish.

Businesses and philanthropists often adopt schools and, with the principal, work out ways to help them. Corporations, too, sponsor a variety of arts in education programs. Illustrative is Colgate-Palmolive's assistance for the Wadley Junior High School in New York.

In many schools, basic concerns such as finding space and time for dance education require resolution. Dance classes are often sandwiched into a cafeteria/utility room or gym, sometimes while several other activities are underway. Collaborative arrangements between the school and the community's resources often resolve such problems.

Community resources include individual dancers, performance companies, artists' collectives, arts councils, theaters, museums, broadcast and print media, libraries, and businesses. Students benefit from exposure to a variety of performances, including live and videotaped concerts; contacts with visiting dancers; internships; and paid jobs in institutions that present dance to the public. Partnerships work best when each partner's responsibilities are spelled out.

RESEARCH AND NEW STEPS

Good teachers research their own teaching methods (see Wong 1995 on challenges involved with teacher-conducted research). For self-appraisal they may keep a journal to document activities, problems, and solutions. The journal helps them keep track of whether they are meeting their goals. Finding time to reflect on one's work is important.

Quantitative and qualitative research are necessary in dance and dance education to advance the dance discipline and pedagogy. Stinson cautions the dancer as researcher to be aware of the extant residue of dancers' suspicion of dancers who write rather than move. As a dancer and researcher, she conceptualizes the researcher as choreographer (1994b).

Early research on arts education focused on the psychological controlled experiments of science to probe aspects of children's artistic development. The precepts of science aim toward "objectivity," validity, reliability, and statistical distributions. This quantitative focus continues alongside new research methods and topics. The 1970s saw the development of theoretical, historical, and philosophical foundations of aesthetic education. The 1980s witnessed an increase in histories, surveys of existing dance education, and different types of qualitative (often called interpretative) methods (Gottschild 1997; Stinson and Anijar 1993).

The qualitative first-hand documentary field work, or ethnography, of anthropology looks at the connectedness, the holism of dance as "text" in its "context." Taking the approach of intensive observation and informal interviewing has debunked many myths about dances (Hanna 1987). For example, African dances had been dismissed fallaciously as merely "fits, lewd amblings," and "wild hip-swinging orgies."

We learned that with more than 1,000 African language groups and about the same number dance pattern constellations, there are many kinds of dances in Africa with long cultural tradition. Anthropology also debunks myths about students and teaching and learning by trying to discover what people say and do and how their perspectives and actions fit into the broader picture. Anthropology also uses quantitative methods.

Research can help answer key questions, like those shown in the box below. The U.S. Department of Education (1997) report, *Building Knowledge for a Nation of Learners: A Framework for Education*

Key Dance Education Research Questions

» How do dance education programs and practices help meet the nation's educational goals?

» How do students learn best?

» What are the age, gender, and ethnic differences among youngsters that affect teaching and learning?

» What dance curricula and instruction are effective?

» How do dance specialists connect dance instruction with instruction in other subjects?

» How do we assess dance education?

» What kind of preservice and in-service training is needed?

» What dance-specific knowledge and skills must teachers have in order to teach diverse student populations?

» How do different kinds of dance education with various teaching practices affect school attendance, behavior, and academic grades?

» Do dance education practices and programs lead to the acquisition of cognitive skills, subject matter knowledge, and competence in society? How does dance education affect students of varying ability?

» How should we assess student outcomes and evaluate programs?

Research 1997, establishes national priorities. The Goals 2000 Arts Education Partnership (1997) publication, *Priorities for Arts Education Research,* extends this discussion. Research funding comes from universities, foundations, localities, states, and the federal government (Peterson and Howes 1997).

It is difficult for teachers and administrators in the battle trenches to develop dance education programs and teaching practices. To be reflective on paper about student outcomes and program evaluation at the same time compounds the difficulty. This is true even when project directors are encouraged to keep daily or weekly logs and teachers are given reporting forms.

A solution to the problem is to have outsiders conduct applied research that gives practical direction to teaching and learning. For example, evaluators, such as ethnographers, can engage in what is called formative assessment, or action research. This means that observers document what takes place between student and teacher, teacher and administrator, among students, and between school and family and school and community and note problems as they occur so that educators can correct them. The Dance Heritage Coalition's *Beyond Memory* (1994) offers guidelines to document a dancer's development and a school's program.

This ongoing evaluation of a dance education program and specific classroom practices may disclose problems that practitioners and theorists never knew they had. Such an evaluation may also suggest ways for improvement. It is not sufficient to simply know that a dance program or practice works for it to be replicated; educators must also understand *how* it works, that is, the process, its pitfalls, and how problems are resolved or could be prevented (Eisner 1985, Fetterman 1988; Spindler 1982). Professor David Fetterman at Stanford's Graduate School of Education has spelled out the steps of empowerment evaluation (1995a, 1995b). This form of self-evaluation can facilitate transformative learning, that is, the process of reframing reality in ways that facilitate constructive social change and action.

Part of the public image of dance education depends on the quality of dance research. Implicit is dance research that meets the standards of other disciplines that use the same research methods. An invaluable approach is for teachers and dancers to collaborate with well-recognized researchers in dance and in other disciplines. The products of such a collaboration are likely to meet two goals: preservation of the integrity of dance and credibility of the dance research in the broader academic community (see Bickel and Hattrup 1995 for discussion of teachers and researchers in collaboration).

DEEP PLIÉ: GET READY TO SOAR

Yes, dance education is valuable in itself. Often magical in its impact, the art of dance benefits students emotionally, cognitively, and physically. Dance is kinesthetic intelligence and also a physical psychomotor discipline.

The evidence supporting a fuller conceptualization of dance as part of the cognitive domain is irrefutable. Dance is more than valuable in itself: Dance is integrally laced with other aspects of human life, including various academic subjects. And, we know how to implement dance education.

> Dance education is poised, ready to enter the Big Top. It is experiencing a new surge of challenge and a heightened sense of optimism as it moves away from backstage and prepares to enter the Center Ring. A script has been written and rehearsals have taken place. (Hilsendager 1989:1)

Learning in, about, and through dance is a lifelong process. Sometimes dance is controversial. And when dance education is suppressed for religious or political reasons, world history shows that dance recovers, phoenix-like, from the ashes. In a groundswell of educational reform, partnering dance with education and dancing with change are surely intelligent moves. Like the dancer's plié, bending the knees to empower the body to leap forward, current knowledge can empower dance education to soar through the next millennium.

President Clinton, in a speech recognizing the recipients of the National Medal of Arts and Frankel Prize Awards, remarked,

> Today we are on the eve of a new century. The arts and humanities are more essential than ever to the endurance of our democratic values of tolerance, pluralism, and freedom, and to our understanding of where we are and where we need to go. At a momentous time in our history like this when so much is happening to change the way we work and live, the way we relate to one another and the way we relate to the rest of the world, we cannot fully understand the past, nor envision the future we need to pursue without the arts and humanities. (quoted in the President's Committee on the Arts and the Humanities 1997:288-289)

Appendix 1

Discussion Questions

CHAPTER 1: IS DANCE A DISTINCT BODY OF KNOWLEDGE?

What do you think dance is?

What are the stereotypes about dance? What could you do to dispel these stereotypes?

What is the magic of dance?

What brain power is turned on in dance?

CHAPTER 2: THE POWER OF DANCE WELL TAUGHT

Is dance education offered in the schools you know?

In what types of programs? Why?

How can dance education contribute to the school's goals?

CHAPTER 3: SURVIVAL OF DANCE EDUCATION

How do dance educators make sense of, and find their place in, the education world within which they intend to work?

What are you doing to promote dance education?

What could you do in your local area?

What dance education standards do your local schools have?

What do you think the standards should include? Exclude?

How should dance learning be assessed?

CHAPTER 4: WHO SHOULD TEACH DANCE?

Who do you think should teach dance in the different settings it is offered? Why?

What do you think should be the criteria for teaching dance in a private studio? Preprofessional K-12? K-12? Higher education?

What yardsticks should measure the efficacy of teaching?

CHAPTER 5: TEACHING ACADEMIC, CITIZENSHIP, AND WORKPLACE SKILLS THROUGH DANCE

How can dance be a springboard to knowledge and behavior beyond the dance?

How can you educate nondance teachers about the value of dance education to their students?

What decisions do students make in doing dance and creating dance? Why?

CHAPTER 6: DANCE EDUCATION FOR AT-RISK YOUTH

Why do some parents object to their children studying dance in K-12? What would you tell them?

Why do you think dance helps at-risk youth, the disadvantaged, the advantaged?

CHAPTER 7: CHILDREN'S DANCE AT PLAY AS A TEACHING TOOL

How does dance come about?

How do you express your personal identity, gender, ethnicity, and nationality through dance?

What is the role of verbal language in nonverbal dance education?

What are your students' favorite dances? Music, TV Programs? Films? Why? How might you draw upon these in teaching dance?

CHAPTER 8: NATIONAL IDENTITY AND CULTURAL DIVERSITY IN DANCE EDUCATION

What dance activities are unifying? Divisive?

What diverse cultural groups with distinct dances are in your community? Do they want to share their dances? Why? How?

How can you integrate the dances of different cultures into creative/modern dance?

Do your students want to represent their group?

Diversity and Similarity Discussion Questions

(These questions stem from several after-dance concert discussions of multicultural dance.)

I. The dance itself—aesthetics, history, and related literature.

1. What is outstanding about the dance form? Its rivulets and tributaries?
2. What should an audience member see, hear, feel, and understand?
3. Are there many interpretations of the performance?
4. How did the dance form develop?
5. What is the history, philosophy, and related literature?

6. What are the contributions of significant individuals or legendary figures to the dance form?

7. In conveying meaning, which devices and spheres are dominant?

8. What aspects of the dance are considered traditional? Innovative? From the United States?

II. Cultural identity.

1. What identities does the dance reflect?

2. How are these identities reflected (e.g., activity performed or qualities expressed, who participates in bestowing identity on the self)?

3. Does the dance form reflect shifts in social identity?

4. Does the dance reflect a U.S. identity?

III. Values.

1. What ethnic values does the dance convey?

2. Are these values unique or common in the United States?

3. How does the dance form reflect values?

4. How does the dance form, as a venue for presenting things in new ways, influence values?

5. How have the values expressed in immigrants' dances changed since coming to the U.S.? Why?

6. Which dance-related cultural patterns erode and are subsequently replaced by the cultural features of the host society?

7. Is there continuity of older forms along with changed forms?

8. What characterizes appropriateness and excellence in performance?

9. Are there norms on how to treat reality, to challenge or subvert, to idealize, to reproduce and make palatable, to make ambiguous through double meaning?

10. What is the propriety of others borrowing from the ethnic group's dances?

CHAPTER 9: DANCE EDUCATION AND GENDER

What gender patterns in dance education have you observed?

Are these positive or negative?

What patterns should be fostered? How?

Do your colleagues or students think males and females should dance the same way or differently? Why?

Should dance be gender inclusive?

Since boys in the past have responded positively to competitive environments, while girls have responded positively to cooperative environments, what environment should you create for dance education?

How does the teacher's language in dance education classes affect gender?

What does it matter if teachers favor one gender or another in questioning, constructively criticizing, and demonstrating skills?

Chapter 10: Dance Education and Stress

How can you help students work with good stress and bad stress?

What do students do when they're "uptight"? What can they do?

Should you promote dance competitions? Why? How?

Finale: Overcoming Obstacles and Moving Forward

What did you learn about dance in your schooling?

What trend do you need to learn more about?

Where does dance education fit on the map of life and school experiences?

After reading this book, how have your views about dance education changed?

What kinds of dance education resources are there in your community that your school could take advantage of?

Appendix 2

Outline of National Dance Education Standards

- The achievement standard at one level is related to more than one achievement standard at another level.

- The standard appearing at a higher level may not be developmentally appropriate at this level, although learning experiences leading toward the skills associated with the standard are assumed to be taking place.

- The standard appearing at a lower grade level is not repeated, but students at this grade level are expected to achieve that standard, demonstrating higher levels of skill, dealing with more complex examples, and responding to works of art in increasingly sophisticated ways.

Note. Read *across* page spreads (e.g., pp. 200-201) to compare standards from Grades K-4 to Grades 9-12, advanced.

1. Content Standard: Identifying and Demonstrating

GRADES K–4

Achievement Standard:

accurately demonstrate nonlocomotor/axial movements (such as bend, twist, stretch, swing) (a)

accurately demonstrate eight basic locomotor movements (such as walk, run, hop, jump, leap, gallop, slide, and skip), traveling forward, backward, sideward, diagonally, and turning (b)

demonstrate accuracy in moving to a musical beat and responding to changes in tempo (f)

demonstrate kinesthetic awareness, concentration, and focus in performing movement skills (g)

create shapes at low, middle, and high levels (c)

demonstrate the ability to define and maintain personal space (d)

demonstrate movements in straight and curved pathways (e)

———

attentively observe and accurately describe the action (such as skip, gallop) and movement elements (such as levels, directions) in a brief movement study (h)

———

GRADES 5–8

Achievement Standard:

demonstrate the following movement skills and explain the underlying principles: alignment, balance, initiation of movement, articulation of isolated body parts, weight shift, elevation and landing, fall and recovery (a)

accurately identify and demonstrate basic dance steps, positions and patterns for dance from two different styles or traditions (b)

accurately transfer a rhythmic pattern from the aural to the kinesthetic (d)

demonstrate increasing kinesthetic awareness, concentration, and focus in performing movement skills (f)

accurately transfer a spatial pattern from the visual to the kinesthetic (c)

identify and clearly demonstrate a range of dynamics/movement qualities (e)

describe the action and movement elements observed in a dance, using appropriate movement/dance vocabulary (h)

demonstrate accurate memorization and reproduction of movement sequences (g)

MOVEMENT ELEMENTS AND SKILLS IN PERFORMING DANCE

GRADES 9–12, PROFICIENT

Achievement Standard:

demonstrate appropriate skeletal alignment, body-part articulation, strength, flexibility, agility, and coordination in locomotor and non-locomotor/axial movements (a)

identify and demonstrate longer and more complex steps and patterns from two different dance styles/traditions (b)

demonstrate rhythmic acuity (c)

demonstrate projection while performing dance skills (e)

create and perform combinations and variations in a broad dynamic range (d)

demonstrate the ability to remember extended movement sequences (f)

GRADES 9–12, ADVANCED

Achievement Standard:

demonstrate a high level of consistency and reliability in performing technical skills (g)

perform technical skills with artistic expression, demonstrating clarity, musicality, and stylistic nuance (h)

1. CONTENT STANDARD: IDENTIFYING AND DEMONSTRATING

GRADES K–4	GRADES 5–8
Achievement Standard:	**Achievement Standard:**
———	———

2. CONTENT STANDARD: UNDERSTANDING CHOREO-

GRADES K–4

Achievement Standard:

create a sequence with a beginning, middle, and end both with and without a rhythmic accompaniment. Identify each of these parts of the sequence (a)

improvise, create, and perform dances based on their own ideas and concepts from other sources (b)

use improvisation to discover and invent movement and to solve movement problems (c)

create a dance phrase, accurately repeat it, and then vary it (making changes in the time, space and/or force/ energy) (d)

demonstrate the ability to work effectively alone and with a partner (e)

demonstrate the following partner skills: copying, leading and following, mirroring (f)

GRADES 5–8

Achievement Standard:

clearly demonstrate the principles of contrast and transition (a)

effectively demonstrate the processes of reordering and chance (b)

successfully demonstrate the structures or forms of AB, ABA, canon, call and response, and narrative (c)

demonstrate the ability to work cooperatively in a small group during the choreographic process (d)

demonstrate the following partner skills in a visually interesting way: creating contrasting and complementary shapes, taking and supporting weight (c)

———

———

MOVEMENT ELEMENTS AND SKILLS IN PERFORMING DANCE
(CONT.)

GRADES 9–12, PROFICIENT	GRADES 9–12, ADVANCED
Achievement Standard:	**Achievement Standard:**
———	refine technique through self-evalua-tion and correction (i)

GRAPHIC PRINCIPLES, PROCESSES, AND STRUCTURES

GRADES 9–12, PROFICIENT	GRADES 9–12, ADVANCED
Achievement Standard:	**Achievement Standard:**
⟶	⟶

use improvisation to generate move-ment for choreography (a)

demonstrate understanding of struc-tures or forms (such as palindrome, theme and variation, rondo, round, con-temporary forms selected by the stu-dent) through brief dance studies (b)

choreograph a duet demonstrating an understanding of choreographic prin-ciples, processes, and structures (c)

demonstrate further development and refinement of the proficient skills to create a small group dance with coher-ence and aesthetic unity (d)

⟶ ⟶

——— accurately describe how a choreogra-pher manipulated and developed the basic movement content in a dance (e)

3. Content Standard: Understanding dance as

GRADES K–4

Achievement Standard:

observe and discuss how dance is different from other forms of human movement (such as sports, everyday gestures) (a)

take an active role in a class discussion about interpretations of and reactions to a dance (b)

present their own dances to peers and discuss their meanings with competence and confidence (c)

GRADES 5–8

Achievement Standard:

effectively demonstrate the difference between pantomiming and abstracting a gesture (a)

observe and explain how different accompaniment (such as sound, music, spoken text) can affect the meaning of a dance (b)

demonstrate and/or explain how lighting and costuming can contribute to the meaning of a dance (c)

create a dance that successfully communicates a topic of personal significance (d)

---

4. Content Standard: Applying and demonstrating

GRADES K–4

Achievement Standard:

explore, discover, and realize multiple solutions to a given movement problem; choose their favorite solution and discuss the reasons for that choice (a)

observe two dances and discuss how they are similar and different in terms of one of the elements of dance (such as space, through body shapes, levels, pathways) (b)

GRADES 5–8

Achievement Standard:

create a movement problem and demonstrate multiple solutions; choose the most interesting solutions and discuss the reasons for their choice (a)

demonstrate appropriate audience behavior in watching dance performances; discuss their opinions about the dances with their peers in a supportive and constructive way (b)

compare and contrast two dance compositions in terms of space (such as shape and pathways), time (such as rhythm and tempo), and force/energy (such as movement qualities) (c)

GRADES 9–12, PROFICIENT

Achievement Standard:

formulate and answer questions about how movement choices communicate abstract ideas in dance (a)

demonstrate understanding of how personal experience influences the interpretation of a dance (b)

create a dance that effectively communicates a contemporary social theme (c)

GRADES 9–12, ADVANCED

Achievement Standard:

examine ways that a dance creates and conveys meaning by considering the dance from a variety of perspectives (d)

compare and contrast how meaning is communicated in two of their own choreographic works (e)

→   →

CRITICAL AND CREATIVE THINKING SKILLS IN DANCE

GRADES 9–12, PROFICIENT

Achievement Standard:

create a dance and revise it over time, articulating the reasons for their artistic decisions and what was lost and gained by those decisions (a)

establish a set of aesthetic criteria and apply it in evaluating their own work and that of others (b)

GRADES 9–12, ADVANCED

Achievement Standard:

discuss how skills developed in dance are applicable to a variety of careers (d)

4. CONTENT STANDARD: APPLYING AND DEMONSTRATING

GRADES K–4

Achievement Standard:

———

———

GRADES 5–8

Achievement Standard:

identify possible aesthetic creteria for evaluating dance (such as skill of performers, originality, visual and/or emotional impact, variety, and contrast) (d)

———

5. CONTENT STANDARD: DEMONSTRATING AND UNDERSTAND-

GRADES K–4

Achievement Standard:

perform folk dances from various cultures with competence and confidence (a)

learn and effectively share a dance from a resource in their own community; describe the cultural and/or historical context (b)

accurately answer questions about dance in a particular culture and time period (for example, In colonial America, why and in what settings did people dance? What did the dances look like?) (c)

———

GRADES 5–8

Achievement Standard:

competently perform folk and/or classical dances from various cultures; describe similarities and differences in steps and movement styles (a)

competently perform folk, social and/or theatrical dances from a broad spectrum of twentieth-century America (b)

learn from resources in their own community (such as people, books, videos) folk dance of a different culture or a social dance of a different time period and the cultural/historical context of that dance; effectively sharing the dance and its context with their peers (c)

accurately describe the role of dance in at least two different cultures or time periods (d)

———

GRADES 9–12, PROFICIENT

Achievement Standard:

formulate and answer their own aesthetic questions (such as, What is it that makes a particular dance that dance? How much can one change that dance before it becomes a different dance? (c)

————————

GRADES 9–12, ADVANCED

Achievement Standard:

analyze the style of a choreographer or cultural form; then create a dance in that style (e)

analyze issues of ethnicity, gender, social/economic class, age and/or physical condition in relation to dance (f)

ING DANCE IN VARIOUS CULTURES AND HISTORICAL PERIODS

GRADES 9–12, PROFICIENT

Achievement Standard:

perform and describe similarities and differences between two contemporary theatrical forms of dance (a)

perform or discuss the traditions and technique of a classical dance form (b)

⟶

create and answer twenty-five questions about dance and dancers prior to the twentieth century (c)

analyze how dance and dancers are portrayed in contemporary media (d)

GRADES 9–12, ADVANCED

Achievement Standard:

⟶

⟶

⟶

create a time line illustrating important dance events in the twentieth century, placing them in their social/historical/cultural/political contexts (e)

compare and contrast the role and significance of dance in two different social/historical/cultural/political contexts (f)

6. CONTENT STANDARD: MAKING CONNECTIONS

GRADES K–4

Achievement Standard:

identify at least three personal goals to improve themselves as dancers (a)

explain how healthy practices (such as nutrition, safety) enhance their ability to dance, citing multiple examples (b)

––––––––

GRADES 5–8

Achievement Standard:

identify at least three personal goals to improve themselves as dancers and steps they are taking to reach those goals (a)

explain strategies to prevent dance injuries (b)

create their own warm-up and discuss how that warm-up prepares the body and mind for expressive purposes (c)

---

7. CONTENT STANDARD: MAKING CONNECTIONS

GRADES K–4

Achievement Standard:

create a dance project that reveals understanding of a concept or idea from another discipline (such as pattern in dance and science) (a)

respond to a dance using another art form; explain the connections between the dance and their response to it (such as stating how their paintings reflect the dance they saw) (b)

––––––––

GRADES 5–8

Achievement Standard:

create a project that reveals similarities and differences between the arts (a)

cite examples of concepts used in dance and another discipline outside the arts (such as balance, shape, pattern) (b)

observe the same dance both live and recorded on video; compare and contrast the aesthetic impact of the two observations (c)

BETWEEN DANCE AND HEALTHFUL LIVING

GRADES 9–12, PROFICIENT

GRADES 9–12, ADVANCED

Achievement Standard:

reflect upon their own progress and personal growth during their study of dance (a)

Achievement Standard:

effectively communicate how lifestyle choices affect the dancer (b)

analyze historical and cultural images of the body in dance and compare these to images of the body in contemporary media (c)

discuss challenges facing professional performers in maintaining healthy lifestyles (d)

BETWEEN DANCE AND OTHER DISCIPLINES

GRADES 9–12, PROFICIENT

GRADES 9–12, ADVANCED

Achievement Standard:

create an interdisciplinary project based on a theme identified by the student, including dance and two other disciplines (a)

Achievement Standard:

clearly identify commonalities and differences between dance and other disciplines with regard to fundamental concepts such as materials, elements, and ways of communicating meaning (b)

compare one choreographic work to one other art work from the same culture and time period in terms of how those works reflect the artistic/cultural/historical context (d)

demonstrate/discuss how technology can be used to reinforce, enhance, or alter the dance idea in an interdisciplinary project (c)

create an interdisciplinary project using media technologies (such as video, computer) that presents dance in a new or enhanced form (such as video, dance, video/computer-aided live performance, or animation) (e)

Dance Education Resources

(names, addresses, and phone numbers subject to change)

DANCE EDUCATION AND DANCE-RELATED ORGANIZATIONS

Alliance for Arts Education Network
c/o Kennedy Center Education Program
The John F. Kennedy Center for the Performing Arts
Washington, D.C. 20566-001
(202) 416-8845

Americans for the Arts (formerly American Council for the Arts and National Assembly of Local Arts Agencies)
1000 Vermont Avenue, NW, 12th Floor
Washington, D.C. 20005
(202) 371-2830
Satellite Office:
1 East 53rd Street, 7th floor
New York, New York 10022-4201
(212) 223-2787

American Dance Guild
c/o Jana Seinman
Dance Department
Hunter College
THH 616

605 Park Avenue
New York, New York 10021
(212) 772-5010

American Dance Legacy Institute
Box 1897
Providence, Rhode Island 02912
(401) 863-7596
Fax: (401) 863-7529

American Folklife Center
The Library of Congress
101 Independence Avenue, SE
Washington, D.C. 20540-4610
(202) 707-5510

American Dance Therapy Association
200 Century Plaza, Suite 108
10632 Little Patuxent Parkway
Columbia, Maryland 21044
(410) 997-4040

ArtsConnection Young Talent Program
120 West 46th St.
New York, NY 10036
(212) 302-7433
fax: (212) 302-1132

Association for Supervision and Curriculum Development (ASCD) Network in the Arts in Education
Gene Van Dyke, Facilitator
Milton Hershey School
P.O. Box 830
Founders Hall
Hershey, Pennsylvania 17033
(717) 520-2080

Center for the Learning and Teaching of Elementary Subjects
College of Education
Michigan State University
252 Erickson Hall
East Lansing, Michigan 48824
(517) 353-6470
fax: (517) 353-6393

Cecchetti Society, Inc.
c/o Sheila Darby
818 Bell Air Drive

Sacramento, California 95822
(916) 442-2117

Dance and the Child International—daci USA
Dow Center
Hope College Dance Department
P.O. Box 9000
Holland, Michigan 49422
(616) 395-7700

Dance Collection (unique resource; catalog available)
Performing Arts Research Center
New York Public Library
Lincoln Center Plaza
New York, New York 10023
(212) 870-1657

Dance Educators of America
P.O. Box 607
Pelham, New York 10803
(914) 636-3200
(914) 636-5895

Dance Heritage Coalition
DCH: Access Dance Research Resources Project (large database of several libraries)
P.O. Box 15130
Washington, DC 20003
(202) 707-2149

Dance Link
720 Greenwich Street, #7F
New York, New York 10014
(212) 924-8563

Dance Masters of America
Teacher Training School
P.O. Box 620533
214-10 41st Avenue
Bayside, New York 11361
(718) 225-4013

Dancers Over 40, Inc.
P. O. Box 911
New York, New York 10108
(212) 581-4475

Dance/USA (national service organization for professionals in dance)
1156 15th Street, NW

Suite 820
Washington, D.C. 20005-1704
(202) 833-2686
fax: (202) 833-2686

ERIC Clearinghouse for Social Studies/Social Science Education (includes arts education)
Indiana University
Social Studies Development Center
2805 East 10th Street, Suite 120
Bloomington, Indiana 47408-2698
(812) 855-3838
fax: (812) 855-7901

Getty Education Institute for the Arts
1200 Getty Center Drive, Suite 600
Los Angeles, California 90049-1683
(310) 440-7315
fax: (310) 440-7704

Goals 2000 Arts Education Partnership
c/o Council of Chief State School Officers
One Massachusetts Avenue, NW
Suite 700
Washington, D.C. 20001
(202) 326-8693

International Network of Performing and Visual Arts Schools
35 and S Streets, NW
Washington, D.C. 20007
(202) 966-2216
fax: (202) 966-2283

Lincoln Center Institute for Arts Education
70 Lincoln Center Plaza
New York, New York 10023
(212) 875-5535

Magnet Schools of America
Dr. Don Waldrip
2111 Holly Hall, Suite 704
Houston, Texas 77054
(713) 796-9356
fax: (713) 796-1426

National Arts Education Research Center
New York University
32 Washington Place, #41
New York, New York 10003

(212) 988-5060
fax: (212) 995-4048

National Assembly of State Arts Agencies
1010 Vermont Avenue, NW
Suite 316
Washington, D.C. 20005
(202) 347-6352

National Association of Schools of Dance
Samuel Hope
11250 Roger Bacon Drive, Suite 21
Reston, Virginia 22090
(703) 437-0700
fax: (703) 437-6312

National Dance Association
American Alliance for Health, Physical Education, Recreation and Dance
1900 Association Drive
Reston, Virginia 22091
(703) 476-3421

National Dance Education Association
4948 St. Elmo Ave., Suite 207
Bethesda, Maryland 20814
(301) 657-2880
fax: (301) 657-2882

National Endowment for the Arts
Education and Access
Nancy Hanks Center
1100 Pennsylvania Avenue, NW
Washington, D.C. 20506
(202) 682-5426

National Guild of Community Schools of the Arts
P.O. Box 8018
Englewood, New Jersey 07631
(201) 871-3337
fax: (201) 871-7639

National Initiative to Preserve America's Dance
The John F. Kennedy Center for the Performing Arts
2700 F Street, NW
Washington, D.C. 20566
(202) 416-8036

National Registry of Dance Educators
P.O. Box 254
Northport, New York

National Resource Centre for Dance
University of Surrey
Guildford, Surrey GU2 5XH
United Kingdom
(01483) 259316
fax: (01483) 300803

National Task Force on Folk Arts Education
609 Johnston Place
Alexandria, Virginia 22301-2511
(703) 836-7499
fax: (703) 836-4820

Roger Williams Middle School
Susan McGreevy-Nichols
278 Thurbers Avenue
Providence, Rhode Island
(401) 456-9385 or 9355

Royal Academy of Dancing, USA Branch
15 Franklin Place
Rutherford, New Jersey 0707
(201) 438-4400
fax: (201) 438-4552

Smithsonian Institution
Office of Elementary and Secondary Education
Arts and Industries Building, Room 1163
Washington, D.C. 20560
(202) 357-3049
fax: (202) 357-2116

Southern Arts Federation
181 14th Street, NE, Suite 400
Atlanta, Georgia 30309
(404) 874-7244
fax: (404) 873-2148

SPECTRA+ Program
Hamilton Fairfield Arts Association
Fitton Center for Creative Arts
101 South Monument Avenue
Hamilton, Ohio 45011-2833
(513) 863-8873

Very Special Arts
1300 Connecticut Avenue, NW
Washington, D.C. 20036
(800) 933-8721

DANCE EDUCATION UNIVERSITY TRAINING

Preservice Preparation for Dance Specialists (see Clemente 1990)

College Guide (published annually by *Dance Magazine*)
Dance Directory (published periodically by the National Dance Association)
Dance Teacher Now (Dance Career Guide published in December issue)
Stern's Performing Arts Directory (published annually by *Dance Magazine*)

In 1997, seven universities offered doctoral degrees in dance:

Laban Centre for Movement and Dance: B.A., M.A., Ph.D.
New York University Program in Dance Education: B.S., M.A., Ed.D., Ph.D.
Temple University
Texas Women's University
University of California, Riverside
University of Surrey

About 216 colleges offer dance major programs in the United States.

ILLUSTRATIVE K-12 DAN]CE EDUCATION PROGRAMS

Some programs for one or several age groups could be adapted to others; some programs are integrated with other arts and other subjects.

ABC Project (Arts Basic in the Curriculum)
105 McLaurin Hall
Winthrop University
Rock Hill, South Carolina 29733
(803) 323-2451

Aiken Elementary School
2050 Pine Log Road
Aiken, South Carolina 29803
(803) 641-2740
fax: (803) 641-2526

AileyCamp (summer program for at-risk youth)
Dance Theater Foundation, Inc.
211 West 61st Street, 3rd Floor
New York, New York 10023
(212) 767-0590
fax: (212) 767-0625

Kansas City Friends of Alvin Ailey (KCFAA)
218 Delaware, Suite 101
Kansas City, Missouri 64105
(816) 471-6003
fax: (816) 471-6001

ArtsConnection Young Talent Program
505 8th Avenue
New York, New York 10018
(212) 564-5099
fax: (212) 564-5234

Ashley River Creative Arts Elementary School
1871 Wallace School Road
Charleston, South Carolina 29407
(803) 763-1555

Ballet Tech School, The New York City Public School of Dance, Kids Dance
390 Broadway
New York, New York 10003
(212) 777-7710
fax: (212) 353-9036

Boston Ballet Center for Dance Education
19 Clarendon Street
Boston, Massachusetts 02116-6107
(617) 695-6905
fax: (617) 695-6995

City Center—55th Street Theater Foundation Outreach Education
130 West 55th Street
New York, New York 10019
(212) 247-0430

COMPAS (Community Programs in the Arts)
308 Landmark Center
75 West Fifth Street
Saint Paul, Minnesota 55102
(612) 292-3249
fax: (612) 292-3258

Dance Theatre of Harlem
466 West 152nd Street
New York, New York 10031
(212) 690-2800

Duke Ellington School of the Arts (high school)
3500 R Street, NW
Washington, D.C. 20007
(202) 282-0123
fax: (202) 282-1106

Duxbury Park Arts Impact Alternative Elementary School
1779 East Maynard Avenue
Columbus, Ohio 43219
(614) 365-6023

Elm Creative Arts School
900 West Walnut Street
Milwaukee, Wisconsin 53205-1762
(414) 562-1000

Fillmore Arts Center (serves 6 elementary schools)
D.C. Public Schools
35th and S Streets, NW
Washington, D.C. 20007
(202) 625-0341
fax: (202) 625-1543

Highland Park High School
433 Vine Avenue
Highland Park, Illinois 60035-2099
(847) 432-6510
fax: (847) 926-9348

Jefferson High School
5210 North Kerby Avenue
Portland, Oregon 97217
(503) 916-2607
fax: (503) 916-2697

Karl H. Kellogg Elementary School
229 East Naples Street
Chula Vista, California 91911
(619) 420-4151

Kennedy Center Education Program
The John F. Kennedy Center for the Performing Arts
Washington, D.C. 20566-001
(202) 416-8800

The Kirov Academy of Ballet
4301 Harewood Road, NE
Washington, D.C. 20017-1558
(202) 832-1087
fax: (202) 526-4274

Learning to Read through the Arts (LTRTA)
Business for the Arts in Education
P. O. Box 52
Glen Rock, New Jersey 07452
(201) 445-5359
fax: (201) 445-6389

Learning Through an Expanded Arts Program
580 West End Avenue

New York, New York 10024
(212) 769-4160

Lincoln Center Institute for the Arts in Education
Lincoln Center for the Performing Arts, Inc.
70 Lincoln Center Plaza
New York, New York 10023-6594
(212) 875-5535
fax: (212) 875-5539

Minnesota Center for Arts Education
Arts High School and Resource Center
6125 Olson Memorial Highway
Golden Valley, Minnesota 55422
(612) 591-4700
Toll-free: (800) 657-3515; (800) 657-3515
fax: (612) 591-4747

Montgomery County Public Schools (interrelated arts activities and
sample lesson plans)
850 Hungerford Drive, Room 255
Rockville, Maryland 20850
(301) 279-3250
fax: (301) 279-3072

National Dance Institute (NDI)
594 Broadway, Room 805
New York, New York 10012
(212) 226-0083
fax: (212) 226-0761

Neshaminy High School
2001 Old Lincoln Highway
Langhorne, Pennsylvania 19047-3295
(215) 752-6435
fax: (215) 752-6374

North Carolina A+ Schools
Thomas S. Kenan Institute for the Arts
P.O. Box 10610
Winston-Salem, North Carolina 27108
(910) 722-0030

North Carolina School of the Arts
School of Dance
P.O. Box 12189
Winston-Salem, North Carolina 27117
(910) 770-3208

St. Augustine School of the Arts
Principal
1176 Franklin Avenue
Bronx, New York 10456
(212) 542-3633
fax: (212) 542-7871

Vancouver School of Arts and Academics
P.O. Box 8937
Vancouver, Washington 98668-8937
(360) 696-7143

Walnut Hill School
12 Highland Street
Natick, Massachusetts 01760
(508) 653-4312
(508) 653-9593

Young Audiences
115 E. 92nd Street
New York, New York 10023
(212) 831-8110

NONACADEMIC DANCE EDUCATION PROGRAMS

Listings of nonacademic dance programs can be found in these publications:

DanceMagazine
Dance Teacher Now
Dancing (see Jacob 1996)

STATES WITH DANCE TEACHER CERTIFICATION REQUIREMENTS

(Changes occur as states introduce or withdraw dance certification.)

Arizona (secondary level)
Florida
Idaho
Maryland
Massachusetts
Michigan
Mississippi
New York
North Carolina
Ohio
Pennsylvania
Rhode Island
Texas
Utah
Vermont
Wisconsin

Selected Readings

Curriculum Frameworks/Guides

Mirus, Judith, Elena White, Loren E. Bucek, and Pamela Paulson. 1996. *Dance Education Initiative Curriculum Guide,* 2nd ed. Golden Valley, MN: Minnesota Center for Arts Education.

California Department of Education, History–Social Science and Visual and Performing Arts Unit. 1991. *United States History and Geography: Making A New Nation,* Course Models for the History–Social Science Framework, Grade 5. Sacramento: California Department of Education. (Available from Bureau of Publications, Sales Unit, California Department of Education, P.O. Box 271, Sacramento, CA 95812-0271, $7.00.)

Fine Arts Curriculum, Kindergarten through Sixth Grade. 1990. National City, California: National School District.

Visual and Performing Arts Essential Learnings Curriculum. 1995. (Available from the Vancouver School District, 605 North Devine Road. P.O. Box 8937, Vancouver, WA 98668)

Dance Education History and Life (see References for a complete citation)

Jacob

Kraus, Hilsendager, and Dixon

White, Friedman, and Levinson

Dance and Health

Fitt

Hamilton 1998

Hanna 1988a

Ryan

Solomon

Thomasen

Wright

Dance Instruction

Andrews

Benzwie

Blom and Tarin

Cheney

Diamondstein

Focus on Dance Education Conference Proceedings, 1996, Minnesota Center for Arts Education

Fortin and Siedentop

Gilbert

Grody and Lister

Joyce

Lavender

Lawson

McGreevy-Nichols

Mettler
Minton
Murray
Penrod and Plastino
Pica 1991, 1993
Purcell
Rowan
Russell
Schlaich and DuPont
Schneer
Schrader
Stinson 1988
Taylor and Taylor
Wright

Dance Linkages to Other Core Curricula

Blatt and Cunningham
Boorman
Cambigue
Clark
Countryman
Dean and Gross
Gilbert
Gray
Katz
Laws
Lee
McQuade
Pauly and Parker
Taylor, Vlastos, and Marshall
Teck
Troxell

Dance for People With Disabilities

AAPHERD
Benari
Canner
Levete

Dance Research Methods

Booth 1995
Dance Heritage Coalition
Dell 1970
Fetterman 1998
Gottschild 1997
Hanna1979b, 1983, 1987, 1988b, 1988c, 1989a, 1989b

Hutchinson
Krebs
Stinson and Anijar

Finance and Partnership

Hanna 1991
Katz
Urban and State Initiatives
Wolf

General Learning

Banks
Bloom
Brophy and Good
Dryfoos
Eisner
Gardner 1983, 1991, 1992, 1998
Gray
Moles
National Roundtable on Folk Arts in the Classroom
Ogbu
Perkins
Resnick
Sizer
Smelser
Swartz and Perkins
Vygotsky

Movement Analysis

Dell
Hanna
Hutchinson
Krebs

PERIODICALS AND NEWSLETTERS

Afterimages: Newsletter of Performing Arts Documentation and Preservation
American Dance Guild Newsletter
Arts Education Policy Review (formerly Design for Arts in Education)
Attitudes and Arabesques
Dance: Current Selected Research (annual)
Dance Directory of Ballet Companies (see Petrides 1996a, 1996b, 1996c)
This directory provides information for beginning career dancers for America and for Europe, including an audition calendar; a list of dance companies; their history; predominant type of repertory; touring program; school affiliations; whether the companies are professional, regional, or civic; and audition requirements. This publication also has background on the artistic director and ballet master or mistress, salary, guaranteed weeks for dancers, number of

performances per year, and if the company provides health benefits and hires foreign dancers.

Dance Magazine

Dance Research Journal

Dance Teacher Now

Dance USA

Journal of Aesthetic Education

JOPERD (Journal of Physical Education, Recreation and Dance)

Minnesota Center for Arts Education Articulars

Southern Arts Education Connections

Spotlight on Dance (National Dance Association Newsletter)

INTERNET AND OTHER COMPUTER RESOURCES

Americans for the Arts/Arts USA, http:/www.artsus.org/index

GettyArtsEdNet, http://artsednet.getty.edu

Goals 2000 Arts Education Partnership, http://www.artsedge.kennedy-center.ort/aep

Kennedy Center/ArtsEdge, http://www.artsedge.kennedy-center.org

National Assembly of State Arts Agencies, http://www.nasaa-arts.org

National Dance Association, http://www.aapherd.org/nda/nda.html

National Endowment for the Arts, http://www.arts.endow.gov

Schools, Communities, and the Arts: A Research Compendium, http:// aspin.asu.edu/~rescomp/

U.S. Department of Education, http://www.ed.gov

Dance on Disc (for CD-ROM players used with Windows on IBM PC and compatibles, provides access to catalogue of the dance collection of the New York Public Library) G.K. Hall & Co., CD-ROM Inside Sales, P.O. Box 99, Thorndike, ME 04986, (800) 223-1244, ext. 282

Dance/USA (dance education databank can link potential artist–school partners)

Electronic/school on the Web www.access.digex.net/nsbamags/e-school.html

Goals 2000 Arts Education Partnership, http://artsedge.kennedy-center.org/ aep/aep,.html

Internet ArtsResources, http://www.ftgi.com/

National Endowment for the Arts, http://arts.endow.gov

World Arts Resources, http://wwar.world-arts-resources.com/index.html

VISUAL RESOURCE GUIDES

Credo Multimedia Software, Inc. (dance animation). 8900 Nelson Way, Suite 270, Burnaby, BC Canada V5A lS6

Dance Films Association. 1991.

Dance Film and Video Guide. Comp. Deirdre Towers. Princeton: Dance Horizons/Princeton.

Extension Media Center Catalogue. Berkeley: University of California.

JVC Smithsonian Folkways Video Anthology, Multicultural Media, RR3, Box 6655, Granger Road, Barre, Vermont 05641, (800) 550-9675

References and Suggested Readings

References with an asterisk (*) have been cited in the text.

Acer, C.C. 1987. *Crime, Curriculum and the Performing Arts: A Challenge for Inner City Schools to Consider Integrated Language, Music, Drama and Dance Experiences as Compensatory Curriculum for At-Risk Urban Minorities in Elementary School.* Unpublished doctoral dissertation, State University of New York at Buffalo.

*Achenbach, Joel. 1995, February 24. "What Did You Say?" *Washington Post*, p. C 5.

*Anderson, J. 1997, March 15. Musings on Mortality and Courage. *New York Times*, p. B10.

*Andrews, Gladys. 1954. *Creative Rhythmic Movement for Children.* Englewood Cliffs, NJ: Prentice Hall.

*Arkin, Lisa C. 1994. Dancing the Body: Women in Dance Performance. *Journal of Physical Education, Recreation & Dance*, 65(2):36-39.

*Arnheim, Rudolf. 1966. *Toward a Psychology of Art: Collected Essays.* Berkeley: University of California Press.

*Arts in Education Programs. 1996. New York: Alvin Ailey Dance Theater Foundation. Mimeograph.

*Avison, William R. and Ian H. Gotlib, Eds. 1984. *Stress and Mental Health: Contemporary Issues and Prospects for the Future.* New York: Plenum Press.

*Bandura, Albert. 1986. *Social Foundations of Thought and Action: A Social Cognitive Theory.* Englewood Cliffs, NJ: Prentice Hall.

*Bandura, Albert. 1997. *Self Efficacy: The Exercise of Control.* East Lansing, MI: Freeman Press.

*Banes, Sally. 1980. *Terpsichore in Sneakers: Post-Modern Dance.* Boston: Houghton Mifflin.

*Banks, James A. 1997. *Educating Citizens in a Multicultural Society.* New York: Teachers College Press.

*Barboza, Steven. 1990. The Man Who Is Called the Pied Piper of Dance. *Smithsonian*, 20(12):84-95.

*Barko, Carol. 1977. The Dancer and the Becoming of Language. *Yale French Studies*, 54:173-187.

Barron, Randy. 1996. *Scientific Thought in Motion*. Washington, DC: John F. Kennedy Center, Professional Development Opportunities for Teachers.

Barryte, Marcia A. and Valena B. Dismukes. 1988. A Dance Ethnology Approach to Teaching in a Junior High School. *UCLA Journal of Dance Ethnology*, 12:8-11.

*Baumeister, Roy F. 1996, Summer. Should Schools Try to Boost Self-Esteem? *American Educator*, pp. 14-19, 43.

*Bean, Martha S. 1997. Talking with Benny: Suppressing or Supporting Learner Themes and Learners' Worlds? *Anthropology and Education Quarterly* 28(1):50-69.

Beech, Tamara. 1997. Concensus: Yes, We Need a Preschool Syllabus. *Dance Teacher Now*, 19(4):88-92. 94-95.

Benari, Naomi. 1995. *Inner Rhythm: Dance Training for the Deaf*. New York: Gordon.

Benzwie, T. 1987. *A Moving Experience: Dance for Lovers of Children and the Child Within (Pre-K Through 6th Grade)*. Reston, VA: National Dance Association.

Benzwie, T. 1994. *More Moving Experiences: Connecting Arts, Feelings and Imagination (Grades K-12)*. Reston, VA: National Dance Association.

*Bergonzi, Louis and Julia Smith. 1996. *Effects of Arts Education on Participation in the Arts* (Research Division Report #36). Washington, DC: National Endowment for the Arts.

Bernstein, Penny Lewis. 1981. *Theory and Methods in Dance-Movement Therapy* (3rd ed.). Dubuque, IA: Kendall/Hunt.

Beyond Fred Astaire: Gill Stresses Totality of Dance. 1972, December 6. *Daily Record,* p. 47.

Beyond Memory. 1994. Washington, DC: Dance Heritage Coalition.

Bickel, William E. and Rosemary A. Hattrup. 1995. Teachers and Researchers in Collaboration: Reflections on the Process. *American Educational Research Journal*, 32(1):35-62.

Blaine, Vera J. and Loren E. Bucek. 1988. Creating a Public Image for Dance Education. *Design for Arts in Education*, January/February, 38-40.

Blatt, Gloria T. and Jean Cunningham. 1981. *It's Your Move: Expressive Movement Activities for the Language Arts Class*. New York: Teachers College, Columbia University.

Blau, Eleanor. 1991. Arts Gets A in Looks, F in Leaks. *New York Times*, August 17, pp. A11, 14.

Blom, Lynne Anne and Tarin Chaplin L. 1982. *The Intimate Act of Choreography*. Pittsburgh: University of Pittsburgh Press.

*Bloom, Benjamin S., M.D. Engelhart, E.J. Frost, W.H. Hill, and D.R. Krathwohl. 1956. *Taxonomy of Educational Objectives, Handbook I: Cognitive Domain*. New York: McKay.

*Blumenthal, Ralph. 1996. Arts Backed as Aid for Troubled Youths. *New York Times*, April 26, p. C3.

*Bonbright, Jane. 1995. Meet the NDA Triad: National Dance Standards, Opportunity-to-Learn Standards, and Dance Assessment. *Spotlight*, 21(2):12.

*Bond, Karen E. 1994. How "Wild Things" Tamed Gender Distinctions. *Journal of Physical Education, Recreation & Dance*, 65(2):23-35.

Boorman, Joyce. 1969. *Creative Dance in the First 3 Grades.* Don Mills, ON: Longman.

Boorman, Joyce. 1971. *Creative Dance in Grades 4-6.* Don Mills, ON: Academic Press Canada.

Boorman, Joyce. 1973. *Dance and Language Experience with Children.* Don Mills, ON: Longman.

Booth, Wayne C., Gregory G. Colomb, and Joseph M. Williams. 1995. *The Craft of Research.* Chicago: University of Chicago Press.

*Boston, Bruce O. 1996, October 28. Educating for the Workplace through the Arts. *Business Week* (Special Advertising Section).

Boyer, Ernest. 1983. *High School: A Report on Secondary Education in America.* New York: Harper & Row.

*Brandt, Ron. 1987-1988. On Discipline-Based Art Education: A Conversation with Elliot Eisner. *Educational Leadership*, 45(4):6-16.

Bresler, Liora. 1992. Dance Education in Elementary Schools. *Design for Arts in Education*, 93(5):13-20.

*Brittain, Harriet B. 1988. Discipline-Based Art Education. Educational Researcher 17(3):55.

*Brooks, Bonnie. 1998. Here and Now. *Dance Magazine*, 72(2):92.

BrooksSchmitz, Nancy. 1990a. Key Education Issues: Critical to Dance Education. *Journal of Physical Education, Recreation & Dance*, 61(5):59-61.

*BrooksSchmitz, Nancy. 1990b. *Young Talent Research Project: An Analysis of the Effect of Arts-in-Education Programming on the Motivation, Academic Performance, and Personal Development of Inner City Youth Involved in the Young Talent Program.* New York: ArtsConnection.

*BrooksSchmitz, Nancy. 1992. Influences Affecting Dance Education in the United States: 1950-1980. In Lynette Overby and James H. Humphrey (Eds.), *Dance: Current Selected Research. Volume III.* (pp. 27-38). New York: AMS Press.

Brophy, Jere E. and Thomas L. Good. 1974. *Teacher-Student Relationships: Causes and Consequences.* New York: Holt, Rinehart & Winston.

*Brown, Ann L. 1994. The Advancement of Learning. *Educational Researcher*, 23(8):4-12.

Bucek, Loren E. 1992. Constructing a Child-Centered Dance Curriculum. *Journal of Health, Physical Education, Recreation & Dance*, 63(9):39-41.

Building Knowledge for a Nation of Learners: A Framework for Education Research. 1997. Washington, DC: U.S. Department of Education.

*Calabria, Frank M. 1993. *Dance of the Sleep-Walkers: The Dance Marathon Fad.* Bowling Green, OH: Bowling Green State University Popular Press.

Cambigue, Susan. 1981. *Learning Through Dance/Movement*. Los Angeles: Performing Tree.

Canner, Norma. 1968. *And a Time to Dance*. Boston: Beacon Press.

Carnegie Council on Adolescent Development. 1989. *Turning Points: Preparing American Youth for the 21st Century*. Washington, DC: Carnegie Corporation of New York.

*Carr, John C. and Lynne Silverstein. 1994. *Artists as Educators: Becoming Effective Workshop Leaders for Teachers*. Washington, DC: The John F. Kennedy Center.

*Cashion, Susan V. 1989. Continuity and Change: Dance in Higher Education. *Liberal Education*, 75(2):18-22.

*Catteral, James S. 1995. *Different Ways of Knowing: 1991-1994 National Longitudinal Study Final Report. Program Effects on Students and Teachers*. Los Angeles: UCLA Graduate School of Education and Information Studies Galef Institute.

Catteral, James S. 1997. Involvement in the Arts and Success in Secondary School. *Americans for the Arts Monographs* 1(9).

*Cawelti, Gordon and Milton Goldberg. 1997. Imagination in Education. Preliminary Draft of Final Report and Meeting, May 7, Task Force on Research, Goals 2000 Arts Education Partnership.

*Cerulo, Karen A. 1995. *Identity Designs: The Sights and Sounds of a Nation*. New Brunswick, NJ: Rutgers University Press.

*Chalmers, F. Graeme. 1996. *Celebrating Pluralism: Art, Education, and Cultural Diversity*. (Occasional Paper 5). Los Angeles: The Getty Education Institute for the Arts.

*Chase, Jill. 1995. Teacher Training and the DMA. *Dance Teacher Now*, 17(2):32-37.

Cheney, Gay. 1989. *Basic Concepts in Modern Dance: A Creative Approach* (3rd ed.). Princeton, NJ: Princeton Book.

*Christopher, Luella Sue. 1979. *Pirouettes with Bayonets: Classical Ballet Metamorphosed as Dance-Drama and Its Use in the People's Republic of China as a Tool of Political Socialization*. Unpublished doctoral dissertation, American University.

Chuck Davis: Peace, Love and Respect for Everybody. 1998. *Dance Teacher Now*, 20(1):48-52, 54.

Clark, Dawn. 1994. What's in a Name? A Creative Dance Lesson. *Strategies*, 7(7):10-12.

*Clemente, K. 1990. *Dance in the Public Schools: Implementing State Policies and Curricular Guidelines for Dance in Education—A Nationwide Survey*. Unpublished doctoral dissertation, Temple University.

College Entrance Examination Board. 1983. *Academic Preparation for College: What Students Need to Know and Be Able to Do*. Princeton.

College Entrance Examination Board. 1985. *Academic Preparation in the Arts: Teaching for the Transition for High School to College*. Princeton.

College Entrance Examination Board. 1987, 1988, 1989. *Profile of SAT and Achievement Test Takers*. Princeton.

*Collen, Robin. 1997. Uncovering Personal Pedagogy: The Congruence Between Self and Action. In *Dance, Culture & Art-Making Behavior* (pp. 73-110). Proceedings, 30th Annual Conference, Congress on Research in Dance. New York: Congress on Research in Dance.

Comer, James P. 1980. *School Power: Implications of an Intervention Project.* New York: Free Press.

Company History. 1989. New York: Alvin Ailey Dance Theater Foundation. Mimeograph.

*Conference Report on H.R. 1804, Goals 2000: Educate America Act. 1994. *Congressional Record*, 140(32), H1625-H1684.

*Cooper, Cary, Ed. 1996. *Handbook of Stress, Medicine, and Health.* Boca Raton, FL: CRC Press.

*Cordiero, Paula, Ed. 1997. *Boundary Crossings: Educational Partnerships and School Leadership.* San Francisco: Jossey-Bass.

*Cormier, Stephen M. and Joseph D. Hagman, Eds. 1987. *Transfer of Learning: Contemporary Research and Application.* San Diego: Academic Press.

Council of Chief State School Officers (with the College Board and the Council for Basic Education). 1994. *Arts Education Assessment Framework.* Washington, DC: National Assessment Governing Board.

*Crain, Robert L., Rita E. Mahard, and Ruth E. Narot. 1982. *Making Desegregation Work: How Schools Create Social Climates.* Cambridge, MA: Ballinger.

*Crawford, Donna and Richard Bodine. 1996. *Conflict Resolution Education: A Guide to Implementing Programs in Schools, Youth-Serving Organizations, and Community and Juvenile Justice Settings.* Washington, DC: U.S. Department of Justice and the U.S. Department of Education.

*Crawford, John R. 1994. Encouraging Male Participation in Dance. *Journal of Physical Education, Recreation & Dance*, 65(2):40-43.

Creative America: A Report to the President. 1997 President's Committee on the Arts and the Humanities. Washington, D.C.

*Cunningham, Jean. 1991. *Classical Dance of India in Canada: School, Play and Adaptation.* Unpublished doctoral dissertation, William Lyon University.

*d'Amboise, Jacques. 1989, August 6. I Show a Child What Is Possible. *Parade Magazine*, pp. 4-6.

*d'Amboise, Jacques, Hope Cooke, and Carolyn George. 1983. *The Magic of Dance.* New York: Simon & Schuster.

Dalcroze, Emile Jacques. 1930. *Eurhythmics: Art and Education.* London: Constable.

*Dalva, Nancy Vreeland. 1988. The I Ching and Me: A Conversation with Merce Cunningham. *Dance Magazine,* 62(3): 58-61.

*Daly, Ann. 1994. Gender Issues in Dance History Pedagogy. *Journal of Physical Education, Recreation & Dance*, 65(2):34-35, 39.

Dance Film Directory: An Annotated and Evaluative Guide to Films on Ballet and Modern Dance. Mueller, John. 1979. Princeton, NJ: Princeton University Press.

*Dance Masters Move Forward. 1997. *Dance Teacher Now*, 19(5):26.

Dancers in Cap and Gown: Northeast College Dance Festival. 1995. *Dance Magazine*, 69(12):82-84.

*Daniel, Yvonne. 1995. *Rumba: Dance and Social Change in Contemporary Cuba*. Bloomington: Indiana University Press.

Deacon, Terrence W. 1997. *The Symbolic Species: The Co-Evolution of Language and the Brain*. New York: Norton.

Dean, Jodi and Ila Lane Gross. 1992. Teaching Basic Skills Through Art and Music, *Phi Delta Kappan*, 73:613-618.

*Delandshere, Ginette and Anthony R. Petrosky. 1998. Assessment of Complex Performances: Limitations of Key Measurement Assumptions. *Educational Researcher* 27(2):14-24.

*Dell, Cecily. 1970. *A Primer for Movement Description Using Effort-Shape and Supplementary Concepts*. New York: Center for Movement Research and Analysis, Dance Notation Bureau.

*Dennett, Daniel. 1991. *Consciousness Explained*. New York: Little, Brown.

*Deutsch, Claudia H. 1991, September 8. What Art Can Teach Business. *New York Times*, p. F23.

*Dewey, John. 1913. *Interest and Effort in Education*. Boston: Houghton Mifflin.

*Dewey, John. 1915. *Schools of Tomorrow*. New York: Dutton.

Dimondstein, Geraldine. 1971. *Children Dance in the Classroom*. New York: Macmillan.

*Dionne, Alexandria. 1997. National Dance Institute. *Dance Magazine*, 71(5):104-105.

Dionne, E.J., Jr. 1997, February 14. Bringing a Little Balance to the Simpson Case. *Washington Post*, p. A21.

*Dobbs, Stephen Mark. 1998. *Learning in and Through Art: A Guide to Discipline-Based Art Education*. Los Angeles: The Getty Institute for the Arts.

Dryfoos, Joyce. 1990. *Adolescents at Risk*. New York: Oxford University Press.

"Duel Over Turkey Trot." 1913, July 26. *New York Times*, p. 7.

*Dunning, Jennifer. 1997a, May 21. Telling Stories on Flying Feet. *New York Times*, pp. B1, B6.

*Dunning, Jennifer. 1997b, November 4. A Dancer Returns, Abstract and Storied. *New York Times*, pp. B1, B4.

*Dunning, Jennifer. 1998. To See, Even to Enjoy, But Perhaps Not to Understand. *New York Times,* April 6, p. B2.

*Durr, Dixie, Feature Ed. 1993. Developing Dance Teachers' Competencies. *Journal of Physical Education, Recreation & Dance*, 64(9):32-48.

Durr, Dixie. 1998, January 4. Dancing Permitted. *New York Times*, p. 24.

Eisner, Elliot W. 1982a. *The Art of Educational Evaluation*. Philadelphia: Falmer Press.

*Eisner, Elliot W. 1982b. *Cognition and Curriculum*. New York: Longman.

*Eisner, Elliot W. 1985. *The Educational Imagination* (2nd ed.). New York: Macmillan.

Eisner, Elliot W. 1990. A Developmental Agenda: Creative Curriculum Development and Practice. *Journal of Curriculum and Supervision*, 6(1):62-73.

Eliade, Mircea, Ed. 1987. *The Encyclopedia of Religion*. New York: Macmillan.

*Eller, Jack David. 1997. Anti-Anti-Multiculturalism. *American Anthropologist*, 99(2):249-260.

*Ensman, Richard G., Jr. 1995. The Basics of Navigating the Internet: What Is the Information Superhighway? And Can You Dance on It? *Dance Teacher Now*, 17(1):47-50, 52-53, 57.

*Ensman, Richard G., Jr. 1998. Styling Your Web Site. *Dance Teacher Now*, 20(4):45-48, 49.

*Entwisle, Doris R. and Karl L. Alexander. 1992. Summer Setback: Race, Poverty, School Composition and Mathematics Achievement in the First Two Years of School. *American Sociological Review*, 57:72-84.

Epskamp, Kees. 1984. Going "Popular" with Culture: Theatre as a Small-Scale Medium in Developing Countries. *Development and Change*, 15:43-64.

*Faber, Rima. 1994. *The Primary Movers: Kinesthetic Learning for Primary School Children*. Master of Arts in Performing Arts: Dance.

*Favors, Ronnie. 1996. AileyCamp. *Choreography and Dance*, 4(1):41-46.

Feldman, Robert S. and Bernard Rimé, Eds. 1991. *Fundamentals of Nonverbal Behavior*. Cambridge, England: Cambridge University Press.

*Ferdun, Edrie. 1990. *Moving Dance: Poetics and Praxis*. Reston: National Dance Association Dance Scholar Lecture.

*Ferdun, Edrie. 1994. Facing Gender Issues Across Curricula. *Journal of Physical Education, Recreation & Dance*, 65(2):46-48.

*Ferguson, Suanne. 1992. Dance as a Means of Teaching Science. *Dance Teacher Now*, 14(7):51-52, 54-56.

*Fetterman, David M., Ed. 1988. *Qualitative Approaches to Evaluation in Education*. New York: Praeger.

*Fetterman, David M. 1995a. *Empowerment Evaluation: Knowledge and Tools for Self-Assessment & Accountability*. Thousand Oaks, CA: Sage Publications.

*Fetterman, David M. 1995b. In Response. *Evaluation Practice*, 16(2):179-99.

Fetterman, David M. 1998. Webs of Meaning: Computer and Internet Resources for Educational Research and Instruction. *Educational Researcher*, 27(3):22-30.

Fichter, Nancy Smith. 1989. Stalking in Deep Coherence: Curricular Design in the Arts. *Design for Arts Education*, 91(1):2-10.

*Fineberg, Carol. 1995. *AileyCamp 1995, Evaluation Report*. New York: C.F. Associates.

*Fineberg, Carol and Charles E. Wilson. 1996. *AileyCamp VIII Evaluation Report*. New York: C.F. Associates.

Finn, Chester E, Jr. 1989. The Pitfalls of School Reform. *The Public Interest*, 94:114-120.

Fitt, Sally Sevey. 1988. *Dance Kinesiology*. New York: Schirmer Books.

*Fletcher, Heather. 1998. *Does a Connection Exist Between Ballet Training and*

Academic Performance? Paper presented at the Society for Research on Adolescence, March, San Diego.

*Fong, David. 1996. March 1, Letter to National Endowment for the Arts.

Fortin, Sylvie and Daryl Siedentop. 1995. The Interplay of Knowledge and Practice in Dance Teaching: What We Can Learn from a Non-Traditional Dance Teacher. *Dance Research Journal,* 27(2):3-15.

*Foster, John. 1977. *The Influences of Rudolph Laban.* London: Lepus Books.

*Fowler, Charles. 1988. *Can We Rescue the Arts for America's Children? Coming to Our Senses—10 Years Later.* New York: American Council for the Arts.

*Fowler, Charles. 1996. *Strong Arts, Strong Schools: The Promising Potential and Shortsighted Disregard of the Arts in American Schooling.* New York: Oxford University Press.

*Frangione, Danna. 1988. *The Bodies of Change: Dance and Women in Higher Education.* Paper presented at the International Conference for Women in Higher Education.

*Fratzke, Beth. 1990. Get the Message? Communications Skills Are Integrated Across the Arts High School's Curriculum. *Articulars,* 5(4):2-3.

Frosch-Schroder, Joan. 1991. A Global View: Dance for the 21st Century. *Journal of Physical Education, Recreation & Dance,* 62(3):61-66.

Gallas, Karen. 1991. Arts as Epistemology: Enabling Children to Know What They Know. *Harvard Educational Review,* 61(1):40-50.

*Gardner, Howard. 1983. *Frames of Mind: A Theory of Multiple Intelligences.* New York: Basic Books.

*Gardner, Howard. 1991. *The Unschooled Mind: How Children Think, How Schools Should Teach.* New York: Harper Collins.

Gardner, Howard. 1992. *Multiple Intelligences: The Theory in Practice.* New York: Basic Books.

*Gardner, Howard. 1998. Extraordinary Cognitive Achievements (ECA): A Symbol Systems Approach (pp. 415-466). In William Damon and Richard M. Lerner (Eds.), Handbook of Child Psychology. Fifth Edition. New York: Wiley & Sons, Inc.

*Gaunt, Krya D. 1997. *The Games Black Girls Play: Music, Body, and "Soul."* Unpublished doctoral dissertation, University of Michigan.

*Gazzaniga, Michael. 1985. The Social Brain. *Psychology Today,* 19(1):29-30, 32-34, 36-37.

Geis, Gilbert. 1968. Slum Art, Shoestrings, and Bootstraps. In Joan Grant (Ed.), *The Arts, Youth, and Social Change* (pp. 42-77). Washington, DC: Dept. of Health, Education, and Welfare, Office of Juvenile Delinquency and Youth Development.

Gilbert, Anne Green. 1977. *Teaching the Three Rs Through Movement Experiences.* New York: Macmillan.

Gilbert, Anne Green. 1992. *Creative Dance for All Ages.* Reston, VA: National Dance Association.

*Giles, Raymond H., Jr. 1972. *Black and Ethnic Studies Programs at Public*

Schools: Elementary and Secondary. Ph.D. dissertation, University of Massachusetts (University Microfilms 73 6465).

*Gilmore, Perry. 1983. Spelling "Mississippi": Recontextualizing a Literacy-Related Speech Event. *Anthropology & Education Quarterly*, 14(4):235-255.

Gingrasso, Susan. 1991. North Carolina: State of the Arts—A Report on the Implementation of K-12 Dance Education. *Design for Arts in Education*, 93(1):9-20.

Gladstone, Roy. 1989. Teaching for Transfer Versus Formal Discipline. *American Psychologist*, 44(8):1159.

Glaser, Robert. 1984. Education and Thinking: The Role of Knowledge. *American Psychologist*, 39:93-104.

*Glaser, Robert. 1987. Thoughts on Expertise. In C. Schooler and W. Schale (Eds.), *Cognitive Functioning and Social Structure Over the Life Course* (pp. 81-94). Norwood, NJ: Ablex.

*Goals 2000: Educate America Act of 1994, PL 103-227, 20 U.S.C. § 5801 *et seq.*

*Goellner, Ellen W. and Jacqueline Shea Murphy, Eds. 1995. *Bodies of the Text: Dance as Theory, Literature as Dance*. New Brunswick, NJ: Rutgers University Press.

*Goldin, Augusta R. 1979. *The Shape of Water*. Garden City, NY: Doubleday.

*Goleman, Daniel. 1995. *Emotional Intelligence*. New York: Bantam.

Goodlad, John I. 1990. *Teachers for Our Nation's Schools*. San Francisco: Jossey-Bass.

*Goodwin, Marjorie. 1991. *He-Said-She-Said: Talk as Social Organization Among Black Children*. Bloomington: Indiana University Press.

*Gottschild, Brenda Dixon. 1996. *Digging the Africanist Presence in American Performance: Dance and Other Contexts*. Westport, CT: Greenwood Press.

*Gottschild, Brenda Dixon. 1997. Some Thoughts on Choreographing History. In Jane C. Desmond (Ed.), *Meaning in Motion: New Cultural Studies of Dance* (pp. 167-178). Durham, NC: Duke University Press.

*Gould, Stephen Jay. 1996 (October). Creating the Creators. *Discover*, pp. 43-44, 48, 50, 52, 54.

*Graham, Martha. 1985, March 31. Martha Graham Reflects on Her Art and a Life in Dance. *New York Times*, pp. HI, H8.

Grant, Joan, Ed. 1968. *The Arts, Youth, and Social Change*. Washington, DC: Dept. of Health, Education, and Welfare, Office of Juvenile Delinquency and Youth Development.

Gray, Judith A. 1989. *Dance Instruction: Science Applied to the Art of Movement*. Champaign, IL: Human Kinetics.

Gray, Judith A. 1989. *Dance Technology: Current Applications and Future Trends*. Reston, VA: AAHPERD.

*Greene, Maxine. 1995. *Releasing the Imagination: Essays on Education, the Arts, and Social Change*. San Francisco: Jossey-Bass.

*Greenberg, J. 1979. The Child's Capacity to Perceive Metaphor in Art Objects: A Paradigmatic Case of Aesthetic Development. *Journal of Creative Behavior*, 13(4):232-246.

Greeno, James G. 1997. On Claims That Answer the Wrong Questions. *Educational Researcher*, 26(1):5-17.

Grody, Svetlana McLee and Dorothy Daniels Lister. 1996. *Conversations with Choreographers*. Portsmouth, NH: Heinemann.

*H'Doubler, Margaret Newell. 1925. *The Dance*. London: Cape.

H'Doubler, Margaret Newell. 1927. *Dance and Its Place in Education*. New York: Harcourt Brace.

H'Doubler, Margaret Newell. 1940. *Dance: A Creative Art Experience*. New York: F. S. Crofts.

Haass, Richard N. 1994. *The Power to Persuade*. Boston: Houghton Mifflin.

Haberman, Martin and Tobie Meisel, Eds. 1970. *Dance: An Art in Academe*. New York: Teachers College Press.

*Halpern, Diane F. 1996. *Thought and Knowledge: An Introduction to Critical Thinking* (3rd ed.). Hillsdale, NJ: Erlbaum.

Hamblen, Karen A. 1989. Research in Art Education as a Form of Educational Consumer Protection. *Studies in Art Education: A Journal of Issues and Research*, 31(1):37-45.

*Hamilton, Linda. 1997. The Dancers' Health Survey Part II: From Injury to Peak Performance. *Dance Magazine*, 71(2):60-65.

*Hamilton, Linda. 1998. *Advice for Dancers: Emotional Counsel and Practical Strategies*. San Francisco: Jossey-Bass.

Hanna, Judith Lynne. 1965. African Dance as Education. *Impulse: Dance and Education Now*, pp. 48-52.

Hanna, Judith Lynne. 1970. Dance Mobilization as Therapy in the Inner City. In *Workshop in Dance Therapy: Its Research Potentials* (Proceedings of a Joint Conference of Research Department of Postgraduate Center for Mental Health, Committee on Research in Dance, American Dance Therapy Association, November 10, 1968, New York) (pp. 37-42, 62-63). New York: Committee on Research in Dance.

Hanna, Judith Lynne. 1979a. Movements Toward Understanding Humans Through the Anthropological Study of Dance. *Current Anthropology*, 20(2):313-339.

Hanna, Judith Lynne. 1979b. Toward Semantic Analysis of Movement Behavior. *Semiotica*, 25(1-2):77-110.

Hanna, Judith Lynne. 1982a. Public Social Policy and the Children's World: Implications of Ethnographic Research for Desegregated Schooling. In George D. Spindler (Ed.), *Doing the Ethnography of Schooling* (pp. 316-355). New York: Holt, Rinehart and Winston.

*Hanna, Judith Lynne. 1982b. Tempest in a Toeshoe: Public Policy and the Performing Arts. *Practicing Anthropologist*, 4(1):14-15.

*Hanna, Judith Lynne. 1983. *The Performer-Audience Connection: Emotion to Metaphor in Dance and Society*. Austin: University of Texas Press.

*Hanna, Judith Lynne. 1986. Interethnic Communication in Children's Own Dance, Play, and Protest. In Young Y. Kim (Ed.), *Interethnic Communication*.

Vol. 10: International and Intercultural Communication Annual (pp. 176-198). Newbury Park, CA: Sage.

*Hanna, Judith Lynne. 1987. *To Dance Is Human: A Theory of Nonverbal Communication* (rev. ed.). Chicago: University of Chicago Press.

*Hanna, Judith Lynne. 1988a. *Dance and Stress*. New York: AMS Press.

*Hanna, Judith Lynne. 1988b. *Dance, Sex, and Gender: Signs of Identity, Dominance, Defiance, and Desire*. Chicago: University of Chicago Press.

*Hanna, Judith Lynne. 1988c. *Disruptive School Behavior: Class, Race and Culture*. New York: Holmes & Meier.

*Hanna, Judith Lynne. 1988d. Theories and Realities of Emotion in Performance. *Polish Art Studies*, 9:44-66; *Gestos*, 3(6):27-51.

*Hanna, Judith Lynne. 1989a. African Dance Frame by Frame: Revelation of Sex Roles through Distinctive Feature Analysis and Comments on Field Research, Film, and Notation. *Journal of Black Studies*, 19(4):422-441.

*Hanna, Judith Lynne. 1989b. The Anthropology of Dance. In Lynnette Y. Overby and James H. Humphrey (Eds.), *Dance: Current Selected Research. Vol.I* (pp. 219-237). New York: AMS Press.

*Hanna, Judith Lynne. 1989c. Dance in Public Education. *Dance Teacher Now*, 11(2):25-26, 28, 32.

Hanna, Judith Lynne. 1990a. Dance and Stress: Good or Bad? *Dance Teacher Now*, 12(1):27-28, 30, 32, 34, 36.

*Hanna, Judith Lynne. 1990b. AileyCamp Promotes Literacy for At-Risk Youth. *Dance Teacher Now*, 12(4):38-40.

Hanna, Judith Lynne. 1990c. Anthropological Perspectives for Dance/Movement Therapy. *American Journal of Dance Therapy*, 12(2):115-126.

*Hanna, Judith Lynne. 1991a. Advantages of Bharata Natyam. *Dance Theatre Journal*, 9(1):14-15.

*Hanna, Judith Lynne. 1991b. Using the Arts as a Dropout Prevention Tool. *Child Behavior and Development Letter*, 7(3):1-2.

Hanna, Judith Lynne. 1992a. Tradition, Challenge, and the Backlash: Gender Education Through Dance. In Laurence Senelick (Ed.), *Gender and Performance* (pp. 223-238). Hanover, NH: University Press of New England.

*Hanna, Judith Lynne. 1992b. Moving Messages: Identity and Desire in Dance. In James Lull (Ed.), *Popular Music and Communication* (2nd ed.) (pp. 176-195). Newbury Park, CA: Sage.

*Hanna, Judith Lynne. 1992c. Connections: Arts, Academics, and Productive Citizens. *Phi Delta Kappan*, 73(8):601-607.

*Hanna, Judith Lynne. 1992d. Shock Troupes: Helms, Kitty Kat, and So What? *Ballet Review*, 20(3):85-93.

Hanna, Judith Lynne. 1993a. Classical Indian Dance and Women's Status. In Helen Thomas (Ed.), *Dance, Gender and Culture* (pp. 119-127). London: Macmillan.

Hanna, Judith Lynne. 1993b. Education and Social Change. In John U. Ogbu (Sect.

Ed.), Anthropology of Education; T. Husen and T.N. Postelthwaite (Eds.-in-chief), *International Encyclopedia of Education, Research and Studies* (2nd ed) (pp. 5508-5510). Oxford: Pergamon Press; 2nd ed., 1997.

Hanna, Judith Lynne. 1994a. Issues in Supporting School Diversity: Academics, Social Relations, and the Arts. *Anthropology & Education Quarterly*, 25(1):1-20.

*Hanna, Judith Lynne. 1994b. Arts Education and the Transition to Work. *Arts Education Policy Review*, 96(2):31-37.

*Hanna, Judith Lynne. 1994c. Kennedy Center's Programs Reach the Nation. *Dance Teacher Now*, 16(4):63-66.

*Hanna, Judith Lynne. 1994d. What Is Black Dance? *Dance Teacher Now*, 16(8):69-72, 74, 76.

*Hanna, Judith Lynne. 1995a. Moving With the Arts: The Getty Center for Education in the Arts' National Conference Defines the Year's Benchmarks and Cries "Forward." *Dance Teacher Now*, 17(8):55-58, 60.

Hanna, Judith Lynne. 1995b. The Power of Dance: Health and Healing. *Journal of Alternative and Complementary Medicine*, 1(4):323-327.

*Hanna, Judith Lynne. 1996a. The Private Studio's Role in Educational Reform. *Dance Teacher Now*, 18(1):61, 63-64, 66-67, 68.

Hanna, Judith Lynne. 1996b. Rhythm and Choreography. *Degrés*, (87, Autumn):65-80.

Hanna, Judith Lynne. 1997a. Problems and Dilemmas in Classifying African Dances. In Ester Dagan (Ed.), *The Spirit's Dance In Africa* (pp. 210-215). Montreal: Galerie Amrad.

*Hanna, Judith Lynne. 1997b. "Ubakala, We Are Coming": Searching For Meaning In Dance. In Ester Dagan (Ed.), *The Spirit's Dance In Africa* (pp. 90-93). Montreal: Galerie Amrad.

Hanna, Judith Lynne. 1997c. Creativity in Ubakala, Dallas Youth, and Exotic Dance. In R. Keith Sawyer (Ed.), *Creativity in Performance* (pp. 143-167). Norwood, NJ: Ablex.

*Hanna, Judith Lynne. 1997d. "Nilimma Devi's Touch of India in America," *Dance Teacher Now*, 19(2):97-100, 102.

*Hanna, Judith Lynne. 1997e. Rasta Thomas: Extraordinary Boy Next Door," *Dance Teacher Now*, 19(1):65-72.

*Hanna, Judith Lynne. 1997f. What Can Students Get From Dance Competitions? (Guest Editorial), *Dance Teacher Now*, 19(3):100.

Hanna, Judith Lynne. 1998a. "Cultural Context," Vol. 4:362; "Ubakala," Vol. 6:219; "West Africa," Vol. 6:381-385. In Selma Jeanne Cohen (Ed.), *International Encyclopedia of Dance*. New York: Oxford University Press.

*Hanna, Judith Lynne. 1998b. "Undressing the First Amendment and Corsetting the Striptease Dancer," *The Drama Review* (T158) 42(2):38-69, Summer.

Hanna, Judith Lynne. 1998c. Feminist Perspectives on Classical Indian Dance. In David Waterhouse (Ed.), *Dance of India* (pp. 169-202). Toronto: University of Toronto Graduate Centre for South Asian Studies.

Hanna, Judith Lynne. 1998d. "Learning Ballet the Russian Way." *Dance Teacher Now* 20(9).

*Hanna, Judith Lynne. 1999. Toying with the Striptease Dancer and the First Amendment. In Stuart Reifel (Ed.), *Play and Culture Studies*, Vol. 2. Greenwich, CT: Ablex.

*Hansen, C. 1967. Jenny's Toe: Negro Shaking Dances in America. *American Quarterly*, (19):554-563.

Harris, Louis. 1992. *Americans and the Arts VI*. New York: American Council for the Arts.

Harvey, Steve. 1989. Creative Arts Therapies in the Classroom: A Study of Cognitive, Emotional, and Motivational Changes. *American Journal of Dance Therapy*, 11(2):85-100.

Hawkins, Erick, 1992. *The Body Is a Clear Place and Other Statements on Dance*. Pennington, NJ: Princeton Book Company.

*Hazzard-Gordon, Katrina. 1983. Afro-American Core Culture Social Dance: An Examination of Four Aspects of Meaning. *Dance Research Journal*, 15(2):21-26.

Hegel, G.W.F. 1975. *Aesthetics* (T. M. Knox, Trans.). Oxford: Clarendon Press. (Original work published 1835)

*Hilsendager, Sarah. 1989. *Under the Big Top: Dance Education Moves Toward a New Era* (lecture). Reston, VA: National Dance Association.

*Hilsendager, Sarah. 1992. *Preservice Preparation for Dance Specialists*. Paper presented at "The Arts in American Schools: Setting a Research Agenda for the 1990s," conference sponsored by the National Endowment for the Arts' Arts in Education Program and the U.S. Department of Education, Office of Educational Research and Improvement.

*Hinde, R.A., Ed. 1972. *Nonverbal Communication*. Cambridge: Cambridge University Press.

*Hipple, John. 1996, Spring. Performance Anxiety May Be More Than Stage Fright. *Performance Pulse: A Newsletter for Wellness*, pp. 1-2, 4.

*Hoberman, John. 1997. *Darwin's Athletes: How Sport Has Damaged Black America and Preserved the Myth of Race*. New York: Houghton Mifflin.

*Hodes, Stuart. 1995. Dance and Essence: Reflections on Morality and Education. *Arts Education Policy Review*, 97(2):2-13.

*Hoffman, Diane M. 1996. Culture and Self in Multicultural Education: Reflections on Discourse, Text, and Practice. *American Educational Research Journal*, 33(3):545-569.

Hoover, Carolyn Faye. 1980. *The Effectiveness of a Narrated Dance/Pantomime Program in Communicating Selected Basic Health Concepts of Third Graders*. Unpublished doctoral dissertation, University of Oregon.

Hope, Samuel. 1989. On National Conditions and Policy Imperatives. *Design for Arts in Education*, 91(1):15-35.

*Howe, Dianne S. and Mary Maitland Kimball. 1994. What National Dance Standards Mean to You. *Dance Teacher Now*, 16(7):32-34, 36, 38, 40-41, 44-45.

*Hutchinson, Ann. 1970. *Labanotation* (rev. and exp. Ed.). New York: Theatre Arts Books.

*Hymes, Dell. 1974. *Foundations in Sociolinguistics*. Philadelphia: University of Pennsylvania Press.

*Interdisciplinary Approach Highlights Open House. 1989. *Articulars* 5(2):1.

*Ijaz, A.M. 1980. *Ethnic Attitudes of Elementary School Children Toward Blacks and East Indians and the Effect of a Cultural Program on These Attitudes*. Unpublished doctoral dissertation, University of Toronto, Ontario Institute for Studies in Education.

**An Invitation to Your Community: Building Community Partnerships for Learning*. 1995. Washington, DC: U.S. Department of Education.

*Isaacs, Harold R. 1975. *Idols of the Tribe*. New York: Harper & Row.

Jacob, Ellen. 1996. *Dancing: The All-In-One Guide for Dancers, Teachers, and Parents* (rev. ed.). Reading, MA: Addison-Wesley.

*Jacques-Dalcroze, Emile. 1930. *Eurhythmics: Art and Education*. New York: A.S. Barnes.

*Jones, Bessie and Bess Lomax Hawes. 1972. *Step It Down: Games, Plays and Stories from the Afro-American Heritage*. New York: Harper & Row.

Joyce, Mary. 1994. *First Steps in Teaching Creative Dance to Children* (3rd ed.). Mountain View, CA: Mayfield.

*Joyner, Will. 1996, March 10. The Maturing of an Investment in Ballet's Future. *New York Times*, p. H10.

*Kaagan, Stephen S. 1990. *Aesthetic Persuasion: Pressing the Cause of Arts Education in American Schools*. Los Angeles: Getty Center for Education in the Arts.

*Kahlich, Luke. 1993. Educating Dance Educators. *Bulletin of the Council for Research in Music Education*, 117:136-151.

Katz, Jonathan, Ed. 1988. *Arts and Education Handbook: A Guide to Productive Collaborations*. Washington, DC: National Assembly of State Arts Agencies.

Katz, Phyllis. 1990. *Exploring Science Through Art*. New York: Franklin Watts.

*Kaufman, Sarah. 1995, February 26. D.C. Barre Association, *Washington Post*, p. G1.

*Kaufman, Tanya. 1996. February 28, Letter to National Dance Institute.

*Kerr-Berry, Julie A. (Feature Ed.). 1994a. African Dance; Enhancing the Curriculum. *Journal of Physical Education, Recreation & Dance*, 65(5):25-47.

*Kerr-Berry, Julie A. 1994b. Using the Power of West African Dance to Combat Gender Issues. *Journal of Physical Education, Recreation & Dance*, 65(2):44-45.

Kidd, Ross. 1982. *The Popular Performing Arts, Non-Formal Education and Social Change in the Third World: A Bibliography and Review Essay*. The Hague: Centre for the Study of Education in Developing Countries (CESO).

*Kirkland, Gelsey, with Greg Lawrence. 1986. *Dancing on My Grave*. Garden City, NY: Doubleday.

*Kisselgoff, Anna. 1980. Maverick of the Dance. *Harvard Magazine*, 82(5):42-46.

*Kisselgoff, Anna. 1997, March 9. Masters of the Grammar of Movement. *New York Times*, p. H10.

*Kramer, Jill. 1991. Movement Classes for 14,000 Children. *Dance Teacher Now*,

13(5):34-40.

*Kraus, Richard, Sarah Chapman Hilsendager, and Brenda Dixon. 1991. *History of the Dance in Art and Education* (3rd ed.). Englewood Cliffs, NJ: Prentice Hall.

Krebs, Stephanie. 1975. The Film Elicitation Technique: Using Film to Elicit Conceptual Categories of Culture. In Paul Hockings (Ed.), *Principles of Visual Anthropology* (pp. 283-302). The Hague: Mouton.

*Laban, Rudolf. 1948. *Modern Educational Dance*. London: Macdonald & Evans.

Lane, Robert Wheeler. 1995. *Beyond the Schoolhouse Gate: Free Speech and the Inculcation of Values*. Philadelphia: Temple University Press.

*Langer, Susanne K. 1953. *Feeling and Form: A Theory of Art Developed From Philosophy in a New Key*. New York: Scribner's.

*Langer, Susanne. 1957. *Philosophy in a New Key: A Study of the Symbolism of Reason, Rite and Art* (3rd ed.). Cambridge, MA: Harvard University Press.

Lavender, Larry. 1992. Critical Evaluation in the Choreography Class. *Dance Research Journal*, 24(2):33-39.

*Laws, Kenneth and Cynthia Harvey. 1994. *The Physics of Dance* (rev. ed.). New York: Schirmer.

*Lawson, Joan. 1989. Teaching Technical Differences to Boys and Girls. *Dancing Times*, 80(949):55-57.

*Lawson, Joan. 1994. *Beginning Ballet*. New York: Theatre Arts Books/Routledge.

Lee, Mary Ann. 1993. Learning Through the Arts. *Journal of Physical Education, Recreation & Dance*, 64(5):42-46.

*Lemay, Paul H. 1990. Rudolf Nureyev. *Dance Magazine*, 64(5):35-36.

Levete, Gina. 1995. *No Handicap to Dance: Creative Improvisation for People With and Without Disabilities*. Lower Lake, CA: Souvenir-Atrium.

*Levine, Lawrence W. 1977. *Culture and Black Consciousness: Afro-American Folk Thought From Slavery to Freedom*. New York: Oxford University Press.

*Levine, Mindy L. 1994. *Widening the Circle: Towards a New Vision for Dance Education (A Report of the National Task Force on Dance Education)*. Washington, DC: Dance/USA.

Levy, Carla. 1992. Performing Arts: An Example of Excellence in Vocational Arts Education. *Journal of Physical Education, Recreation & Dance*, 63(2):36-38.

*Loyacono, Laura. 1992. *Reinventing the Wheel: A Design for Student Achievement in the 21st Century*. Washington, DC: National Conference of State Legislatures.

*Luftig, Richard L. 1994. *The Schooled Mind: Do the Arts Make a Difference? An Empirical Evaluation of the Hamilton Fairfield SPECTRA+ Program, 1992-93*. Oxford, OH: Miami University, Center for Human Development, Learning, and Teaching.

*Lyman, Rick. 1997, July 16. Finding Government Profit in Aid to the Arts. *New York Times*, p. B1.

McGreevy-Nichols and Helene Scheff. 1995. *Building Dances: A Guide to Putting Movements Together*. Champaign, IL: Human Kinetics Press.

McGreevy-Nichols and Helene Scheff. 1996. The Roger Williams Middle School

Dance Program. *Teaching Secondary Physical Education*, 2(3):22-24.

McQuade, Finlay. 1986. Interdisciplinary Contours: Art, Earth Science, & Logo. *Science and Children*, 24(1):25-27, 85.

*Martin, Barbara. 1994. *Dance Marathons: Performing American Culture in the 1920s and 1930s*. Jackson: University Press of Mississippi.

Mason, Rachel. 1988. *Art Education and Multiculturalism*. London: Croon Helm.

*Meglin, Joellen A. (Feature Ed.). 1994. Gender Issues in Dance Education. *Journal of Health, Education, Recreation & Dance*, 25-47.

Mettler, Barbara. 1960. *Materials of Dance as a Creative Art Activity*. Tucson, AZ: Mettler Studios.

Minton, Sandra Cerny. 1986. *Choreography: A Basic Approach Using Improvisation*. Champaign, IL: Human Kinetics Press.

Mirus, Judith. 1994. *Dance Resource Collection: An Annotated Bibliography* (videotapes and books). Golden Valley, MN: Minnesota Center for Arts Education.

Modgil, S., G. Verma, K. Mallick, and C. Modgil, Eds. 1986. *Multicultural Education: The Interminable Debate*. Philadelphia: Falmer Press.

*Moffatt, Michael. 1989. *Coming of Age in New Jersey: College and American Culture*. New Brunswick, NJ: Rutgers University Press.

Moles, Oliver C., Ed. 1990. *Student Discipline Strategies: Research and Practice*. Albany: State University of New York Press.

Moore, Carol-Lynne and Kaoru Yamamoto. 1988. *Beyond Words: Movement Observation and Analysis*. New York: Gordon & Breach.

Murname, Richard J. and Frank Levy. 1997, February 17. Clinton Is Half-Right on Schools. *Washington Post*, p. A25.

Murray, Ruth Lovell. 1975 (3rd ed.). *Dance in Elementary Education*. New York: Harper and Row.

*Myerson, Allen R. 1996, January 30. For the First Time in 151 Years, Baylor Puts a Bounce in Its Step. *New York Times*, p. A 8.

*National Arts Education Associations, Consortium of. 1994. *National Standards for Arts Education: Dance, Music, Theatre, Visual Arts—What Every Young American Should Know and Be Able to Do in the Arts*. Reston, VA: Music Educators National Conference.

*National Arts Education Associations, Consortium of. 1995. *Opportunity-to-Learn Standards for Arts Education*. Reston, VA: Author.

National Assembly of Local Arts Agencies (NALA). 1994. *Arts in the Local Economy*. Washington, DC: Author.

*National Assembly of Local Arts Agencies. 1995. *Working Relationships: The Arts, Education, and Community Development*. Washington, DC: Author.

*National Board for Professional Teaching Standards. 1994. *What Teachers Show Know and Be Able to Do*. Washington, DC: NBFTS.

*National Center for Education Statistics. 1995. *Arts Education in Public Elementary and Secondary Schools: Statistical Analysis Report*. Washington, DC: U.S. Department of Education, Office of Educational Research and Improvement.

*National Commission on Excellence in Education. 1983. *A Nation at Risk: The Imperative for Educational Reform.* Washington, DC: Government Printing Office.

*National Commission on Teaching and America's Future. 1996. *What Matters Most: Teaching for America's Future.* New York: Teachers College Press.

*A National Dance. 1884, December 21. *New York Times* Editorial, p. 8.

National Dance Association Conference: Dancers in Cap and Gown. 1995. *Dance Magazine*, 69(7):56-58.

National Dance Association and The Minnesota School and Resource Center for the Arts. 1989. *Dance Directions: 1990 and Beyond* (Conference Proceedings). Reston, VA: National Dance Association.

*National Endowment for the Arts. 1988. *Toward Civilization: A Report on Arts Education.* Washington, DC: Government Printing Office.

*National Endowment for the Arts. 1994. *Arts Education Research Agenda for the Future.* Washington, DC: NEA and U.S. Office of Education.

*National Endowment for the Arts. 1995. *The Arts and Education Partners in Achieving Our National Goals.* Washington, DC: NEA and U.S. Office of Education.

National Roundtable on Folk Arts in the Classroom. 1993. *Folk Arts in the Classroom: Changing the Relationship Between Schools and Communities.* Washington, DC: National Endowment for the Arts.

*Newman, Barbara. 1982. *Striking a Balance: Dancers Talk About Dancing.* Boston: Houghton Mifflin.

*Nigles, Lynda. 1996, October. Ingredients for a Gender Equitable Physical Education Program. *Teaching Elementary Physical Education*, pp. 28-30.

*Nketia, J.H. Kwabena. 1974. *The Music of Africa.* New York: Norton.

*North, Marion. 1971. *Body Movement for Children.* London: MacDonald & Evans.

*North, Marion. 1972. *Personality Assessment Through Movement.* London: MacDonald & Evans.

*Northrop, F.S.C. (Filmer Stuart Cuckow). 1949. New York: Macmillan.

*Nowicki, Stephen, Jr., and Carolyn Oxenford. 1989. The Relation of Hostile Nonverbal Communication Styles to Popularity in Preadolescent Children. *Journal of Genetic Psychology*, 150(1):39-44.

*Ogbu, John U. 1986. The Consequences of the American Caste System. In Ulric Neisser (Ed.), *The School Achievement of Minority Children* (pp. 14-56). Hillsdale, NJ: Erlbaum.

*O'Harrow, Robert, Jr. 1995, January 18. Fairfax Plan Requires All Students Be Schooled in World of Work. *Washington Post*, pp. A1, A10.

*O'Neil, John. 1994. Looking at Art Through New Eyes. *Curriculum Update*, January.

*Oreck, Barry. 1997. A New Process for Identifying Potential Talent in the Performing Arts: A Valid, Reliable and Unbiased Assessment Approach. Mimeograph. New York: ArtsConnection.

Overby, Lynnette Young. 1990. The Use of Imagery by Dance Researchers. *Journal of Health, Physical Education, Recreation & Dance,* 61(2):24-27.

Overby, Lynnette Young. 1993. Motor Learning Knowledge in the Dance Education Curriculum. *Journal of Physical Education, Recreation & Dance,* 64(9):42-44, 48.

Paulson, Pamela. 1993. New Work in Dance Education. *Arts Education Policy Review,* 95(1):30-35.

Pauly, Nancy and Janet Parker. 1990. Nancy Engen-Wedin, Ed., *Interdisciplinary Learning and the Arts: An Annotated Bibliography.* Golden Valley, MN: Minnesota Center for Arts Education.

Penrod, James and Janice Gudde Plastino. 1970. *The Dancer Prepares: Modern Dance for Beginners.* Palo Alto, CA: National Press Books.

People for the American Way. 1994. Artistic Freedom Under Attack. Washington, DC: Author.

Perkins, David N. 1994. *The Intelligent Eye: Learning to Think by Looking at Art* (Occasional Paper #4). Santa Monica, CA: Getty Center for Education in the Arts.

*Perkins, David N. and Gavriel Salomon. 1988. Teaching for Transfer. *Educational Leadership,* 46(1):22-32.

*Peterson, Terry and Sarah Howes. 1997. *Arts Education & School Improvement Resources for Local and State Leaders.* Washington, DC: U.S. Department of Education.

Petrides, Faith Shaw. 1996a. *The Dance Directory of Ballet Companies, 1997, American Companies.* P.O. Box 904, New York, New York 10023.

Petrides, Faith Shaw. 1996b. *The Dance Directory of Ballet Companies, 1997, Audition Calendar.* P.O. Box 904, New York, New York 10023.

Petrides, Faith Shaw. 1996c. *The Dance Directory of Ballet Companies, 1997, European Companies.* P.O. Box 904, New York, New York 10023.

*Piaget, Jean. 1929. *A Child's Conception of the World* (J. & A. Tomlinson, Trans.). New York: Harcourt Brace.

*Piaget, Jean. 1955. *The Language and Thought of the Child.* New York: New World.

*Piaget, Jean. 1962. *Play, Dreams and Imitation in Childhood* (C. Gatetegno & F. M. Hodgson, Trans.). New York: Norton.

Pica, Rae. 1991. *Early Elementary Children Moving and Learning* (notebook and 5 cassettes). Champaign, IL: Human Kinetics Press.

Pica, Rae. 1993. *Upper Elementary Children Moving and Learning* (notebook and 2 cassettes). Champaign, IL: Human Kinetics Press.

Plastino, Janice Gudde. 1991. *Dance and Science: Melding, Molding, and Moving.* Reston, VA: National Dance Association Dance Scholar Lecture.

Portes, Alejandro and Rubén G. Rumbaut, Eds. 1996. *Immigrant America: A Portrait* (2nd ed.). Berkeley: University of California Press.

Presseisen, Barbara Z., Ed. 1988. *At-Risk Students and Thinking: Perspectives from Research.* Washington, D.C. and Philadelphia: National Education Association and Research for Better Schools.

Preston-Dunlop, Valerie, Comp. 1996. *Dance Words: A Dictionary of Western Dance Practice and Research*: Vol. 8. *Choreography and Dance Studies.* London: Harwood Academic Press.

Priorities for Arts Education Research. Washington, DC: Goals 2000 Arts Education Partnership.

Purcell, Theresa. 1994. *Teaching Children Dance.* Champaign, IL: Human Kinetics Press.

Purcell, Theresa. 1996. *Teaching Children Dance: Becoming a Master Teacher* (Pre-K-6). Reston, VA: National Dance Association.

Ramsey, Kate. 1997. Vodou, Nationalism, and Performance: The Staging of Folklore in Mid-Twentieth-Century Haiti. In Jane C. Desmond (Ed.), *Meaning in Motion; New Cultural Studies of Dance.* Durham, NC: Duke University Press.

*Rauscher, Frances H., Gordon L. Shaw, Linda Levine, Eric L. Wright, Wendy R. Dennis, and Robert L. Newcomb. 1997. Music Training Causes Long-Term Enhancement of Preschool Children's Spatial-Temporal Reasoning. *Neurological Research*, 19(1):2-8.

Remer, Jane. 1990. *Changing Schools Through the Arts* (rev. ed.). New York: American Council for the Arts.

Remer, Jane. 1996. *Beyond Enrichment: Building Effective Arts Partnerships with Schools and Your Community.* New York: American Council for the Arts.

*Resnick, Lauren B., Ed. 1989. *Knowing, Learning, and Instruction: Essays in Honor of Robert Glaser.* Hillsdale, NJ: Erlbaum.

Richards, David. 1997, January 29. A Clash of Theater Titans. *Washington Post*, pp. D1, D8.

The Road to City Center: Moving in New Directions. Per annum. (Young People's Dance Series Study Guide). New York, New York: City Center.

Rogoff, Barbara and Jean Lave, Eds. 1984. *Everyday Cognition: Its Development in Social Context.* Cambridge, MA: Harvard University Press.

Rogoff, Barbara, Jean Lave, and William Gardner. 1984. Adult Guidance of Cognitive Development. In Barbara Rogoff and Jean Lave (Eds.), *Everyday Cognition: Its Development in Social Context* (pp. 95-116). Cambridge, MA: Harvard University Press.

Root-Bernstein, Robert. 1987. *Education and the Fine Arts from a Scientist's Perspective: A Challenge.* White paper written for the College of Fine Arts, UCLA.

*Root-Bernstein, Robert. 1997. For the Sake of Science, the Arts Deserve Support. *Chronicle of Higher Education*, 43(44):B6.

Rosow, Jerome M. and Robert Zager. 1988. *Training—The Competitive Edge.* San Francisco: Jossey-Bass.

*Ross, Janice. 1994. The Right Moves: Challenges of Dance Assessment. *Arts Education Policy Review*, 96(1):11-17.

Rothman, Robert. 1995. *Measuring Up: Standards, Assessments, and School*

Reform. San Francisco: Jossey-Bass.

Rowen, Betty. 1994. *Dance and Grow: Developmental Activities for 3-8 Year Olds.* Reston, VA: National Dance Association.

Rubel, Robert J. 1977. *The Unruly School: Disorders, Disruptions, and Crimes.* Lexington, MA: Heath.

*Russell, Joan. 1965. *Creative Dance in the Primary School.* London: Macdonald & Evans.

Russell, Joan. 1969. *Creative Dance in Secondary School.* London: Macdonald & Evans.

Ryan, Allan J., and Robert E. Stephens. 1988. *The Dancer's Complete Guide to Healthcare and a Long Career.* Chicago: Bonus Books.

*Sachs, Curt. 1937. *World History of the Dance.* Bessie Schoenberg, Trans. New York: Norton.

*Safire, William. 1991, April 29. On Language. *New York Times Magazine*, p. 16.

*Salomon, Gavriel and David N. Perkins. 1989. Rocky Roads to Transfer: Rethinking Mechanisms of a Neglected Phenomenon. *Educational Psychologist*, 24(2):113-143.

*Salzer, Beeb. 1995, December 1. Good Art Asks Tough Questions. *Chronicle of Higher Education*, pp. B1-B2.

*Schiffman, Jan. 1993. Anyone Can Write a Grant Proposal. *Dance Teacher Now*, 15(9):91-92, 94, 96-98.

Schlaich, Joan and DuPont, Betty 1993. *The Art of Teaching Dance Technique.* Reston, VA: National Dance Association.

Schmais, Claire. 1966. Learning Is Fun When You Dance It. Dance Helps to Prepare Slum Children for Reading. *Dancemagazine*, 40(1):33-35.

Schneer, Georgette. 1994. *Movement Improvisation: In the Words of a Teacher and Her Students.* Champaign, IL: Human Kinetics Press.

Schneider, David J. 1991. Social Cognition. In Mark R. Rosenzweig and Lyman W. Porter (Eds.), *Annual Review of Psychology*, 42:527-561.

Schoenberg, Lelia W. 1988. *Arts Education Programs in Five Illinois School Districts: Report on the Illinois Arts Education Pilot Study.* Springfield, IL: Illinois Alliance for Arts Education.

School Success for Students At Risk: Analysis and Recommendations of the Council of Chief State School Officers. 1988. Orlando, FL: Harcourt Brace Jovanovich.

Schrader, Constance A. 1996. *A Sense of Dance: Exploring Your Movement Potential.* Champaign, IL: Human Kinetics Press.

Schwager, Susan and Cathy Labate. 1993, May/June. Teaching For Critical Thinking in Physical Education. *Journal of Physical Education, Recreation & Dance*, pp. 24-26.

*Schwartz, Peggy. 1992. Dance Teacher Certification in Massachusetts: A Cautionary Tale. *Design for Arts in Education*, 93(5):34-40.

Scribner, Sylvia. 1984. Studying Working Intelligence. In Barbara Rogoff and Jean Lave (Eds.), *Everyday Cognition: Its Development in Social Context* (pp. 9-40). Cambridge, MA: Harvard University Press.

*Sebeok, Thomas A. 1986. *Encyclopedic Dictionary of Semiotics.* Berlin: Mouton-Degruyter.

*Shawn, Ted. 1954. *Every Little Movement: A Book About François Delsarte.* New York: Dance Horizons reprint.

*Siegel, Bernard. 1970. Defensive Structuring and Environmental Stress. *American Journal of Sociology*, 76(1):11-23.

*Sims, Caitlin. 1996. Competing at Conventions. *Dance Magazine*, 70(7):41-43.

Sinatra, Richard. 1986. *Visual Literacy Connections to Thinking, Reading and Writing.* Springfield, IL: Charles C. Thomas.

*Singley, Mark K. and John T. Anderson. 1989. *The Transferability of Cognitive Skills.* Cambridge, MA: Harvard University Press.

Sizer, Theodore R. 1984. *Horace's Compromise: The Dilemma of the American High School.* Boston: Houghton Mifflin.

*Smelser, Neil J. 1989. Self-Esteem and Social Problems: An Introduction. In Andrew M. Mecca, Neil J. Smelser, and John Vasconcellos (Eds.), *The Social Importance of Self-Esteem* (pp. 1-23). Berkeley: University of California Press.

Smith, Ralph. 1983. Forms of Multi-Cultural Education in the Arts. *Journal of Multi-Cultural and Cross-Cultural Research in Art Education*, 1(1):23-32.

*Smith-Autard, Jacqueline M. 1994. *The Art of Dance in Education.* London: A & C. Black.

*Solomon, John and Ruth Solomon, Eds. 1995. *East Meets West in Dance: Voices in the Cross-Cultural Dialogue. Vol. 9: Choreography and Dance Studies.* London: Harwood Academic.

Solomon, Ruth, Sandra C. Minton, and John Solomon, Eds. 1990. *Preventing Dance Injuries: An Interdisciplinary Perspective.* Reston, VA: American Alliance for Health, Physical Education, Recreation and Dance.

*Solway, Diane. 1988, April 24. City Ballet Moves in an American Beat. *New York Times,* p. H1, 40.

Soundpost. 1986. *Grades of High School Arts Students Compare Favorably with Other Students.* Reston, VA: Music Educators National Conference.

*Spalding, Susan Eike and Jane Harris Woodside, Eds. 1995. *Communities in Motion: Dance, Community, and Tradition in America's Southeast and Beyond.* Westport, CT: Greenwood.

*Spindler, George D., Ed. 1982. *Doing the Ethnography of Schooling.* New York: Holt, Rinehart and Winston.

*Sternberg, Robert. 1996. *Successful Intelligence.* New York: Simon & Schuster.

*Stinson, Susan W. 1985. Piaget for Dance Educators: A Theoretical Study. *Dance Research Journal*, 17(1):9-15.

*Stinson, Susan W. 1987. *Gender Issues in Dance Education.* In M. M. Carnes and P. Stueck, pp. 33-43, (Eds.), *Proceedings of the Fifth Conference on Curriculum Theory in Physical Education* (pp. 33-59). Athens: University of Georgia.

Stinson, Susan W. 1988. *Dance for Young Children: Finding the Magic in Movement.* Reston, VA: American Alliance for Health, Physical Education, Recreation and Dance.

Stinson, Susan W. 1990. Dance as Curriculum, Curriculum as Dance. In G. Willis and W. H. Schubert (Eds.), *Reflections From the Heart of Curriculum Inquiry: Understanding Curriculum and Teaching Through the Arts* (pp. 190-196). Albany: State University of New York Press.

*Stinson, Susan W. 1991. Reflections on Teacher Education in Dance. *Design for Arts in Education*, 92(3):23-30.

*Stinson, Susan W. 1992. Reflections on Student Experience in Dance Education. *Design for Arts in Education*, 93(5):21-27.

*Stinson, Susan W. 1993a. Journey Toward a Feminist Pedagogy for Dance. *Women in Performance,* 6(1):131-146.

*Stinson, Susan W. 1993b. Meaning and Value: Reflections on What Students Say About School. *Journal of Curriculum & Supervision*, 8(3):216-238.

Stinson, Susan W. 1993c. Realities, Myths, and Priorities: Teacher Competencies in Dance. *Journal of Physical Education, Recreation & Dance*, 64(9):45-48.

*Stinson, Susan W. 1993d. Voices from Schools: The Significance of Relationship to Public School Dance Studies. *Journal of Physical Education, Recreation & Dance*, 64(5):46-52.

*Stinson, Susan W. 1994. *Research as Choreography*. Reston, VA: National Dance Association Scholar Lecture.

Stinson, Susan W. 1995. Body of Knowledge. *Educational Theory*, 45(1):43-54.

*Stinson, Susan W. and Karen Anijar. 1993. Interpretive Inquiry in Dance Education. *Impulse*, 1(5):52-64.

Stinson, Susan W., Donald Blumenfeld-Jones, and Jan Van Dyke. 1990. Voices of Young Women Dance Students: An Interpretive Study of Meaning in Dance. *Dance Research Journal*, 22:13-22.

Strickland, Carol. 1990, February 12. Young Achievers: Art and Ambition in Action. *Christian Science Monitor*, pp. 12-13.

Stuart, Otis. 1995. *Perpetual Motion*. New York: Simon & Schuster.

* *Survey of the Condition of Arts Education in American Schools*. 1995. Washington, DC: U.S. Department of Education.

*Svien, Rik. 1989. De-Exclusifying Science. *Articulars*, 5(2):2.

Swartz, Robert and David Perkins. 1989. *Teaching Thinking: Issues and Approaches*. Pacific Grove, CA: Midwest.

*Talbert, Joan E. 1993. Constructing a School-Wide Professional Community: The Negotiated Order of a Performing Arts School. In Judith Warren Little and Milbrey W. McLaughlin (Eds.), *Teachers' Work: Individuals, Colleagues and Context* (pp. 164-184). New York: Teachers College Press.

Tanenbaum, Morris. 1989. *Why We Need the Arts: 8 Quotable Speeches by Leaders in Education, Government, Business and the Arts*. New York: American Council for the Arts.

Taylor, Jim and Ceci Taylor. 1995. *Psychology of Dance*. Champaign, IL: Human Kinetics Press.

*Taylor, Anne, George Vlastos, and Alison Marshall. 1991. *Architecture and Children: Teacher's Guide, Interdisciplinary Learning Activities of the Architecture and Children Curriculum.* Seattle: Architecture and Children Institute.

Teck, Katherine. 1994. *Ear Training for the Body: A Dancer's Guide to Music.* Pennington, NJ: Princeton Book Co.

Thomasen, Eivind. 1996. *Anatomy and Kinesiology for Ballet Teachers.* London: Dance Books. (Available from Princeton Book Co.)

Thorndike, E. L. and R. S. L. Woodworth. 1901. The Influence of Improvement in One Mental Function Upon the Efficiency of Other Functions. *Psychological Review,* 8:247-61.

*Trescott, Jacqueline. 1994, April 16. For Artists, A Call for Creative Community: NEA Meeting Stresses Social Role, *Washington Post,* pp. C1, C5.

Troxell, Kay (Ed.), 1991. *Resources in Sacred Dance: Annotated Bibliography from Christian and Jewish Traditions.* Peterborough, NH: Sacred Dance Guild.

Trueba, Henry, George Spindler, and Louise Spindler. 1989. *What Do Anthropologists Have to Say About Dropouts*? London: Falmer Press.

*Trujillo, Lorenzo Alan. 1979. *The Effect of a Hispanic Ethnic Dance Curriculum Upon High School Students' Self Concept and Academic Performance.* Unpublished doctoral dissertation, University of San Francisco.

*U.S. Congress. 1994a. Public Law 103-227. Goals 2000 Educate America Act. 103rd Congress, March 31, Title I, Sect. 102, B3.

*U.S. Congress. 1994b. Public Law-103-382. Improving America's Schools Act. 103rd Congress, October 20.

*U.S. Department of Education. 1995. *An Invitation to Your Community: Building Community Partnerships for Learning.* Washington, DC: Author.

U.S. Department of Education. 1995. *Survey of the Condition of Arts Education in American Schools. Urban and State Initiatives: Case Studies of Two Successful Arts Education Advocacy Initiatives in Chicago and the State of South Carolina.* 1995. Los Angeles: Getty Center for Education in the Arts.

*Verhovek, Sam Howe. 1997, October 5. Stardom Seasoned With a Yearning for Home and Kin. *New York Times,* p. AR6.

*Vorrath, Harry H. and Larry R. Brendtro. 1985. *Positive Peer Culture* (2nd ed.). New York: Aldine.

*Vygotsky, L.S. 1978. *Mind in Society.* Cambridge, MA: Harvard University Press.

*Weinraub, Judith. 1995, December 3. Jacques d'Amboise: Steps in the Right Direction. *New York Times,* p. G6.

*Weitz, Judith Humphreys. 1996. *Coming Up Taller: Arts and Humanities Programs for Children and Youth at Risk.* Washington, DC: President's Committee on the Arts and Humanities.

Welch, Nancy. 1995. *Schools, Communities, and the Arts: A Research Compendium.* Washington, DC: National Endowment for the Arts.

Wenner, Gene C. 1973. Project IMPACT: Designing an Arts-Centered Curriculum. *Music Educators Journal,* 59(5):26-31.

White, David R., Lise Friedman, and Tia Tibbitts Levinson. 1993. *Poor Dancer's Almanac: Managing Life and Work in the Performing Arts*. Durham, NC: Duke University Press.

*Wiggins, Grant P. 1993. *Assessment of Student Performance: Exploring the Purpose and Limits of Testing*. San Francisco: Jossey-Bass.

*Wiley, Hannah C. 1990. Changing the Fate of the Retiring Dancer. *Dance Teacher Now*, 12(5):35-37.

*Willis, Cheryl M. 1995a. Creative Dance—How to Increase Parent and Teacher Awareness. Journal of Physical Education Recreation and Dance, 66(5):48-53.

Willis, Cheryl M. 1995b. Factors that Affect Dance Programs. Journal of Physical Education Recreation and Dance, 66(4):58-63.

*Wilson, Brent. 1997. *The Quiet Evolution: Changing the Face of Arts Education*. Los Angeles: The Getty Education Institute for the Arts.

*Wilson, Bruce, Dick Corbett, Amee Adkins, and George Noblit. 1996. *Valuing A+: Assessing the First Year 1995-96*. A Report on the North Carolina A+ Schools Program.

* *Window on the Work*. New York: Winston-Salem: Thomas S. Kenan Institute for the Arts. Lincoln Center Institute. 1996.

Wolf, Thomas, Ed. 1983. *The Arts Go to School: An Arts-in-Education Handbook*. New York: American Council for the Arts, and Cambridge, MA: New England Foundation for the Arts.

*Wolfgang, Aaron, Ed. 1984. *Nonverbal Behavior: Perspectives, Applications, Intercultural Insights*. Toronto: Hogrefe.

*Wong, E. David. 1995. Challenges Confronting the Researcher/Teacher: Conflicts of Purpose and Conduct. *Educational Researcher*, 24(3):22-28.

Wright, Judy Patterson. 1992. *Social Dance: Steps to Success*. Champaign, IL: Human Kinetics Press.

Wright, Stuart. 1985. *Dancer's Guide to Injuries of the Lower Extremity: Diagnosis, Treatment, and Care*. New York: Cornwall Books.

*Yamamoto, Kaoru. 1987. Voices in Unison: Stress Events in the Lives of Our Children in Six Countries. *Journal of Child Psychology and Psychiatry*, 28(6):855-64.

*Youskevitch, Igor. 1969. The Male Image. *Dance Perspectives*, 40:13-23.

*Zamdmer, Mona. 1994. *Learning to Read Through the Arts: Its Emergence in Context*. (Educational Resources Information Center [ERIC] Document Reproduction Service No. 378103)

*Zullinger, Chip. 1990. Letter and Key Performance Indicators, sent to the Hon. N. Leo Daughtry, June 21.

*Zweig, Connie. 1986, February 7. Exploring the Link Between Arts and Sciences. *Los Angeles Times*, p. V6.

Index

mastery
dance forms. *See* ballet, creativity, Graham
  African 21-22, 121, 137, 145-147, 156,
    158-159, 161, 192
  Asian 16, 147-148, 150
  belly 148
  Caribbean 121, 126
  Charleston 139-140
  country/western dance 54
  courtship 22
  creative 46, 51, 55, 74, 100
  diversity of 3, 5
  doing steps 151
  flamenco 148
  folk and national 51, 82
  fox trot 147
  Haitian 22
  hip hop 54, 82, 147
  Irish 161
  house 54
  improvisation 19, 40, 46, 51
  Indian 16, 19, 143
  jazz 47, 82, 85, 94, 107, 113, 121, 126,
    128, 147
  jitterbug 147
  marathon 147
  modern 19, 51-54, 79, 82, 85, 94, 107,
    121, 126, 144, 153, 162
  Morris 148
  play 5, 134-135, 151
  post-modern 53
  religious 10-11, 21, 82, 145, 151
  ring and line play 137
  social 54, 59, 144
  Spanish 121
  square dance 54, 144
  street 54, 129
  striptease 146
  tap 47, 82, 85, 94, 161
  theatrical 145-147, 161
  Tongan 24
  turkey trot 147
  warrior 22
Dance Heritage Coalition 193
Dance Masters of America 62, 81-82, 85
dancer 2-4, 17, 19, 23-24, 26, 52, 81, 90, 92,
  112, 168, 187
  retired 78
Dance Theatre of Harlem 44, 73-74, 114,
  122, 140, 161
Dance/USA 71, 188
Aaron Davis Hall 122
Davis, Chuck 9, 135
Davis, Thulani 110
Delsarte, François 14, 54
Dennett, Daniel 17
Devi, Nilimma 143
Dewey, John 57
Discipline-based Arts Education 45, 60, 79, 85
District of Columbia Public Schools

Superintendent's Academy for Humani-
  ties and Arts 190
"Dr. Schaffer and Mr. Stern" 74
Duncan, Isadora 11, 51-52, 146, 186
Dudley, Jane 53
Dunham, Katherine 44, 53, 147
Dunning, Jennifer 12
Duxbury Park Arts IMPACT Elementary
  School 45, 95
E
economy 2, 26, 32-35, 60-61, 149, 152, 184-
  185
education
  decision-makers 1, 4
  reform 2, 47, 58-68
effort element of dance 13, 33
Eilber, Janet 53
Eisner, Elliot 32, 65
Eller, Jack 149
Ellington, Duke, School of the Arts 42, 97
emotion 10, 13-18, 53-54, 58, 167-168, 171-
  172, 175, 179
  multiple ways of expression 15
  performer-audience connection 14-17,
    149
English 90, 95-96, 113, 115, 118-120, 124,
  126, 128-129
F
Fairfield, Hamilton, Arts Association 43
Faison, George 53
Federal Register 190
feeling. *See* emotion.
Feld, Eliot 41
Ferri, Alessandra 12
Fetterman, David 193
Fillmore Arts Center 45-46
First Amendment 186
Fitton Center for Creative Arts 43
Fletcher, Heather 36
Fonseca, Hortensia 164, 175
Fonseca, Peter 164
Foundation Center 190
foundations 4, 59, 190
Frames of Mind 17
Frangione, Danna 162
French 95
Frick International Studies Academy 73
Froebel, Friedrich 54
G
The Galef Institute's Different Ways of Know-
  ing in the Classroom (DWOK) 39-40
Gannett Foundation 123, 190
Gardner, Howard 2, 58, 135
Gaunt, Kyra 134, 137-138
Giles, Raymond 152
Goldberg, Milton 49
Goleman 14
Graham, Martha 9, 18-19, 52, 135, 146, 162
  technique 19, 52, 75, 94, 121
grammar. *See* dance as language-like

About the Author

Judith Lynne Hanna has spent a half-century dancing, researching, writing, and teaching others about dance in community centers, schools, and universities. After teaching English and social studies for the Los Angeles City School System, she held positions at Michigan State University, American University, Fordham University, and the University of Texas at Dallas. She has conducted field research all over the world on different forms of dance. Currently, she is a Senior Research Scholar at the University of Maryland and an expert court witness nationwide concerning freedom of expression through dance.

Hanna has long been a leading advocate to make dance an essential component of children's education. In 1972, at Gill/St. Bernard's Upper School in Bernardsville, NJ, she offered an interdisciplinary dance-centered course. Between 1989 and 1993, Hanna worked for the United States Department of Education, where she was able to assess what is happening in dance education throughout the United States.

Hanna received her PhD in anthropology from Columbia University in 1976. She has explored how knowledge in the arts, humanities, and social and behavioral sciences helps us understand dance. Her books include *To Dance Is Human: A Theory of Nonverbal Communication; Dance, Sex, and Gender: Signs of Identity, Dominance, Defiance, and Desire; The Performer–Audience Connection: Emotion to Metaphor in Dance and Society; Dance and Stress: Resistance, Reduction, and Euphoria;* and *Disruptive School Behavior: Class Race and Culture.* Hanna's articles have appeared in *Dance Teacher Now, Ballet Review, Stagebill, Education Week, Dance Magazine, Anthropology and Education,* and *The Washington Post.*

Hanna's numerous awards include a National Endowment for the Humanities Fellowship and the American Alliance for Health, Physical Education, Recreation and Dance's Anderson Award for significant publications.